THE STATE OF THE
SCOTTISH WORKING-CLASS
IN 1843

THE STATE OF THE
SCOTTISH WORKING-CLASS
IN 1843

A statistical and spatial enquiry
based on the data from the Poor Law
Commission Report of 1844

IAN LEVITT
and
CHRISTOPHER SMOUT

1979

SCOTTISH ACADEMIC PRESS
EDINBURGH

Published by
Scottish Academic Press Ltd,
33 Montgomery Street
Edinburgh EH7 5JX

SBN 7073 0247 1

© 1979 Scottish Academic Press Ltd

Printed in Great Britain
by R. & R. Clark Ltd, Edinburgh

CONTENTS

A Note on References

References to the volumes of the *Report of the Royal Commission on the Poor Law* P.P. 1844 Vol. 20–25, are given in the body of the text in this form: (20.215), meaning Vol. 20, p. 215. References to the *New Statistical Account of Scotland* (15 Vols, Edinburgh, 1845) are similarly given in this form: (*NSA*, V, Ayr, 260).

TABLES

MAPS and DIAGRAMS

Chapter 1

INTRODUCTION

This book is based on data embedded in the appendices to the *Report of the Royal Commission on the Poor Law (Scotland)*, published as a Parliamentary Paper in 1844. The appendices fill 6 large volumes, three of which are occupied by the replies to a questionnaire, with 70 questions on it, sent to the minister or some other qualified person in all the 906 parishes of Scotland; 93 per cent. of those asked responded by filling it in, producing over 60,000 individidual answers.[1] It is these that form the raw material for the tables and maps in our study.

The richness and abundance of the material is the main reason why it has lain unused so long. Historians have scarcely attempted to use the replies except occasionally as a quarry for an illustrative fact. It appears that the Commissioners themselves made no systematic use of them either, being equally daunted by the volume of the information they had succeeded in collecting. Yet even a cursory examination showed us that the data were more systematic and more structured than in the more familiar *New Statistical Account* of the same period.[2] With the help of the SPSS package computer programme for the tables and the CAMAP 6 computer mapping programme to produce draft working maps we have set out to produce a quantitative and spatial account of the condition of Scotland in 1843, as it was portrayed by the respondents to the Poor Law Inquiry.

Funds to do the work were forthcoming in a generous grant from the Social Sciences Research Council, to whom we express our thanks. Help was also forthcoming from many sides, but our greatest debt is to the other members of our Economic History Department and Geography Department at the University of Edinburgh (especially to Barbara Morris who drew the final maps), and to the Edinburgh Regional Computing Centre. The serious work of coding, analysis by computer and printing rough working maps began in September 1975 and was completed within two years. Ian Levitt was responsible for the computing side and for writing Chapter 8, Christopher Smout for the general planning and writing the remainder, but we have worked so closely together throughout that it can only be considered an inseparably joint venture.

We hope the book would have pleased those early Victorians who were trying to pierce the darkness of insufficient knowledge in their own day. It is a snapshot at one point in time, in the tradition of the *Statistical Accounts*, trying to explain through text, maps and tables in as much detail as possible for each region the basic conditions for the common man in respect of food, prices, wages, possibilities for saving and squandering, the patterns of poor relief if he became destitute and the patterns of emigration if he wished to get away from it all. We have tried to write it in the spirit of the great eighteenth-century pioneer Sir John Sinclair to whom the idea of a 'statistical inquiry' meant presenting social information systematically but in a way that any interested reader could follow. If our fellow social scientists find our treatment inadequate for their purposes they can re-work the original data from the computer tapes deposited with the SSRC Survey Archive at the University of Essex.

The character of the source explains both its strengths and its weaknesses. The questionnaire was sent out in order to help the Royal Commission assess the need for a reform of the Scottish Poor Law, which had been under increasing fire from critics like W. P. Alison, Professor of Medicine at the University of Edinburgh, whose writing had stressed the inability of the traditional system based on distributing voluntary contributions through the kirk sessions to cope with the problems of poverty in an industrialising society.[3] The intense urban distress of 1841–2, especially in the stricken, shawl-making town of Paisley, had convinced the government that the swelling tide of criticism should at least be heard.[4] The problems of the traditional system were further exacerbated in the course of the investigation by the Disruption of the Church of Scotland, which sundered the principal body responsible for relief in the parishes.

When the Commission was appointed one of its first acts in the early months of 1843 was to prepare the questionnaire and to send it to the ministers of the established church in every parish. It was fortunate that the Disruption had not yet occurred, so they had the benefit of putting the questions to men who were often of long experience as pastors in the same parish. In March they began hearing other expert witnesses in the cities and large towns of the central belt. Between June and September they split into two parties to tour the parishes of the north, including Orkney, Shetland and the Hebrides; in the autumn they came down through the north-east, down the east coast and into the western Lowlands and Galloway; in January and February 1844 they finished off in the Lothians and the south-east corner. Wherever they went they called the men to whom they had sent the questionnaires before them and, if possible, collected the answers in person, making the ministers testify to their accuracy – a fact which must surely account for the very high response rate. They then proceeded to examine them and any other local witnesses individually on general matters relating to poor relief in the locality, a procedure that filled three volumes of Parliamentary Papers with evidence. The fact of the Disruption probably made very little difference to the inquiry, as they were usually successful in contacting the man who had been in office until June: 95 per cent. of the respondents were ministers, and those who were not were generally session clerks or heritors' clerks who had had long experience of the parish poor. The Commissioners considered they had been well served by the clergy: 'We consider that we should not be doing justice to that most useful body of men, were we to neglect to state that, with scarcely any exceptions, there has been manifested on their part a most praiseworthy zeal to furnish us with information.' They went on: 'From some parishes we have not yet procured any satisfactory returns; the answers which we have received will, we fear, in no small number of cases, show that the questions have been imperfectly understood; but upon the whole the returns will be found to contain a mass of valuable statistical information relative to the Parochial Economy of Scotland.'

But what about the calibre of the respondents and the nature of the questions? Church of Scotland ministers were not, it must be recalled, like Anglican rectors – often absentee, or in other ways basically out of touch with the facts of their working-class parishioners' lives. The presbyterian system enforced a degree of conscientiousness in their performance of ministerial duties and a close acquaintance with the way the common people lived, at least in farming and crofting parishes and in small towns. This was less often true in the cities, from which, as we shall see, there was a poor response rate. It was not always true in populous parishes with a predominantly industrial work force of miners, iron-workers or factory hands, yet even here ministers often seem to have been closely acquainted with the details of economic and social life.

Those unacquainted with the Scottish tradition may be surprised that the ministers made such an effort to collect the facts and get them right, but the idea of using the church for a centrally directed inquiry into local affairs went back to Webster's enumeration of the Scottish population in 1755 and Sinclair's first *Statistical Account* of the 1790s. Still more relevant is the fact that the Church of Scotland was just completing the *New Statistical Account*, begun in 1832 and eventually published in 15 volumes in 1845. The *NSA* was also based on a questionnaire sent to every parish, though the questions have been lost and can scarcely be reconstructed from the replies. Those who had laboured conscientiously to reply to that inquiry would find it less strange or forbidding to provide the information for the Poor Law Commissioners. The essential difference between them was that the *NSA* questions evidently invited long and diffuse (and very uneven) replies that do not yield easily to attempts at systematic analysis or summary, while the 1843 questions were specific and the replies short and usually to the point. There is for us, however, still a great advantage in having the *NSA* to turn to, for the long descriptions for each parish can often amplify the background into which we need to fit the 1843 data.

However careful the ministers might be to provide accurate information they could only hope to do so if the questions were of a type that they could answer. Of the 70 questions we decided to ignore no fewer than 33. Some we disregarded on the grounds that they were not of great moment, others because the information asked for was replicated in the 1841 census or in other Parliamentary inquiries of the time. A number more we rejected because, although the answers would have been worth knowing, either the questions were unanswerable given the contemporary level of knowledge or they were so poorly framed as to invite pointlessly vague replies. One of the questions, for instance, was: 'Are the heritors absentee or resident? If absentee, do they reside in any other part of Scotland?' The answers were worthless for bulk analysis because no definition was attempted of what an 'absentee' or a 'resident' was – the replies tended to run: 'Some absentee, some resident, some residing partly in Scotland, partly in England.' Another question was 'What is the average age at which males in your parish have married during the last five years?' The very first reply to this (from Colinton) explained why it was usually unanswerable before the establishment of the Registrar General for Scotland's office in 1855: 'As the ages are not entered in the register of marriages it is impossible to give the real averages.'

The 37 remaining questions we subjected to analysis. Even these often presented particular problems of interpretation, and it is by no means clear that every minister was equally well informed or answered them in the same way. The peculiar difficulties of each are discussed in turn in one of the relevant chapters below. They were, however, all about subjects on which the ministers could gather good information if they chose – common foodstuffs, prices, wages, saving institutions, public houses, pawn shops, the poor law and migration. They were all fairly clearly framed – which is not to say they are totally free of ambiguities or put in the way that a modern social investigator would find optimal. Above all, trial runs on the computer yielded internally consistent and meaningful results. These, then, are the hard kernels of data that we accept as grist for the mill.

Next there is the problem of geographical coverage. While it is true that 845 parishes out of 906 responded to the questionnaire (93 per cent.), not every individual question was so thoroughly covered – only 693 parishes (76 per cent.) gave, for instance, a numerical answer to the question on how many emigrants had left in the previous three years. More serious is the absence of answers to the questionnaire from many of the largest towns: there is no reply for Edinburgh, Glasgow, Paisley or Perth, though there is an answer for Aberdeen, Dundee, Greenock, Inverness, Ayr, Stirling, Arbroath, Dumfries, and Hamilton. Thus while 93 per cent. of the parishes replied these contained 75 per cent. of the population of Scotland but only 43 per cent. of the population of towns of over 5000 inhabitants. On many occasions we have been able to use supplementary information on the large towns from the other three volumes of evidence to amplify what the questionnaire said, and have discussed this evidence at length in the text. But our main tables and the maps are derived from the answers to the questionnaire alone. These must be considered strongest and most reliable for the rural parishes.

Any study of regions and regional differences is a work of economic geography as well as of economic history. In order to present our data in maps, however, we had to decide on the best method of dividing Scotland into spatial units that could be readily comprehended. It would have been ridiculous to reproduce the data on a parish-by-parish basis in the tables, which are intended to be summaries that can be assimilated by the reader. It would also have been misleading to use the parish as the basic unit for most of the maps if only because of the discrepancies in size between individual parishes: one parish in Highland Perthshire covers the same extent as 40 in Lowland Fife, and mapping a response from such a parish would give a visual impact on the map out of all proportion to its real significance. One alternative would have been to aggregate the parishes on a conventional county basis for both tables and maps. This would have had the advantage of referring to familiar units: but Scottish counties in many cases are very inconvenient and unnatural ones. Perthshire, for example, is half barren Highland and half fertile Lowland. Inverness-shire is nearly 200 miles wide from St. Kilda in the Atlantic to the Banffshire border in the east; Kinross is only 15 miles wide. Aberdeenshire has 83 parishes, Selkirk has only 7 parishes.

As an alternative, we arranged the 906 parishes into 43 districts chosen after a careful inspection of a physical map of Scotland and after examining by eye a series of large-scale computer-drawn working maps to make sure we were following the edges of consistent discontinuities in several of the variables we analysed first – rent, food and the price of coal being examples. We also took account of traditional administrative boundaries, and of our knowledge of the types of farming and degree of industrialisation within the areas. Each of these districts contained between 10 and 40 responding parishes, usually towards the lower end in upland areas and towards the upper end in east-coast low-lying areas. Sometimes such districts coincided with the traditional counties – e.g., Orkney, Shetland and Kincardineshire: often they did not do so exactly, yet formed a division that was readily identifiable as part of a county. Map 1.1 shows how the district boundaries have been drawn and Appendix I lists all the parishes in Scotland and shows to which district they have been assigned. Where we use the term 'Highland' in this book it means the area covered by districts 4–14, i.e., excluding Caithness and the northern isles and also excluding the low-lying lands of the north-east.

For some purposes, however, it is not adequate to classify the parishes by geographical position alone. It is, for instance, interesting to know whether prices for certain goods were higher in towns than in country, or whether migrants for America were more prone to leave a locality with an industrial or a crofting economy. We therefore also classified the parishes into three main economic types, each sub-divided into two as follows:

1.1 Urban-industrial: large towns. Parishes containing or part of a town of over 5000 inhabitants (e.g., Glasgow, Montrose, Alloa).

1.2 Urban-industrial: small towns etc. Parishes containing a town of fewer than 5000 inhabitants, but having an industrial base (e.g., Dalkeith, Irvine) and country parishes with clearly more industrial than agricultural workers, generally with factory, weaving or mining villages (e.g., Kilbarchan, Bothwell).

2.1 Mixed economy: rural parishes. Country parishes with significant industrial employment, often in domestic textiles or small mines, where industrial workers do not outnumber agricultural workers (e.g., Cumbrae, Edzell, Midcalder).

2.2 Mixed economy: country towns. Parishes containing a town of fewer than 5000 inhabitants having a non-industrial base and servicing the countryside around (e.g., Haddington, Turriff, Kirkcudbright).

3.1 Agricultural: farming. Country parishes in which the great majority of the inhabitants were clearly the families of farmers or farm-workers (e.g., Aberlady, Crathie and Braemar, Stichill).

3.2 Agricultural: crofting. West Highland parishes in which the great majority of the inhabitants were clearly the families of small tenants, crofters or cottars (e.g., Lochs, Barra, Ardnamurchan).

Only the last sub-category has any geographical cohesion: the remainder were scattered through many different regions and districts. We allocated each parish after reading their replies to the 1843 questionnaire and checking the *New Statistical Account* and the 1841 census. In some cases it inevitably remained difficult to decide on the correct category, since not even the *NSA* invariably provided a breakdown of the population between agricultural occupations and others.

What kind of country was Scotland in 1843? The answer will become clearer as we proceed with the book, but by way of background we thought it worth analysing two other statistical Parliamentary Papers of the time, the census of 1841[5] and the income tax assessments of 1842–3[6] to delineate the demographic and economic structure of the country. In both of these the coverage of Scotland is complete, and the under-representation of urban areas mentioned in respect to the Poor Law Inquiry returns does not apply.

The historian is accustomed to thinking of Scotland as an industrialising and urbanising country from 1780 onwards, which is, of course, perfectly correct. The 1841 census shows, however, that even after sixty years of this process Scotland was still by modern standards very imperfectly urbanised. Only 35 per cent. of the population lived in towns of 5000 inhabitants or more, compared with 74 per cent. in 1971. Map 1.2 shows the distribution of these towns, 30 in all. By far the biggest burgh was the megapolis of Glasgow, 275,000 strong, a by-word even then for urban and industrial problems: it contained only a little over a tenth of the Scottish population of 2,620,184 and was predominantly a textile town with an interest in heavy engineering. Edinburgh was only half the size; it lived from being the capital and thereby was a centre of consumer goods and service industries. Aberdeen, Dundee and Paisley, each 60–65,000, were in turn half the size of Edinburgh but depended mainly on textiles like Glasgow. Greenock reached 36,000 and depended on engineering. Leith reached 26,000; Perth 19,000; eight towns (Dumfries, Ayr, Kilmarnock, Arbroath, Montrose, Airdrie, Stirling and Inverness) hovered around the 11–13,000 mark; the remainder were all below 10,000. None of the towns was in the Highlands, except Campbeltown and Inverness which sat on the edges. The majority were ancient burghs that had been among the largest towns a hundred years earlier, but some, like the iron town of Airdrie, were mushroom growths of the first phase of Scottish industrialisation. All, old and new alike, had grown very rapidly since the start of the century. They worried the social reformer with their high death rates, low standards of public health, their illiteracy, their drunkenness, their prostitution and their crime, and the larger or newer they were the more appalling and intractable their problems seemed. Nevertheless, two Scots out of three lived outside them.

Map 1.2 also shows where the remainder of the population lived, and should be considered in conjunction with maps 1.3–1.6 which show the distribution of four important industries: the latter are based on replies to the 1843 questionnaire supplemented by the tax assessment data in the case of the coalmines. A population density outside the large towns of over 80 people per square kilometre was only achieved in six districts on or near to extensive coalfields: the population here was not merely mining but also iron-working (in North Lanarkshire and North Ayrshire) or involved in textile manufacture (especially cotton, but also linen in Fife) as well as in agriculture. The next highest densities (around 50) occurred in the textile districts (mainly linen) of east-central Scotland, especially in Angus and Perthshire where the ground was also fertile enough to support a large farming population. Elsewhere in the Lowlands, districts where there was little besides extensive fertile land reached densities in the 40s or 30s dropping to the 20s or even lower if there was a high proportion of infertile uplands. The manufacture of woollen cloth, more diffused geographically than cotton or linen but employing many fewer hands, had little obvious effect on population. Densities were also in the 20s in the Northern Isles; in the Highlands they never achieved even this, although the Hebrides and the southern and north-eastern fringes were over twice as densely populated as the central and western mainland bloc, where densities fell to as little as 4 or 5 people per square kilometre.

The proximity of coal, the possibility of cotton and linen trades and the fertility of the land, then, were the main elements determining the density of population outside the large towns, but the industrial elements had by 1843 a greater effect than the agricultural. One could be misled by the low level of urbanisation into thinking Scotland was not yet an industrial country, but in fact there were considerably more people living in parishes classified as urban industrial than in those classified as agricultural. 52 per cent. of the population lived in urban-industrial parishes (including 17 per cent. outside the large towns); 20 per cent. lived in mixed economy parishes; 28 per cent. lived in agricultural parishes.

Much industry was semi-rural. Coalmining was almost always carried out in clusters of villages occupied by a few score of miners. Even iron works might have a rural site, the richness of the ores tempting exploitation before the infrastructure of a large town had emerged. Many spinning mills were still turned by water wheels on fast-flowing country streams, like the cotton factories at New Lanark, Stanley and Deanston or the woollen factories at Galashiels.

Even as late as the 1830s and 1840s there was also surprisingly extensive country employment in handloom weaving. In 1835, for example, Glasgow merchants employed 18,500 handloom weavers within the city and 13,500 outside (*NSA*, VI, 958) – the tentacles of their business stretched at least as far as south Lanarkshire, south Ayrshire, Perth and Fife. Flowering muslins (embroidering fine cottons) and sewing also employed thousands of women in the western counties. In Fife, Perthshire, Angus and as far north as Kincardineshire handloom weaving in linen was still important; there were relatively new manufacturing villages like Friockheim in Angus, where there were said in 1840 to be 'about 789 manufacturing operatives, employed in spinning flax and weaving osnaburgh cloth, two-thirds of whom are females, and of these nearly four fifths are weavers on the hand-loom'. The writer continued with this significant observation: 'This resource makes female farm servants very independent in their own eyes, because the equally lucrative employment of the loom or mill is at their acceptance' (NSA, XI, 389). In Aberdeenshire and the north-east generally the domestic linen industry had already decayed, but knitting woollen stockings for low wages remained a source of supplementary earnings for many old people. In Orkney, the recent collapse of the old trade of straw plaiting in the face of foreign competition was frequently cited as a local cause of depression.

In sum, the jam of industrial activity, though thinner on the bread than today, was spread widely into many corners that have since reverted to being entirely agricultural. This was, however, only true of the Lowlands, and was mainly true of a central belt running from Dunbartonshire and Ayrshire to Angus and Fife. Outside that zone the logic of high distribution costs made it hard to make a success of manufacturing except in favoured pockets like Hawick and Aberdeen.

The tax assessment data (see Table 1.A and Map 1.7) throw light on, among other things, the geographical variations in the value of the land itself. The authorities assessed land, under Schedule 'A' of Sir Robert Peel's new Income Tax, by its annual value, or the actual rent a tenant would pay for its occupancy. The resulting values per kilometre measure not merely natural fertility but also proximity to markets and development potential in urban areas. There is a close relationship between these values and the incomes of the landlords and of the total agricultural sector in these areas. The natural poverty of the Highlands and the far north at once meets the eye. Nowhere did the annual value of land reach £50 per square kilometre, and in three western areas it was below £10. At the other extreme lay a group of five east-coast districts on the Firths of Tay and Forth, all with values exceeding £250 per kilometre, favoured by a combination of extremely fertile land, advanced capitalist farming and ready access to markets. Between the two lay a spectrum that tended to higher values in the proximity of cities and coalfields (though mineral rights were not counted into the land assessment) and lower in remoter counties like Nairn and Wigtownshire, again emphasising the fact that in a country still substantially without railways (except for a few short-haul lines) the worth of a farm often depended on how close it was to the industrial consumer.

Some indication of regional variations in the distribution of personal wealth comes from the income tax assessment data of the annual value of houses — 'annual value' again means here the rent such property reached or would reach on the open market. It cannot, of course, be read as a simple proxy for the distribution of wealth since the rent of a house is compounded of two elements that are difficult to separate. One is the niceness of the house – a pleasant home reflects the personal wealth as well as the taste of the owner. The other is its scarcity – a rotting slum can be made valuable by the shortages of a city, yet be occupied by poverty-stricken tenants.

Variations in annual value of houses per capita are also shown in Table 1.A and on Map 1.8. The highest values are reached in five districts containing the seven largest towns where demand for housing of any kind was greatest. The Edinburgh district comes out top; the capital was both a slum city and the site of the New Town, the finest middle-class housing area in Scotland. But the slums of Edinburgh were not worse than the slums of Glasgow, so it is reasonable to suppose that the differential that separates average house value in the Edinburgh district from that in North Lanarkshire reflects a similar differential in average per capita wealth in their respective cities.

Similarly, in rural areas where there was no obvious pressure on house sites, at least the rank order of annual values may reflect the rank order of differences in wealth per head. There is a striking, if rough, continuum from north-west to south-east. At one extreme stands the extremely low values of the western Highlands where many homes were black houses or hovels of turf often described in the 1843 Poor Law Report as having no worth at all. At the other stands a group of districts in the south-east quarter of the country, Peebles, Kelso, Dunbar, East Fife and South Dumfries, where the values approached those in some of the more urban districts. It was not just because the Highland working-class was composed of desperately poor crofters and cottars and the working-class of the south-east had a large number of skilled and better paid members; the south-east also had a much larger upper class of resident gentry and prosperous farmers. The placing of some of the intermediate districts is also interesting. South Argyll district, for instance, appears much better off than anywhere else in the Highlands, perhaps because this district contained Campbeltown and Rothesay: the north-east and districts south of the Ayr coalfield, on the other hand, have strikingly low values compared with other parts of the Lowlands, though they exceeded all the Highlands except South Argyll and North-east Inverness.

It would have been useful to be able to use the entire tax data to give a more accurate regional breakdown of incomes. Unfortunately this is impossible since the only readily available figures relate to assessment under Schedule 'A' and measure annual value of land and houses, as discussed, along with feudal burdens, mines, iron works, quarries, canals and railways: there are no data at all on a parish basis for industrial, commercial and professional incomes under Schedule 'D' and even if we had them the problems of Victorian tax evasion would nullify their usefulness. For the sake of completeness Table 1.A does, however, also include the aggregate valuation of each district under Schedule 'A' per square kilometre: it contains no surprises – the wealthiest districts are the most industrialised and urbanised, an effect which could only be magnified if we had good information on Schedule 'D' since industrial and professional incomes are bound to have been concentrated in the same localities. It would be more misleading to present the same data on a per capita basis, since the absence of Schedule 'D' makes the crowded towns seem relatively poor compared with the countryside, an impression that is almost certainly wrong.

What conclusions can be drawn so far? Firstly, Scotland in 1843 occupied an intermediate position between an undeveloped and a modern economy, perhaps not so far along the road to modernity as is sometimes assumed. Relatively limited urbanisation was one sign of this; the dependence of much industry on cheap labour of low productivity (in, for instance, rural mining, handloom weaving, muslin flowering and knitting) was another. A poor transport network still limited the value that could be placed on her resources, though agriculture was nevertheless dependent on a burgeoning local industry. Secondly, regional differences appear to have been striking. There was an enormous gulf in development and wealth between the Highlands and the Lowlands, with a particular zone of economic under-development along the western Highland coast. Within the Lowlands, the north-east and the south-west were backward compared to the central industrial triangle bounded by the Firth of Clyde, Edinburgh and the Angus coast, while the Eastern Borders, though rural, were better off than any other area of comparable economic structure.

Theoretically it is reasonable to suppose that regional differences in income per head will reach their maximum at an early stage in industrialisation.[7] In preindustrial economies all areas are of uniformly low income since all mainly rely on near-subsistence forms of farming. Travellers in Scotland before 1750 seem to have noticed no great difference in private wealth whether they were trudging through the Borders, the Lothians or the Highland edges. Today, regions are likely to be relatively uniform in terms of income per capita, partly because trade unions keep wages up to standard national rates, partly because of government welfare intervention, partly because modern communications and selling techniques have perfected the market for commodities and labour. By 1843, however, rapid, if primitive, economic growth had already created limited areas of great opportunity without everywhere creating concomitant superstructures to iron out regional differences. Such differences were not necessarily at their maximum — we shall present evidence later to suggest that they may have subsided since the 1790s, but were not as small as they became by 1900 (see below pp. 80–1). What the data from the 1843 questionnaire do allow us to examine, however, is the magnitude and extent of regional differences at one particular and significant point in the transition of an economy.

REFERENCES

1. *Report of the Royal Commission on the Poor Law (Scotland)* P.P. 1844, vols. 20–25. The replies to the questionnaire fill vols. 23–25.
2. *The New Statistical Account of Scotland* in 15 volumes (Edinburgh, 1845).

3. Alison's most influential attack was *Observations on the Management of the Poor in Scotland* (Edinburgh, 1840).

4. T. C. Smout, 'The Strange Intervention of Edward Twistleton', in *The Search for Wealth and Stability: Essays in Economic and Social History presented to M. W. Flinn* (ed. T. C. Smout, London, 1979).

5. *Population in 1841 of each County of Great Britain*, P.P. 1841, vol. 2.

6. *Return showing the Total Annual Value of Real Property in each Parish for each County of (Scotland) assessed to the Property and Income Tax, for the Year ending April 1843*, P.P. 1845, vol. 38.

7. H. W. Richardson, *Regional Economics* (London, 1969), especially chapter 13.

TABLE 1.A
Value of Land and Houses according to Income Tax Returns
1842–3, by District

	Annual value (£) of land (per sq. kilometre)	Annual value (£) of houses (per head)	Annual value (£) of total Schedule 'A' assessment (per sq. kilometre)
1. Shetland	13·0	0·10	15·5
2. Orkney	19·8	0·05	20·2
3. Caithness	17·3	0·18	19·8
4. East Sutherland	7·1	0·04	7·7
5. East Ross	24·0	0·15	27·8
6. N.-E. Inverness	34·3	0·30	42·3
7. North-west coast	5·7	0·02	6·2
8. Skye and Outer Hebrides	10·0	0·02	10·3
9. West Argyll	19·6	0·90	20·9
10. North Argyll	68·5	0·16	25·9
11. South Argyll	41·3	0·52	51·7
12. Highland Inverness, Banff, Moray	10·9	0·06	11·4
13. Highland Perth, Aberdeenshire	16·3	0·04	16·4
14. N.-W. Perth	39·9	0·07	40·4
15. Nairn, Lowland Moray	61·8	0·18	70·9
16. Lowland Banff	77·3	0·19	87·3
17. Buchan	113·2	0·13	122·7
18. S.-E. Aberdeenshire	150·1	1·41	333·4
19. Inner Aberdeenshire	67·7	0·08	69·2
20. Kincardine	130·6	0·07	136·7
21. Inner Angus	150·9	0·37	167·1
22. Coastal Angus	275·2	1·25	531·5
23. East Perthshire	300·6	1·18	411·4
24. South Perthshire	120·2	0·10	123·3
25. East Fife	301·8	0·52	358·2
26. West Fife	246·4	0·39	359·4
27. North Stirling-Clackmannan	163·2	0·80	242·5
28. West Lothian, East Stirling	233·5	0·65	331·2
29. Edinburgh area	367·7	3·43	1628·3
30. Dunbarton, Renfrewshire	192·9	1·67	529·8
31. North Ayrshire	205·7	0·63	310·5
32. South Ayrshire	88·8	0·28	101·0
33. North Lanarks.	223·9	2·47	1642·2
34. South Lanarks.	90·8	0·68	115·6
35. Peeblesshire	83·2	1·18	99·1
36. Dunbar area	288·0	0·91	327·9
37. South Berwick	195·2	0·49	211·8
38. Kelso area	186·1	1·23	221·1
39. Hawick area	104·6	1·07	134·0
40. Inner Dumfries, Kirkcudbright	51·3	0·26	54·9
41. South Dumfries	144·2	0·81	185·3
42. South Kirkcudbright	115·0	0·24	122·5
43. Wigtown and south tip of Ayr	83·5	0·25	90·2

1.1 DISTRICT AND PARISH BOUNDARIES

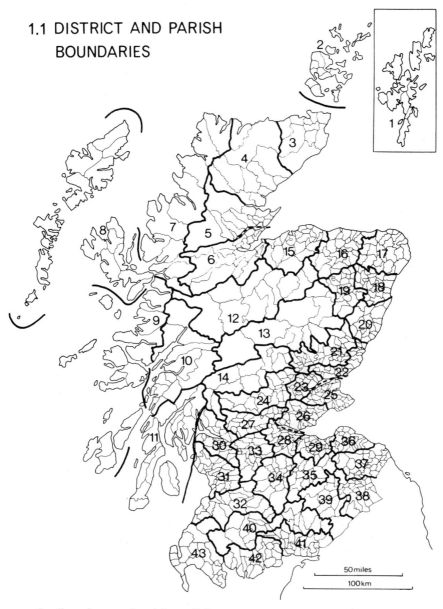

See discussion on p. 5, and Appendix I.
The districts are those used throughout the tables.
For key, see facing page.

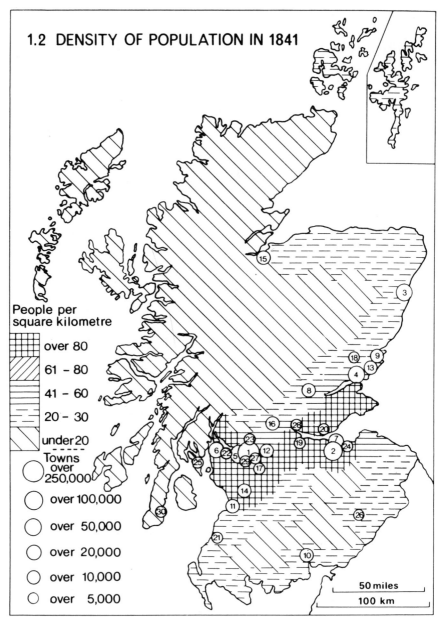

1.2 DENSITY OF POPULATION IN 1841

People per
square kilometre

over 80
61 – 80
41 – 60
20 – 30
under 20

Towns
over
250,000

over 100,000
over 50,000
over 20,000
over 10,000
over 5,000

50 miles
100 km

See discussion on pp. 6–7.
The density of population is exclusive of the numbered towns.
For key, see facing page.

KEY to MAP 1.2

TOWNS OVER 5,000 INHABITANTS IN 1941

1.	Glasgow	274,533
2.	Edinburgh	138,182
3.	Aberdeen	64,778
4.	Dundee	60,553
5.	Paisley	60,487
6.	Greenock	36,135
7.	Leith	26,433
8.	Perth	19,293
9.	Montrose	13,402
10.	Dumfries	13,299
11.	Ayr	12,746
12.	Airdrie	12,418
13.	Arbroath	12,313
14.	Kilmarnock	12,232
15.	Inverness	12,100
16.	Stirling	11,699
17.	Hamilton	8,876
18.	Forfar	8,362
19.	Falkirk	8,209
20.	Dunfermline	7,865
21.	Girvan	7,424
22.	Port Glasgow	6,973
23.	Kirkintilloch	6,698
24.	Musselburgh	6,331
25.	Rothesay	5,789
26.	Hawick	5,770
27.	Rutherglen	5,623
28.	Alloa	5,434
29.	Pollockshaws	5,283
30.	Campbeltown	5,028

N.B. It is sometimes difficult to decide on the natural boundaries of towns: normally the definitions of the 1841 census have been followed, but Ayr includes Newtown, Dumfries Maxwelltown, Arbroath St Vigeans and Inverbrothock, Stirling St Ninians: and 3,000 has been added to the burgh of Inverness from the very populous enveloping parish. Paisley is the entire parish, not merely the Parliamentary burgh.

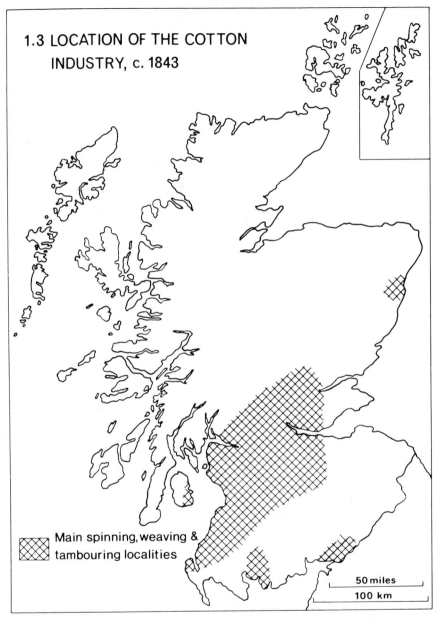

1.3 LOCATION OF THE COTTON
    INDUSTRY, c. 1843

Main spinning, weaving &
tambouring localities

50 miles
100 km

See discussion on pp. 7–8.

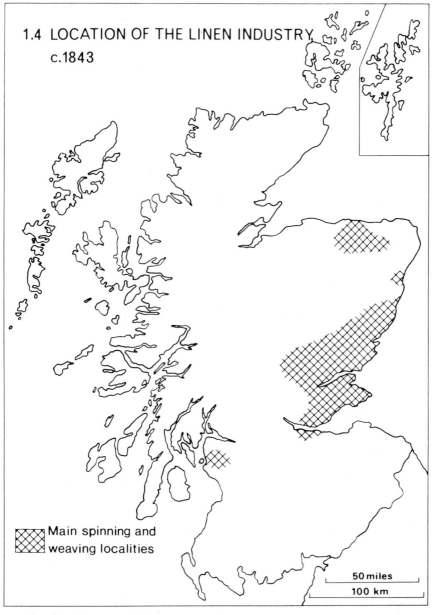

1.4 LOCATION OF THE LINEN INDUSTRY
c.1843

Main spinning and
weaving localities

50 miles
100 km

See discussion on pp. 7–8.

1.5 LOCATION OF THE WOOLLEN
     INDUSTRY, c. 1843

Main spinning, weaving &
knitting localities

50 miles

100 km

See discussion on pp. 7–8.

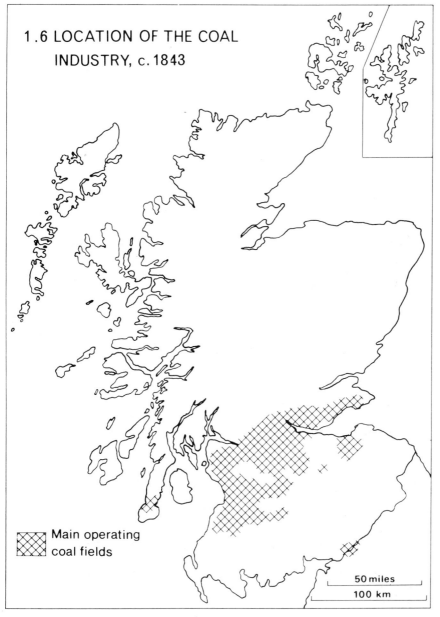

1.6 LOCATION OF THE COAL
INDUSTRY, c. 1843

Main operating
coal fields

50 miles
100 km

See discussion on pp. 7–8.

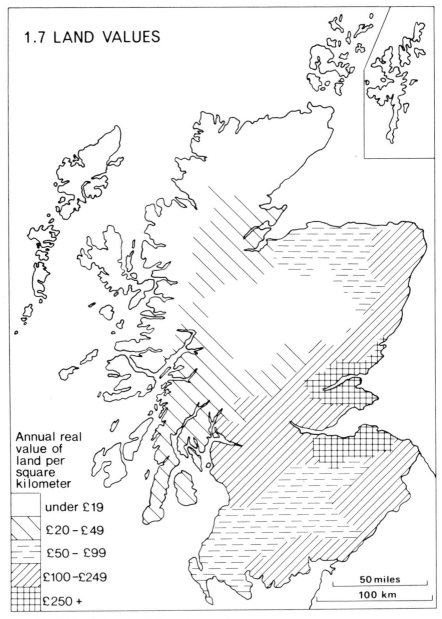

1.7 LAND VALUES

Annual real
value of
land per
square
kilometer

under £19
£20 – £49
£50 – £99
£100 – £249
£250 +

50 miles
100 km

See Table 1.A (p. 12) and discussion on p. 8.
Urban land and mineral rights are excluded.

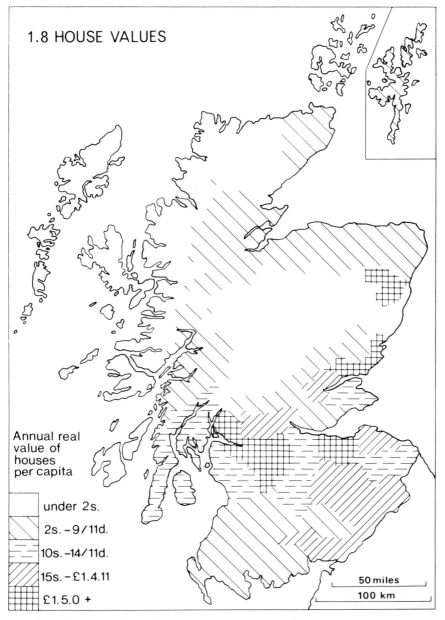

1.8 HOUSE VALUES

Annual real
value of
houses
per capita

under 2s.

2s. – 9/11d.

10s. –14/11d.

15s. – £1.4.11

£1.5.0 +

50 miles

100 km

See Table 1.A (p. 12) and discussion on p. 8.

Chapter 2

FOOD

What was the food of the Scottish working-class in the middle decades of the nineteenth century? Contemporaries gave some generalised accounts, of which that of the lunacy commissioners in 1857 was perhaps the best informed: they were interested in diet because they believed inadequate food to be a common cause of madness.[1]

> The diet of the poor in Scotland varies considerably in different districts. In the Highlands it principally consists of oatmeal and potatoes with the occasional addition of fish; but on the west coast and in the Western Isles the supplies, even of this food, are scanty, and the people are often bordering on starvation. On the whole, the Highland population must be considered as poorly fed. In the rural districts of the Lowlands, also, oatmeal and potatoes constitute the chief part of the diet of the peasantry, with the addition of milk and garden vegetables. Bread is occasionally used, but butcher-meat very seldom forms part of the living. The cottars, generally, both in the Highlands and Lowlands, have small patches of potato or garden ground.
>
> In the manufacturing villages and country towns, bread and tea have, to some extent, especially with the women, taken the place of porridge; but, with the men and children, porridge and buttermilk still constitute the general morning and evening meal. Broth and potatoes, with fish when it is plentiful, or perhaps bread, form the usual dinner of the manufacturing classes in such localities. In the large towns, such as Glasgow, the consumption of butcher-meat has latterly greatly increased, and the high wages of the mechanics are frequently entirely expended on their living.

This broad sketch emphasises the heavy dependence of the population on a limited range of food, especially oatmeal and potatoes, and the relative deficiency in animal protein. It also points to great regional variation both in the items of food eaten and the inadequacy of the diets. We can examine that regional variation in greater detail by using the answers to Question 19 of the Poor Law Inquiry questionnaire, which ran as follows:

> Q. 19. On what articles of food do the labouring classes of your parish principally subsist?

To this they received 821 replies (a 91 per cent. response rate). This can be compared to the responses on food in the *New Statistical Account*, where there were replies from only 119 parishes (13 per cent. of the whole). Plainly analysis of the questionnaire allows for a more subtle study of regional variation, but it is very useful to have supplementary information from the *NSA*.

It is worth pausing to consider the relationship between the two sources. The Poor Law questionnaire gave little space to reply and asked very specifically for the principal items of working-class diet. The *NSA* data were also gathered in response to a questionnaire, though that has been lost and the wording is consequently unknown. We may hazard the guess that it was less specific: perhaps it asked the ministers simply to 'comment on the food eaten in your parish' without any emphasis either on 'principally' or 'the labouring classes'. Certainly if one compares the items mentioned in the two sources (see Table 2.A, columns 1 and 3), although the rank order is remarkably similar (which gives one confidence in the relative national importance of different foods as shown by both) the *NSA* scores higher for virtually every item of food except oatmeal. This exception is probably accounted for by a slight over-representation in the *NSA* of Highland parishes where meal was consumed less often than elsewhere. The higher scores otherwise are due to more items being mentioned for most *NSA* parishes than for 1843 parishes: either the *NSA* respondents were including extra items which the common people fairly often enjoyed but which could not be reckoned as a 'principal food', or they were including items which those slightly higher up the scale than 'the labouring classes' (for instance, farmers) might put on their regular diet. It is as well to remember that the absence of a foodstuff from a district in our tables does not mean that it was never tasted there, though it probably does mean that it was comparatively unimportant. For instance, from the questionnaire answers we can find no tea drinking in the far north, though several ministers in their verbal evidence before the Commissioners referred to it. Indeed, a stray piece of information in the *NSA* tells us that in Shetland $1\frac{1}{2}$ lb. of tea a head were consumed a year: enough, no doubt, to be a comfort, but perhaps not enough to make it a 'principal food' in its own right (*NSA*, XV, Shetland, p. 158).

The 1843 data show many interesting features. To take the farinaceous items of diet first (Table 2.B, Maps 2. 1–4), the dominance of oatmeal is confirmed as virtually universal except in the western Highlands. Taking the country as a whole 'meal' or 'oatmeal' is mentioned in 95 per cent. of the responding parishes – a top score shared only with potatoes. In the Highlands and Islands (beyond Perthshire at least) the percentage drops distinctly, however; and if one excludes the numerous replies in this region which are qualified in a way that implies that oatmeal is eaten only infrequently, at certain times of the year or by a certain minority, the percentage score drops to under half or a third in the Hebrides and along the western seaboard. Oats, of course, grew poorly in this area, the minister of Alvie (Inverness) remarking that 'all the meal' the tenants could raise would not keep them alive for more than a third of the year (*NSA*, Inverness, 90).

Wheat (together with 'loafbread' which seems to imply wheat) was the next most widely consumed grain, but only with 11 per cent. of parishes reporting it. The regional distribution was very striking. All the districts where more than a quarter of the parishes mentioned wheat lay in the central belt, with a particularly heavy concentration of wheat-eaters around the Firth of Forth where most was grown. At Dairsie in Fife the minister said that even the paupers 'all . . . use wheaten bread', and contrasted it with Farr in Sutherland where he had also worked and where 'they subsist principally upon oatmeal and potatoes, and very often no oatmeal' (22.270). There were no wheat-eating parishes at all reported north of Kincardineshire, and in many instances references to wheat-eating were qualified by the remark that it was infrequent.

Barleymeal and barley bread were reported in almost as many parishes as wheat, but their distribution was quite different and more diffuse. Bere (primitive barley) was sometimes used as a bread grain in bleak northern and western localities where even oats had difficulty growing: Barra and Uist were such places (*NSA*, XIV, Inverness, 171–2, 209). More often barley was a supplement to other grains, and the main concentrations of barley-eating parishes were in the far north (especially Orkney) and in the extreme southeast. This pattern, of course, takes no account of the use of 'pot-barley' as a constituent of broth which was probably more widespread: but 'pot-barley' could hardly be described as a principal item of food. The consumption of peasemeal (often in a composite 'mashlem bread' with barleymeal) was entirely restricted in the south of Scotland, and very heavily concentrated in the extreme south-east, in Berwickshire and East Lothian.

Table 2.C (and Maps 2.5–6) show the other vegetable constituents of diet, and fish. Potatoes, like oatmeal, occurred in 95 per cent. of all parishes. There were, however, four contiguous districts in the north-east where the score was distinctly lower – they were a more expensive food here, and it is possible that the more severe climate made them difficult to keep in winter storage.

What the tables do not reveal, however, is the great difference in the relative importance of the potatoes in working-class diets between the western Highlands and the south of Scotland: in the former area, according to the Committee on Famine Relief in 1846, they accounted for 75 per cent. or more of the food eaten; in the latter, only 25 per cent.[2] Although almost all Scots ate potatoes at some point in their daily meals, to rely upon potatoes was everywhere a mark of extreme poverty. Thus at Portree on Skye 'no people on earth live on more simple or scanty diet . . . the greater number of them subsist on potatoes, sometimes with but oftener without fish', and at Bracadale on the same island 'they are generally not considered ill-provided who can feed on potatoes and salt' (*NSA*, XIV, Inverness, 226, 297). In the Small Isles a family would consume 240 to 320 bushels a year: assuming 8 people to a family (the figure given in the *NSA* for neighbouring North Uist) this would work out at $4\frac{1}{2}$ to 6 lbs. a day per head averaged over the adults and the children – a figure consistent with Salaman's estimates of what it takes to keep a person alive on a potato diet (*NSA*, XIV, Inverness, 153).[3] Another estimate, for an able-bodied labourer in full employment in the mainland parish of Urquhart, suggested a more ample daily diet of 8 to 10 lb. of potatoes, plus a half pound of oatmeal and a quart of milk (21.39). Even in the south, though, it was clear that the poorest lived largely on potatoes – as at Arbroath, where 'potatoes with a sprinkling of salt have in many instances been almost the only species of food attainable in families', or in Whithorn where 'potatoes are the principal food of Irish families during three quarters of the year' (*NSA*, XI, Forfar, 85; Wigtown, 36).

Almost the only vegetables specially in the 1843 report apart from potatoes were cabbages and what are variously described as 'greens' and 'kail'. Their consumption, though quite widespread, was not heavy except in the north-east, appropriately the traditional home of the 'kailyard novel'; here the same four districts that report fewer potatoes report eating greenstuffs far more frequently than anywhere else. Four parishes only report turnips – all in the north-east – and one ate onions. The *NSA* certainly gives a more generous overall impression of the consumption of vegetables, and we know that throughout Scotland most farm-workers who lived in cottages also had gardens where they could grow greens and roots apart from potatoes. But (as evidence elsewhere in the 1843 questionnaire shows) the gardens were normally small. Perhaps they provided a few handfuls of food to go in the broth but hardly enough all-round sustenance for the reporters to feel justified in describing vegetables as a 'principal food'. A commentator in Orkney said there was hardly a cottage in the islands without a kailyard, but 'cabbage is not such a very common article of food as formerly. Perhaps to a certain extent, it has been succeeded by potatoes' (21.260).

Fish was an extremely important item of diet from Shetland all the way down the west coast and islands to Argyll, scoring in these districts 90 per cent, on average, much higher than oatmeal or any other food except potatoes. Everywhere else it was widely eaten in coastal parishes, but with comparatively limited inland sales. On the islands it was often extremely cheap. Saithe in Orkney could provide a meal for a family for as little as a halfpenny (in old money); and was sometimes given away (20.727; 21.236). Herring was, however, the usual fish specified, although in the south-east its consumption was said to have fallen, perhaps because it was partly replaced by pork. Highlanders also ate large quantities of cockles and other shellfish – an age-old expedient in famines as far back as the seventeenth century, but one which in some districts now appears to have become general even in ordinary seasons (21.301; 22.394).

Milk, dairy goods and tea are described in Table 2.D and Maps 2.7–9. Most oatmeal was eaten as porridge, which would seem to imply that milk was normally used with it, yet there was much more variation in the percentage of parishes reporting milk as a principal food than there was in those reporting meal. All but one of the districts where more than half the parishes reported milk in this way lay north of a line from Glasgow to Dundee; Argyll, Caithness and the north-east being particularly fond of it. The smallest consumption appears to have been in the Lothians and parts of the Borders, where tea was most popular. It is reasonable to suppose that these dry areas, good for grain and fatstock raised on turnips, had fewest cows. On the other hand references to hinds being allowed to keep cows for their own use are rather commoner in the south-east than in most parts of the Lowlands.

Heavy consumption of cheese and butter, by contrast, lay mainly in the western half of the central belt, especially in North Lanarkshire, North Ayrshire and the adjacent districts, the home of the Ayrshire cow and the Dunlop cheese. It is hard to tell whether most of the milk was manufactured here, or whether workers perhaps drank more fresh milk in these dairy areas than appears from the tables. Cheese and butter were, of course, eaten in other places, but very irregularly in the Highlands even though a good deal was made there. Thus at Alvie it was reported that butter and cheese 'they must sell to pay the rent', at Croy that 'poultry, butter and eggs are all for the market' and at Glenshiel that 'butter and cheese, though favourite articles, they can rarely indulge in' (*NSA*, XIV, Inverness, 91; *ibid.*, Ross and Cromarty, 202). Caithness appears to have been a little better off, but not Orkney.

Tea and coffee are amalgamated in our table: in fact coffee was not mentioned apart from tea, and most of the references are to tea alone. In the 1843 report only one parish in ten considered either to be a 'principal food' of the labouring classes, and they were heavily concentrated south of the Tay. Only in four districts, covering the Edinburgh area and parts of the south-east, did as many as 30 per cent. of the parishes report tea. The *NSA*, on the other hand, reports tea in 24 per cent. of all parishes, and suggests a distribution that included Lowland parishes far to the north – like Knockando in Moray where 'tea and sugar are rapidly gaining ground' and Alvah in Banffshire where tea was used by poor old women 'to a great, perhaps to an injurious extent' (*NSA*, XIII, Elgin, 73; *ibid.*, Banff, 165). Interestingly, too, in the verbal evidence heard before the Commissioners in 1843 there are many references to tea-drinking even by paupers, and some of these come from the north-east – Banchory, Turiff, Aboyne and Deer where 'they cannot do without their tea' (21.634; 21.714; 21.728; 21.730). There are also references to Orkney and Shetland and to the Isle of Arran (21.185–6; 21.236; 21.92; 21.109), but neither source suggests that elsewhere the common Highlander could afford it. In short, there seems to have been a tripartite pattern, with heavy tea-drinking in the south of Scotland, especially in the south-east, moderate tea-drinking elsewhere in the Lowlands and the far north (but not to the extent that it could often be considered a staff of life), and no tea-drinking at all in the Highlands.

It is also interesting how often tea-drinking was associated with women, and sometimes specifically with factory women: but it was also said that the habit was spreading to men and tending to replace the consumption of home-brewed beer. The factor to the Earl of Stair in Wigtownshire even believed that the wives of Irish labourers in the county were so addicted to tea that they 'scrimp their families in food for the purpose of procuring it' (22.525). Sugar was mentioned in 10 parishes in the 1843 questionnaire, all in tea-drinking districts; the relative paucity of references suggests that Scots often took tea as they took porridge, unsweetened. Paupers, however, sometimes used molasses in their tea as a cheap substitute for sugar (21.728).

Beer or ale was mentioned as an item of food in only 13 parishes: all but one of these lay in the north-east, though we know that the old traditions of of home-brewing were also strong in Orkney. The body of the Poor Law Report and the *NSA* also, of course, contain innumerable denunciations of alcoholic drink especially in industrial areas where whisky was regarded as a drug and a threat to working-class happiness. The patterns of licensed drink-sellers' distribution are considered in Chapter 6 below (pp. 135–8).

The consumption of meat (Table 2.E, Maps 2.10–12) provides one of the most intriguing regional distributions of all. The type of meat was itself specified in less than two-thirds of parishes reporting meat-eating, but those reporting pigmeat (generally as pork, sometimes as bacon or ham) outnumbered those reporting beef and those reporting mutton by nine to one. Cows and sheep evidently paid the rent and made a profit for the farmer, but apparently did not feed the working-class except to a minor degree; but the married farm labourer with a garden and a cottage was, in many parts of the eastern Lowlands from Caithness southwards, encouraged to keep a pig and feed it on potato waste. In Orkney and Iona (but not elsewhere) the Commissioners discovered pigs in the homes of the poor. 'They take up their place by the firesides', explained the minister of South Ronaldsay (21.136; 21.226). Pigmeat consumption was reported from all parts of the country except the western Highlands (though they were kept in Argyll – 20.776) and the heartlands of the north-east, but it occurred in over half the parishes only in Fife, East Lothian, and parts of Lanarkshire, Perth and Berwickshire. Beef-eating was relatively most common in industrial North Lanarkshire, where it must have been bought over the counter with high wages: mutton-eating, by contrast, was most common around Peebles and in parts of upland Perthshire where it was farm produce. In some parishes the working-class got only the flesh of dead or diseased sheep, 'braxy mutton' as it was called – 'very wholesome food, though those not accustomed to it would not think so', the minister of Morvern in Argyll assured the Commissioners (21.179). References to poultry are surprisingly unusual, being mentioned in only four parishes (eggs are mentioned in only six); rabbits are also occasional. The *NSA* for Stevenston in Ayrshire refers to 500 dozen rabbits killed in the parish annually, which sounds a lot but works out at less than two a year per head of population (*NSA*, V, Ayr, 460).

Is it true that the Scots as a whole ate little meat, as the comment of the lunacy commissioners with which we began seems to imply? In the 1843 replies meat-eating was reported from almost half the parishes, albeit with wide variations between districts and regions. Low percentages were characteristic of the north-east and the west Highland coast, though they exceeded 40 per cent. in parts of the central Highlands and the far north. High percentages were characteristic of the area south of the Tay and the Firth of Clyde, especially along the east coast and in Lanarkshire where they ranged from 80 to 90 per cent. The south-west hit about the mean. However, meat (like wheat, or oatmeal in the Highlands) was often qualified in the answers to the questionnaire with the comment 'sometimes', 'a little': if one ignores those answers and considers only the replies without qualification as those properly denoting meat as a 'major' foodstuff the picture changes. Only 27 per cent. of parishes report meat in this way. North of Angus the only district with more than 25 per cent. of parishes reporting 'major' meat was Orkney. South of Angus the only districts with more than 50 per cent. reporting 'major' meat were in Fife, East Lothian, Lanarkshire, Berwickshire and parts of Perthshire – broadly, the areas where pig-meat was commonest. In some parts of the south, for instance near Edinburgh, in the east-central Lowlands and in the western Borders, the percentage fell below 20. Considered in this light, it does seem likely that meat was not a prominent part of most people's diet in most parts of the country. It was only where there were concentrations of pig-keepers or affluent workers that this impression needs to be modified.

Local variations in diet, then, were very pronounced: it is worth summarising briefly some of their main features. The far north (Caithness and the northern isles) was palpably better fed than the Highlands, with more meat, two kinds of meal, a lot of fish, and green vegetables to go with their potatoes: Orkney was probably best off in this region, and Shetland worst. The northern Highlands and, particularly, the western Highlands and the Hebrides include the worst-fed districts in the entire country, with little to eat but potatoes and fish, supplemented by milk and a little meal: this was to be the core area of the famine in 1846. Diet distinctly improved throughout Argyll, with more milk and more meat; it was also better in the central Highlands in these respects, and, though they lacked fish, there was distinctly more meal there.

The north-east was different again. It had abundant supplies of oatmeal and drank more milk than anywhere else, but made no use of either barley-meal or wheat and little of cheese or butter, though there was fish for the coastal parishes. It consumed great quantities of green vegetables but relatively fewer potatoes than elsewhere. Home-brewed beer survived as a household food in some localities at least. Tea was not often listed as a principal item of diet here or elsewhere in northern Scotland, though its use may have been spreading.

Descending to lowland Perthshire, Angus and Fife one begins to discover the indications of the typical southern Scottish diet, still basically rooted in oatmeal and potatoes but with more meat, especially pork in southern Perthshire and Fife, and similarly with more parishes reporting tea as important. Wheat becomes significant for the first time in Fife, especially in the west of the county; fish was important on the east side of Fife because so much of it was coastal. Throughout the Lowlands fish was important on the coast.

South of the Forth there are intriguing variations. The Edinburgh area drank a lot of tea and ate a lot of wheat bread (as well as oatmeal and potatoes) but apparently ate little meat. The south-eastern districts had a more varied diet than anywhere else in Scotland, consuming plenty of barleymeal and almost all the peasemeal that was eaten in the country, but wheat was common here only in East Lothian: the south-east also partook generously of meat and tea. Further west along the Borders the consumption of meat (as well as of wheat, barleymeal and peasemeal) thins out quickly: especially in Dumfries and Kirkcudbright food becomes poor and unvaried, more often a matter of oatmeal and potatoes. On the other hand in the west-central industrial belt of Clydeside and the adjacent districts it becomes diversified again: the biggest consumption of cheese and butter is heavily concentrated here, and some districts here eat a lot of meat (though not particularly large quantities of wheat bread or tea).

Was there at this date a special 'urban diet' which differed from that of the countryside? In the early twentieth century, it was commonly stated that the towns ate bread, potatoes and tea, while the countryside kept to a more nutritious diet in which oatmeal still played a large part.[4] The absence of reports in 1843 from the largest burghs, such as Glasgow, Edinburgh and Paisley, makes it difficult to test this proposition directly. On the other hand we do have reports from 20 urban parishes in 14 burghs of 10,000 inhabitants or over, including Aberdeen, Dundee, Greenock and Kilmarnock.[5] In Table 2.A comparison of the first two columns shows how these parishes differed from Scotland as a whole: the towns indeed consumed rather more bread and tea, but neither bread nor tea was of major importance. Oatmeal, on the other hand, and potatoes, were universally consumed in the towns, and generally town diet looks very similar in its overall pattern to country diet in the parishes around. If there was more fish it was because so many towns lay on or near the coast: if there was less meat reported as a 'major' item of diet it was probably because people found it something of a challenge to keep pigs in tenements. Individual towns were, indeed, often more like the surrounding parishes than they were like other communities of a similar size lying at a distance. Ayr, for instance, was typical of Ayrshire in reporting consumption of dairy goods; Hamilton was typical of North Lanarkshire in reporting consumption of beef; Aberdeen (with Old Machar) and Inverness typical of the north in reporting neither bread nor tea.

Some independent confirmation that oatmeal was still more important than bread in town diet comes from institutional diet sheets: Scottish prison food, for example, consisted of oatmeal, potatoes, milk, broth and a portion of wheaten bread. Bread was generally expected to form between a seventh and a third of the total nutrition, but was also sometimes omitted altogether. Oatmeal was never omitted; one of the three meals a day was always porridge, and the other porridge or potatoes.[6] In poorhouses the main item of expenditure on food was meal: at Paisley, for instance, £347 were spent on meal, with £105 on the next most important item, buttermilk, cheese and butter, again reflecting the local character of an important dairy component in the diet (20.573). In lunatic asylums the position was much the same – working-class patients subsisted mainly on porridge with soup and potatoes, but also with some meat, green vegetables, bread and tea: because madness was often associated with under-nourishment, asylum food was reckoned to be better than what the labouring classes lived on outside.[7] Certainly the 'weekly expenditure of a Glasgow weaver' investigated by the handloom weavers' committee in 1834 included nothing for meat or green vegetables, or for bread; two-thirds of the sum allowed for food went on meal, milk and potatoes, and the rest on small quantities of cheese, herrings, sugar, salt and tea. But other Glasgow workers were apparently better off in good times, and particulars given for a weaver in Dundee show that he spent about 60 per cent. of his food budget on meal, milk and potatoes but did manage to include beef and wheat bread in the family diet.[8]

The evidence of the 1903 Glasgow municipal commission on housing the poor provides clear evidence that the change from an oatmeal (porridge) diet to a wheat (and tea) diet came about in that city in the last third of the nineteenth century, and that it was mainly due to price changes. The price of a sack of 280 lb. of oatmeal had fallen from 37 shillings to 31 shillings (by 16 per cent.) between 1857 and 1903, but the price of the same quantity of wheat flour had dropped from 46 shillings to 22 shillings (by 52 per cent.) in the same period; the price of an ounce of tea fell by 64 per cent. As one witness put it in 1903: 'Oatmeal is now a luxury and flour a cheap article ... my friend told me that in Centre Street in a morning he would sell as much as he now sells in a fortnight.'[9]

Recently, it has been suggested that wheat-eating was almost as important as oat-eating in Scotland by 1850, with a ratio of consumption between the two grains of perhaps 44 : 50.[10] The weight of the 1843 evidence and of other contemporary reports is, however, decidedly against so large a role for wheat. It is true that the wheat-eating districts were populous: about 30 per cent. of the total Scottish population lived in the 8 districts where more than a fifth of the parishes reported wheat-eating. It is also true that we have fewer records for the towns than we would like, though this omission can be partially remedied from other sources, as we have seen. But the evidence for anything like parity between wheat-eating and oat-eating is extremely slender. One bald contemporary statement that there were a million wheat-eaters in Scotland can only be a mere guess.[11] The suggestion that in the 1840s fewer people ate wheat bread than in better times before and later, while no doubt true, refers only to a contrast between the worst years of cyclical depressions and the best years of booms, and even then mainly to better-paid workers. Trade conditions at the end of 1843 were much better than they had been in 1842, and at no time was there a hint that people had recently switched from wheat bread to oatmeal or back again. An alternative ratio of wheat consumption to oat consumption of about 25 : 70 would be a better reflection of mid-century conditions.

What were the main determining elements in the patterns of Scottish diet in the 1840s? Perhaps most important was simply what was produced in the neighbourhood. Wheat grew best where most eaten; oats grew worst where eaten least. Ayrshire was the home of the dairy cow and the Dunlop cheese. Fish was eaten in seaside parishes. Pork and bacon were especially eaten in those eastern districts where cottagers kept pigs. Despite the emphasis rightly given by economic historians to the commerce in foodstuffs – the corn trade and the cattle trade – the food of most working-class Scots had probably moved no great distance from producer to consumer. In some districts, indeed, diet was largely a function of how the farmer paid his men: in the south-east hinds were paid in so many bolls of unground oats, barley and peas, along with milk and potatoes, and therefore ate these commodities; in Fife and Angus ploughmen and bothy-workers were paid in oatmeal and milk and sometimes potatoes but not barley or peasemeal – so they consumed the first three commodities but not the last two (see also Chapter 4 below).

Diet was, however, also a matter of the level of wages. The north-west Highlands were worst fed not only because few crops grew in that harsh climate, but also because they had to forgo much of what they produced themselves in meat, cheese and butter in order to pay the rent: and they could seldom afford to enter the market for any external foodstuffs. North Lanark-shire, however, ate relatively heavily of beef and dairy goods not because herds of cattle roamed the industrial belt but because the best-paid workers were concentrated round the iron-works and the coalfields: they could cer-tainly afford to buy butcher meat that might have been raised in those dis-tricts of Aberdeenshire which were also vegetarian because poor. Sometimes one sees a neat combination of locality and income effects: wheat grew best round the Firth of Forth, but most wheat was eaten in the Edinburgh area and in West Fife where there was industry and high incomes; cheese was made in Lanarkshire and Ayrshire but most was eaten in the northern halves of both counties where there was more industrialisation. The information on regional wage levels in the 1843 questionnaire is discussed in Chapters 4 and 5.

Both the 1843 report and the *NSA* frequently remark on the high income elasticity of demand for such items as meat, and on the way certain foods were associated with certain occupations. Thus even in the north at Golspie 'tradesmen and others occasionally use a little wheaten bread, and a little butter, cheese and tea', and at Inverness the 'wealthier tradesmen' ate fish and butcher meat (*NSA*, XV, Sutherland, 35; XIV, Inverness, 19). In the south in mining districts it was often the colliers who ate the meat; they were both well paid compared to other workers and might be said to need it on account of the heavy nature of their work. At Duns it was the artizans who were said to pur-chase beef or mutton occasionally; in Peebles it was a case of 'butcher meat when wages are good'. In Dunbartonshire at Old Kilpatrick it was observed that factory workers both required and obtained better food than agricultural workers; at New Kilpatrick the differences were exemplified in greater detail: 'oatmeal, both in the form of porridge and of cakes, potatoes, milk and cheese, barley broth with butcher meat or herring are the ordinary food of the peasantry. Wheaten bread, butter, tea and coffee are in more common use with the villagers.' In this case the villagers were cotton-spinners and calico-printers (*NSA*, VII, Dumbarton, 24, 52). In Angus at Mains and Strathmartine the farm-workers in their bothies lived on milk and oatmeal, the poor on potatoes alone for half the year, but the 'tradesmen' added fish, butcher meat, pork of their own rearing, sugar and tea (*NSA*, XI, Forfar, 59). At Larbert in Stirlingshire the manufacturing population ate wheat bread but the farm-workers oatcake and barleybread (*NSA*, VIII, Stirling, 365). At Ochiltree in Ayrshire tea-drinking was confined to families of mechanics and not practised by the peasantry; at Leslie and Ruthven in Fife it was the habit of factory women, but at Auchterarder in Perthshire tea was used by the whole population 'as often as they can afford it'; on the other hand at Kirkmaiden in Wigtownshire tea and loaf bread were being consumed only because changes in the local farming system had made it hard for the farm-worker to obtain milk for his porridge, and at Westruther in Berwickshire tea had been introduced during the dearth of 1800 (perhaps as a substitute for ale) and spread since that time (*NSA*, V, Ayr, 110; IV, Wigtown, 210; II, Berwick, 77). In Selkirk old women paupers lived on tea and potatoes – 'they very seldom can afford a dinner. They get tea in the morning and tea in the afternoon, and they can fast longer upon tea than upon porridge' (22.651).

Details of this kind make it clear that there is no single reason why people consumed one foodstuff rather than another. Habit and fashion entered the picture as well as locality and income. Some people went on eating barley fadges mainly because mother used to make them; some spent money on tea, which they could perhaps ill afford, just because they had acquired a taste for it. The argument that by 1900 people had gone onto a bread-and-tea diet instead of one with porridge in it because of the time and trouble it took to cook porridge is plainly wrong. It takes as long and uses as much fuel to make tea as to make porridge; furthermore, bothy workers and others kept cold porridge in a drawer and removed it in slices to eat as occasion required.

In the last analysis, however, locality and income were more important than habit and fashion. As a commentator at Applegarth, Dumfriesshire, put it, the tenantry might be able to enjoy tea and coffee and meat with their dinner, but 'to the man whose day's wages do not exceed 2s. the meal-chest and the potato bing must always be the great resource' (*NSA*, IV, Dumfries, 186).

It is a weakness in both our sources that so little is said about the actual quantities of what was consumed that it is difficult to reach any new conclusions about nutrition. On the other hand they do contain some interesting reports on which items of food were eaten at the different meals: altogether 40 parishes reported in this way, 4 in the western Highlands, 5 on the eastern seaboard between Caithness and Easter Ross, and 31 in the Lowlands south of mid-Angus; to this one can add contemporary descriptions of Orcadian meals, those of a calico-printer at Bonhill north of Glasgow, and those of girls working at the Paisley bleach-fields.

The Highland meals indicate great poverty and lack of variety. That for Ullapool speaks of potatoes and salt herring three times a day (21.423); that for Lochcarron speaks of 'potatoes and herring twice a day, and oatmeal gruel for supper' (*NSA*, XIV, Ross, 111); that for Gigha of 'potatoes and fish or milk, generally twice in a day and often three times'; that for Morvern is even more striking (*NSA*, VII, Argyll, 401, 187):

> There are many, it is feared, much in the predicament of a little boy of the parish, who, on being asked on a certain occasion of what his three daily meals consisted gave the same unvarying answer, 'mashed potatoes', and on being further asked by his too inquisitive inquirer 'what else' replied with great artlessness but with evident surprise, 'a spoon'.

A minister travelling in Skye in July or August 1841 had entered a cottage where a woman was sitting in the middle of the floor with a pot; he was allowed to taste its contents, 'and the impression upon his mind at that time was, and is now, that human creatures could not subsist upon it' (21.761). July and early August was a hungry time in Skye as it was on Iona and Mull, after the old potatoes had been mainly eaten and before the new crop was gathered (21.125; 21.154): roots, cockles and all kinds of semi-edible refuse might have gone into that pot.

Maybe there is so little gratuitous information about meals in the north because in these circumstances one meal was none too clearly differentiated from another. On Tiree in November 1838 the population had resolved to make do with one meal a day to save fuel and food: and though conditions had improved so much on Arran that the population in 1843 had three good varied meals a day like other southern rural parishes, people remembered a time when it was more truly 'Highland' and the tenants had only eaten once (20.730; 21.87).

In Orkney and the five coastal parishes south to the Beauly Firth the structure of meals was broadly as it was further south: breakfast was boiled sowans (an oatmeal-and-water pudding) or porridge and milk; dinner was fish and potatoes, or pork and kail; supper was mashed potatoes and milk, or kail and potatoes or 'knocked' corn.[12] The ingredients of the meals were also very similar along the coast down to Easter Ross (21.13, 21, 37, 56, 343).

The 31 replies from predominantly rural parishes in the south of Scotland are summarised in Table 2.F.[13] They again show three meals, each with a distinct character. Breakfast in every case was dominated by porridge: milk was explicitly mentioned as going with porridge in two-thirds of the instances, though beer and porridge are also mentioned three times; sugar, of course, never occurs. Tea, if it was taken, was generally consumed at this meal: other foods were not very common. Lunch was generally a matter of broth and potatoes, sometimes with bread of one sort or another, and fish or cheese as common alternatives to meat. It is difficult to be sure what went into the broth — presumably a few vegetables from the cottage gardens, pot barley, and small quantities of fat meat or meat-stock. The 1843 report from the weaving town of Dunfermline talks unpleasantly of broth from 'prepared tallow' and from Alford in the north-east there is mention of a soup made from greens, turnips and pot-barley without any meat content (*NSA*, XII, Aberdeen, 501). Supper was either porridge again or potatoes again, frequently with milk but not often with any other items. A fourth meal – tea – is mentioned in three instances: it was a mere cup and snack of bread or oatcakes.

This menu for the day represents, of course, the upper end of the rural working-class diet, with more meat and other protein than the norm. The rural southern Lowlands were in any case better fed than elsewhere, a point which an Orcadian commentator noticed when he compared the lethargy of the peasants around him with the energy of workmen further south – 'I think the want of activity arises partly . . . from the insufficient quality of their food'

(21.263). But even in the south it was common for the poorest to 'have sometimes nothing but potatoes to keep them from starvation' (*NSA*, IV, Dumfries,
251).

Perhaps we can sum up the differences within the working-class itself with
two contrasting quotations. The first is from W. P. Alison's account of how
paupers granted one shilling a week from the kirk session survived at St.
Andrews — 'one or two scanty meals of porridge or potatoes, with now and
then a little tea or thin broth, form the diet of the day with most of these
people'.[14] The other is from the 1843 report itself; a calico-worker at Alexandria in the Vale of Leven was giving evidence of how a skilled worker lived
when times were good (22.467):

> It is to be borne in mind, also, that the occupation of the calico printer
> is exhausting, and requires a better diet than that of the common agri-
> cultural labourer. I myself generally have for breakfast some porridge
> and milk, a little tea, a slice of bread and ham, and, as far as I can afford
> it, a little steak. For dinner I generally have broth; sometimes potatoes
> and milk; and I generally take tea at night, with bread and cheese, or
> bread and butter, with a slice of toast. This is a fair specimen of what
> calico printers would like to have; but I should say that a great number
> of them do not live quite so well . . .

That was rich living indeed; there is no evidence that many of the
working-class approached it very often. No doubt more typical was the food
of Highland girls employed at the bleaching-fields at Paisley — breakfast and
dinner consisted of potatoes with buttermilk or fish, and supper was porridge
and buttermilk. They drank no tea except on pay-day (20.676).

The 1843 data represent a snapshot from one moment in time. How had
things altered since the onset of the industrial and agrarian revolutions? It is
impossible to give a comprehensive answer without a survey in comparable
detail of the earlier period, for which the materials do not exist. Nevertheless
the *NSA* commentators make some comparison with former years, and with
the first *Statistical Account* of the 1790s. It was agreed that potatoes had become much more common, and not only in the Highlands: thus at Mains and
Strathmartine in Angus it was said that 'no article of food has increased so
much in consumption' (*NSA*, XI, Forfar, 59). With potatoes came the possibility of home-fed pork in the eastern Lowlands, which was plainly an
improvement on the eighteenth century. Some commentators said the consumption of butcher meat (more likely to be beef or mutton) had increased
within the last decade or so, the beginning of a trend that had plainly gone
further in 1857, when the lunacy commissioners made their general observation with which this chapter began.[15] Others spoke of greater consumption of
wheat bread and tea.[16]

Nevertheless, one lesson of this study must be that such changes (apart
from the introduction of potatoes) were of limited scope for the bulk of the
working-classes. If, in reply to the question 'on what articles of food do the
labouring classes of your parish principally subsist?' only about one quarter
were able to reply 'meat' without some qualification implying that it was in

some sense exceptional, and only one tenth to reply 'wheat bread', it is difficult to regard the changes as very sweeping. In the 1840s the Scottish working-class was barely beginning to reap any benefit from the modern economy they had done so much to construct: from the point of view of what they ate they had infinitely more in common with the standards of the pre-industrial past than with the standards of the present century.

REFERENCES

1. *Report of the Royal Commission on Lunatic Asylums (Scotland)*, P.P. 1857, vol. 5, pp. 82–3.
2. A. Fenton, *Scottish Country Life* (Edinburgh, 1976), p. 117. This rough proportion is confirmed by evidence on hinds' allowances elsewhere in the 1843 questionnaire.
3. R. N. Salaman, *The History and Social Influence of the Potato* (Cambridge, 1949), pp. 124–5.
4. D. N. Paton, J. C. Dunlop, E. M. Inglis, *A Study of the Diet of the Labouring Classes in Edinburgh* (Edinburgh, n.d.); D. E. Lindsay, *Report upon a Study of the Diet of the Labouring Classes in the City of Glasgow* (Glasgow, 1913).
5. The burghs are Falkirk, Dumfries, Ayr (with St. Quivox and Newton), Kilmarnock, Greenock, Hamilton, Airdrie (New Monkland), Stirling (with St. Ninians), Dunfermline, Dundee, Montrose, Arbroath (with St. Vigeans and Inverbrothick), Aberdeen (with Old Machar) and Inverness.
6. *Fourth Report of the Board of Directors of Prisons in Scotland*, P.P. 1843, vol. 77, Appendix, p. 48.
7. P.P. 1857, vol. 5, Appendix, pp. 184–96.
8. See Norman Murray. *The Scottish Handloom Weavers, 1790–1850*, (Edinburgh, 1978), pp. 100–2.
9. *Glasgow Municipal Commission on the Housing of the Poor, Minutes of Evidence*, vol. I (1903), pp. 337–8.
10. E. J. T. Collins, 'Dietary Change and Cereal Consumption in Britain in the Nineteenth Century', *Agricultural History Review*, vol. 23 (1975), pp. 109–11, 114.
11. J. Dudgeon, 'On a Method of Obtaining Correct Statistics of Agricultural Produce', *Quarterly Journal of Agriculture*, vol. XVII (1849–51), p. 367; Collins, *loc. cit.*, pp. 111–12.
12. Fenton, *op. cit.*, p. 169.
13. The localities concerned are, from 1843 reports, Cameron, Carmyle, Kirkinner, Lanark, Lochwinnoch (also in *NSA*), Ochiltree, Pettinain; from *NSA*, Broughton, Crosshill, Cummertrees, Dalry, Foulden, Innerwick, Kelton, Killearn, Kirkmaiden, Kirkpatrick Fleming, Lauder, Manor, Morham, Newbattle, Penpont, Roxburgh, Stenton, Tibbermore; from the 1843 volumes of spoken evidence, Kilmory and Kilbride (Arran), Carron, Kilwinning (22.497), Foodie by Cupar, and the St. Andrews area.
14. W. P. Alison, 'Illustrations of the Practical Operation of the Scottish System of Management of the Poor', *Journal of the Royal Statistical Society*, vol. III (1840), p. 229.
15. E.g., *NSA*, vol. IX, Fife, 224; vol. X, Perth, 1190; vol. VIII, Stirling, 365.
16. E.g., *NSA*, vol. IX, Fife, 224; vol. X, Perth, 276, 1190; vol. VI, Lanark, 34; vol. IV, Wigtown, 210; vol. II, Berwick, 77.

TABLE 2.A

*Percentages of Parishes naming Certain Foods in 1843 Poor Law Question-
naire and in New Statistical Account, All Scotland*

	In 1843 (all parishes) N = 821	In 1843 (town parishes) N = 20	In *NSA* N = 119
Oatmeal and 'meal'	95	100	83
Wheat and loafbread	11	20	20
Barleymeal and bread	10	—	21
Peasemeal and bread	3	—	3
Unspecified bread	2	5	6
Potatoes	95	100	92
Other vegetables	11	—	12
Fish	35	50	47
Milk	48	40	56
Cheese	8	10	12
Butter	6	15	9
Tea and coffee	10	20	21
Pigmeat	27	5	27
Beef	3	5	10
Mutton	3	—	10
All meat	49	45	55
All meat (major)	27	15	23
'Broth'	—	10	13

TABLE 2.B: GRAINS
Percentages of Parishes in each District reporting Each Food

(Figures in brackets omit all references implying the food was eaten only occasionally, in small quantities, seasonally, or by a minority of the labouring classes)

	Oatmeal or 'meal'	Wheat or loaf bread	Barley-meal or bread	Pease-meal	Unspecified bread	N
1. Shetland	92 (69)	—	15	—	—	13
2. Orkney	78	—	50	—	6	18
3. Caithness	92	—	25	—	—	12
4. East Sutherland	70 (60)	—	30	—	20	10
5. East Ross	93 (85)	—	—	—	—	14
6. N.-E. Inverness	100 (93)	—	—	—	7	15
7. North-west coast	50 (30)	—	8	—	—	10
8. Skye and Outer Hebrides	50 (36)	—	14	—	14	14
9. West Argyll	67 (47)	—	7	—	—	15
10. North Argyll	82 (73)	—	—	—	—	11
11. South Argyll	85	—	—	—	—	20
12. Highland Inverness, Banff, Moray	92	—	17	—	—	12
13. Highland Perth, Aberdeenshire	100 (90)	—	20	—	—	10
14. N.-W. Perth	100	—	14	7	—	14
15. Nairn, Lowland Moray	100 (95)	—	5	—	—	21
16. Lowland Banff	100	—	—	—	—	25
17. Buchan	100	—	—	—	—	25
18. S.-E. Aberdeenshire	96 (92)	—	—	—	—	25
19. Inner Aberdeenshire	100	—	—	—	—	20
20. Kincardine	100	5 (0)	—	—	—	18
21. Inner Angus	100	3	—	—	—	35
22. Coastal Angus	100	4	—	—	—	27
23. East Perthshire	100	14 (5)	5	—	—	19
24. South Perthshire	100	—	5	—	—	22
25. East Fife	94	32 (27)	—	—	—	33
26. West Fife	100	51 (48)	—	—	4	27
27. North Stirling-Clackmannan	100	27 (22)	6	—	—	18
28. West Lothian, East Stirling	100	37 (33)	—	—	—	18
29. Edinburgh area	100	48	5	5	5	21
30. Dunbarton, Renfrewshire	90	29 (25)	—	—	—	20
31. North Ayrshire	100	7 (4)	—	—	—	25
32. South Ayrshire	100	6	—	6	—	17
33. North Lanarks.	100	15	—	—	—	20
34. South Lanarks.	100	6	—	6	—	17
35. Peeblesshire	94	11	18	18	6	17
36. Dunbar area	100	42	42	32	5	19
37. South Berwick	97	26 (13)	73	40	7	30
38. Kelso area	100	4 (0)	33	10	10	21
39. Hawick area	90	18 (10)	30	—	20	10
40. Inner Dumfries, Kirkcudbright	100	—	5	—	—	21
41. South Dumfries	100	4	8	—	4	24
42. South Kirkcudbright	95	—	—	—	5	21
43. Wigtown and south tip of Ayr	94 (91)	6	—	—	6	17
SCOTLAND	95	11	10	3	2	821

TABLE 2.C: VEGETABLES AND FISH

Percentages of Parishes in Each District reporting Each Food.

(N as in Table 2.B)

	Potatoes	Other vegetables	Fish
1. Shetland	100	—	100
2. Orkney	89	22	89
3. Caithness	100	8	100
4. East Sutherland	100	10	90
5. East Ross	100	—	57
6. N.-E. Inverness	100	7	67
7. North-west coast	100	—	100
8. Skye and Outer Hebrides	100	—	86
9. West Argyll	100	—	80
10. North Argyll	100	—	82
11. South Argyll	100	—	80
12. Highland Inverness, Banff, Moray	100	8	25
13. Highland Perth, Aberdeenshire	90	20	—
14. N.-W. Perth	93	—	14
15. Nairn, Lowland Moray	95	14	38
16. Lowland Banff	72	60	20
17. Buchan	80	60	40
18. S.-E. Aberdeenshire	80	64	16
19. Inner Aberdeenshire	85	75	—
20. Kincardine	94	11	39
21. Inner Angus	97	6	3
22. Coastal Angus	100	4	22
23. East Perthshire	100	5	11
24. South Perthshire	96	—	—
25. East Fife	100	3	55
26. West Fife	96	7	33
27. North Stirling-Clackmannan	94	6	17
28. West Lothian, East Stirling	94	6	28
29. Edinburgh area	100	—	24
30. Dunbarton, Renfrewshire	100	—	50
31. North Ayrshire	100	4	16
32. South Ayrshire	100	—	12
33. North Lanarks.	100	—	25
34. South Lanarks.	100	—	24
35. Peeblesshire	94	6	18
36. Dunbar area	90	5	32
37. South Berwick	90	—	23
38. Kelso area	100	—	14
39. Hawick area	90	—	—
40. Inner Dumfries, Kirkcudbright	100	—	19
41. South Dumfries	100	—	29
42. South Kirkcudbright	100	—	24
43. Wigtown and south tip of Ayr	100	6	53
SCOTLAND	95	11	35

TABLE 2.D: DAIRY FOODS AND TEA
Percentages of Parishes in Each District reporting Each Food.
(N as in Table 2.B)

	Milk	Cheese	Butter	Tea and Coffee
1. Shetland	39	—	—	—
2. Orkney	39	—	—	—
3. Caithness	83	17	17	—
4. East Sutherland	50	—	—	—
5. East Ross	29	—	—	—
6. N.-E. Inverness	47	—	—	—
7. North-west coast	30	—	—	—
8. Skye and Outer Hebrides	64	—	—	—
9. West Argyll	60	—	—	—
10. North Argyll	82	—	—	—
11. South Argyll	60	5	5	—
12. Highland Inverness, Banff, Moray	33	—	—	—
13. Highland Perth, Aberdeenshire	90	—	—	—
14. N.-W. Perth	42	7	21	7
15. Nairn, Lowland Moray	47	—	5	—
16. Lowland Banff	76	4	4	4
17. Buchan	80	4	4	—
18. S.-E. Aberdeenshire	64	—	—	12
19. Inner Aberdeenshire	85	10	10	5
20. Kincardine	89	—	—	6
21. Inner Angus	69	—	3	6
22. Coastal Angus	67	4	4	11
23. East Perthshire	21	5	11	21
24. South Perthshire	41	10	5	14
25. East Fife	49	—	3	15
26. West Fife	26	7	4	15
27. North Stirling-Clackmannan	39	33	22	11
28. West Lothian, East Stirling	22	17	17	17
29. Edinburgh area	10	—	—	33
30. Dunbarton, Renfrewshire	40	20	15	20
31. North Ayrshire	36	44	16	12
32. South Ayrshire	53	17	6	6
33. North Lanarks.	40	60	40	10
34. South Lanarks.	35	24	—	12
35. Peeblesshire	41	6	6	24
36. Dunbar area	26	5	5	32
37. South Berwick	40	7	—	30
38. Kelso area	33	—	—	14
39. Hawick area	20	10	10	30
40. Inner Dumfries, Kirkcudbright	33	10	—	5
41. South Dumfries	29	—	13	4
42. South Kirkcudbright	38	10	19	14
43. Wigtown and south tip of Ayr	47	—	6	18
SCOTLAND	48	8	6	10

TABLE 2.E: MEAT

Percentages of Parishes in Each District reporting Each Food (figures in the last column omit all references implying that meat was eaten only occasionally, in very small quantities, or by a minority of the labouring classes)

	Pigmeat	Beef	Mutton	All meat	All meat (major only)
1. Shetland	15	8	8	39	15
2. Orkney	33	—	17	56	33
3. Caithness	17	8	8	42	8
4. East Sutherland	10	—	10	20	—
5. East Ross	—	—	—	—	—
6. N.-E. Inverness	—	—	—	—	—
7. North-west coast	—	—	—	10	—
8. Skye and Outer Hebrides	—	—	—	7	—
9. West Argyll	13	—	7	33	—
10. North Argyll	18	—	9	27	27
11. South Argyll	15	—	—	45	15
12. Highland Inverness, Banff, Moray	—	17	17	25	8
13. Highland Perth, Aberdeenshire	20	—	—	40	—
14. N.-W. Perth	36	—	21	71	50
15. Nairn, Lowland Moray	5	—	—	5	—
16. Lowland Banff	—	—	—	8	4
17. Buchan	—	—	—	16	4
18. S.-E. Aberdeenshire	—	—	—	12	—
19. Inner Aberdeenshire	—	—	—	10	—
20. Kincardine	11	6	—	28	6
21. Inner Angus	26	3	—	31	17
22. Coastal Angus	44	4	—	48	37
23. East Perthshire	42	—	—	58	26
24. South Perthshire	50	5	—	64	50
25. East Fife	79	6	3	82	60
26. West Fife	63	7	4	78	56
27. North Stirling-Clackmannan	11	6	—	67	44
28. West Lothian, East Stirling	22	6	—	72	17
29. Edinburgh area	14	5	—	67	14
30. Dunbarton, Renfrewshire	15	5	—	70	30
31. North Ayrshire	28	4	—	60	28
32. South Ayrshire	24	—	—	41	17
33. North Lanarks.	45	20	—	85	75
34. South Lanarks.	59	6	12	88	53
35. Peeblesshire	35	6	24	71	18
36. Dunbar area	79	—	—	90	74
37. South Berwick	67	3	7	80	60
38. Kelso area	38	—	—	86	48
39. Hawick area	10	—	10	80	20
40. Inner Dumfries, Kirkcudbright	33	—	14	48	38
41. South Dumfries	13	—	—	50	21
42. South Kirkcudbright	14	—	—	48	10
43. Wigtown and south tip of Ayr	41	—	—	53	41
SCOTLAND	27	3	3	48	26

TABLE 2.F: MEALS IN SOUTHERN RURAL PARISHES
Percentages of Parishes naming Certain Foods at Each Meal

	1 At breakfast	2 At dinner	3 At supper
Porridge	100	—	93[1]
Oatcakes	16	6	3
Bread or loafbread	10	10	7
Barley and pease bread	—	13	7
Potatoes	—	68	77[1]
Other vegetables	—	13	—
Fish	—	32	17
Milk	65	13	48
Cheese	10	19	7
Butter	6	3	7
Tea and coffee	26	10	10
Beer	10	3	—
Meat	3	81[2]	—
Broth	—	74	—
N =	31	31	29

[1] In 66 per cent. of parishes potatoes and porridge were given as alternative items for supper.
[2] In 23 per cent. of parishes meat was described as if given infrequently or in small quantities; in another 16 per cent. as an alternative to another item such as cheese or fish.

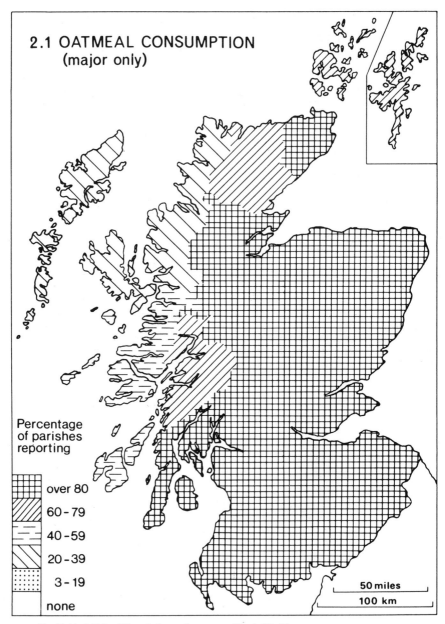

2.1 OATMEAL CONSUMPTION
(major only)

Percentage
of parishes
reporting

over 80

60 - 79

40 - 59

20 - 39

3 - 19

50 miles

100 km

See Table 2.B (p. 37) and discussion on pp. 23–4, 29–30.

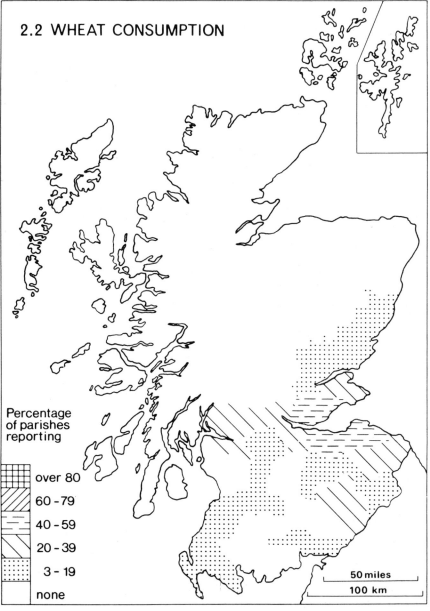

2.2 WHEAT CONSUMPTION

Percentage
of parishes
reporting

over 80
60 - 79
40 - 59
20 - 39
3 - 19
none

50 miles
100 km

See Table 2.B (p. 37) and discussion on pp. 23–4, 29–30.

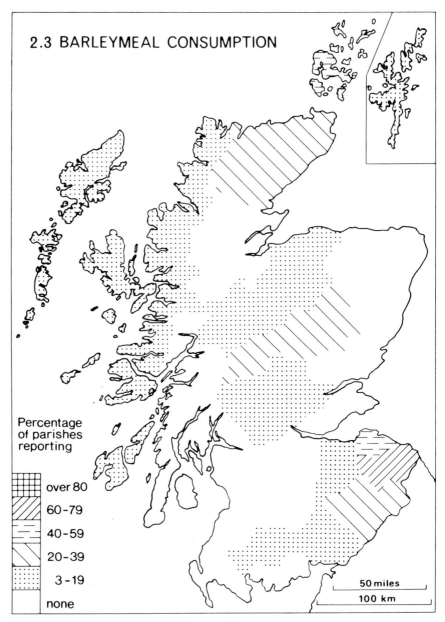

2.3 BARLEYMEAL CONSUMPTION

Percentage
of parishes
reporting

over 80
60-79
40-59
20-39
3-19
none

50 miles
100 km

See Table 2.B (p. 37) and discussion on p. 24.

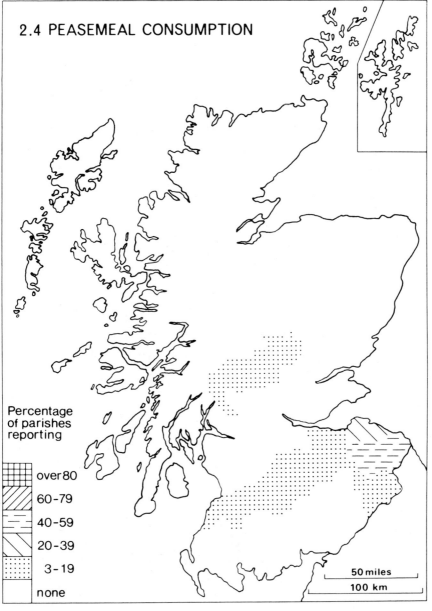

2.4 PEASEMEAL CONSUMPTION

Percentage
of parishes
reporting

over 80

60-79

40-59

20-39

3-19

50 miles

100 km

See Table 2.B (p. 37) and discussion on p. 24.

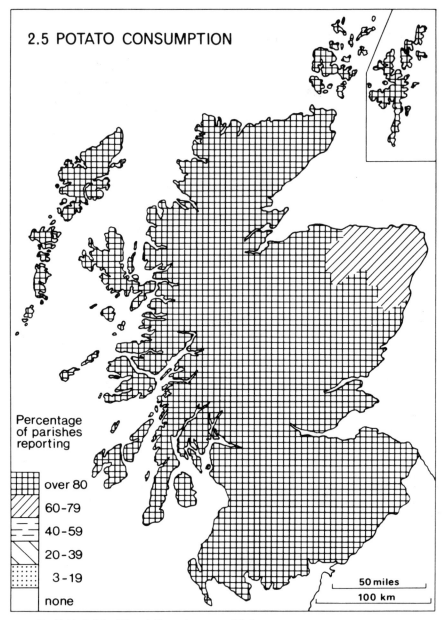

See Table 2.C (p. 38) and discussion on pp. 24–5.

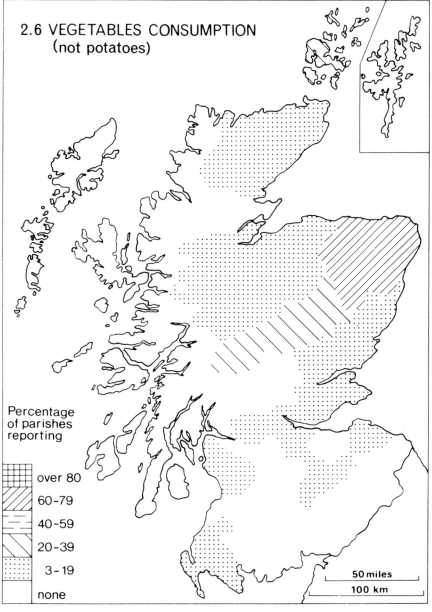

2.6 VEGETABLES CONSUMPTION
(not potatoes)

Percentage
of parishes
reporting

over 80
60-79
40-59
20-39
3-19
none

50 miles
100 km

See Table 2.C (p. 38) and discussion on p. 25.

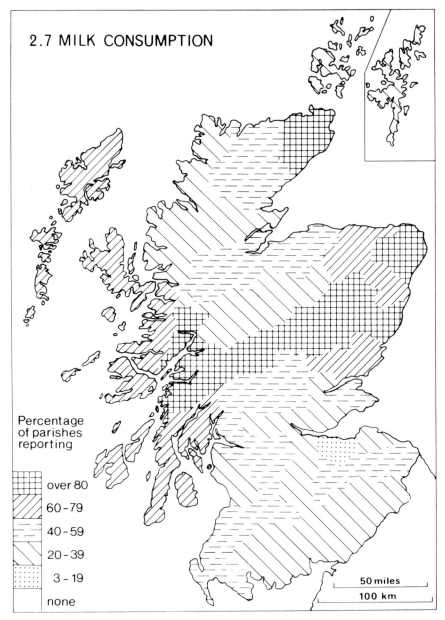

2.7 MILK CONSUMPTION

Percentage
of parishes
reporting

over 80
60 - 79
40 - 59
20 - 39
3 - 19
none

50 miles
100 km

See Table 2.D (p. 39) and discussion on pp. 25–6.

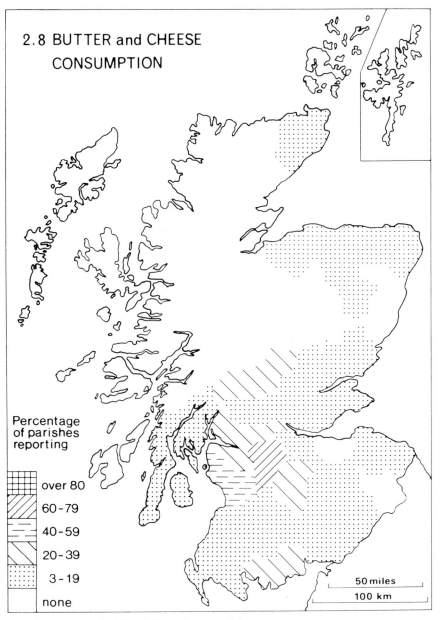

2.8 BUTTER and CHEESE CONSUMPTION

Percentage
of parishes
reporting

over 80
60 - 79
40 - 59
20 - 39
3 - 19
none

50 miles
100 km

See Table 2.D (p. 39) and discussion on pp. 25–6.

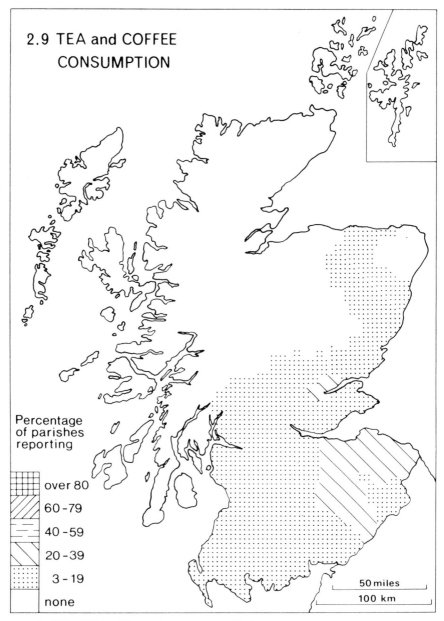

2.9 TEA and COFFEE
CONSUMPTION

Percentage
of parishes
reporting

over 80
60 - 79
40 - 59
20 - 39
3 - 19
none

50 miles
100 km

See Table 2.D (p. 39) and discussion on pp. 25–6.

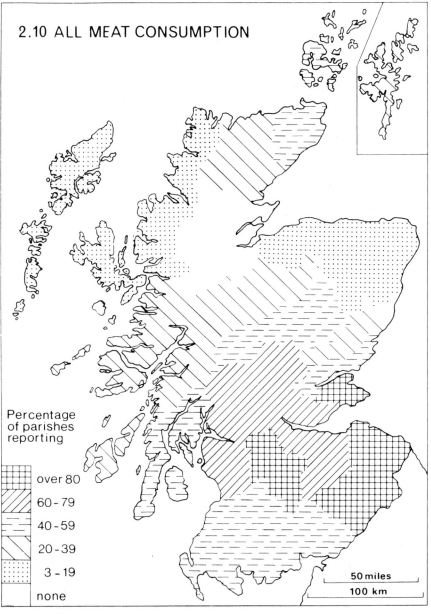

2.10 ALL MEAT CONSUMPTION

Percentage
of parishes
reporting

over 80
60 - 79
40 - 59
20 - 39
3 - 19
none

50 miles
100 km

See Table 2.E (p. 40) and discussion on pp. 27–8.

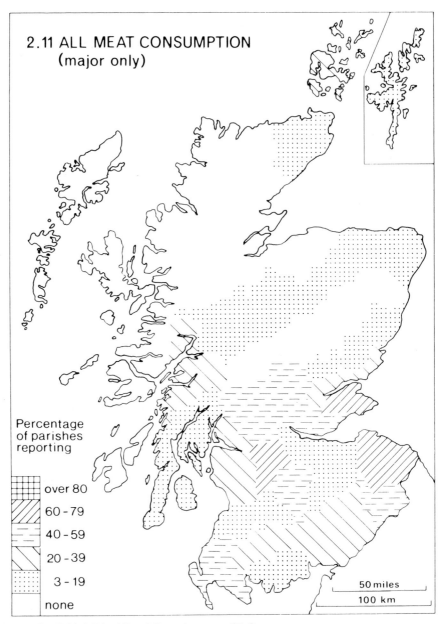

2.11 ALL MEAT CONSUMPTION
(major only)

Percentage
of parishes
reporting

over 80
60 - 79
40 - 59
20 - 39
3 - 19
none

50 miles
100 km

See Table 2.E (p. 40) and discussion on pp. 27–8.

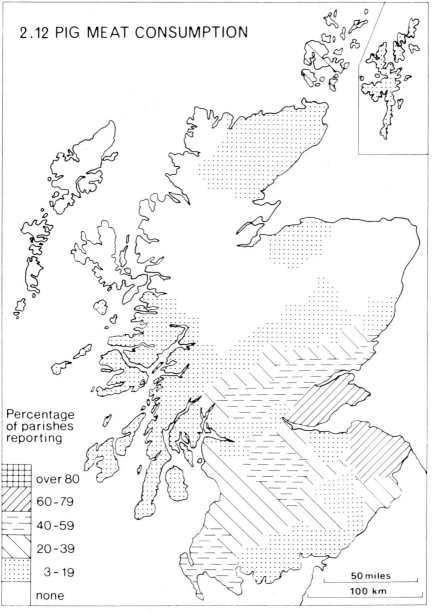

2.12 PIG MEAT CONSUMPTION

Percentage
of parishes
reporting

over 80
60-79
40-59
20-39
3-19
none

50 miles
100 km

See Table 2.E (p. 40) and discussion on pp. 27–8.

Chapter 3

PRICES

The price data in the 1843 questionnaire were contained in two questions dealing with four main commodities: oatmeal, potatoes, coal and cottage rents. The questions were:

Q. 18. What has been the average price of meal, of potatoes, and of coals, or other fuel in your parish during the last five years?

Q. 20. What is the rent usually paid by labourers for a cottage in your parish?

One immediate problem arises with Question 18 – what sort of prices are intended? They were quoted in a wide variety of measurements, but that difficulty, though not a small one, was ironed out by reducing the great majority of quotations to a common standard. We chose the imperial boll (140 lb. avoirdupois), the imperial cwt. (112 lb.) and the imperial ton (2240 lb.) as our standards for oatmeal, potatoes and coal respectively, and have explained elsewhere how we resolved the complications created by a wide variety of local measurements.[1] More intractable is the question as to whether retail or wholesale prices were intended. Common sense suggests that most respondents would name the price at which a rural householder would usually have to pay for goods bought in bulk from the miller, the farmer or the local coal merchant. Plainly in the countryside many working-class families did keep their staple goods in bulk whenever they could, in the meal chest, the potato bing or the coal shed; payment in kind for many workers encouraged the tradition.[2] On the other hand the poorest members of the rural community, dependent on day wages or charity, and town dwellers, may often have been unable to afford to buy and store goods in this way – proportionately they would have had to pay more.

Another problem arises from the request to the respondents to average the prices. Would they have known an 'average' price over a period as long as five years, and what sort of annual variation does this conceal? The problem is probably not important for coal (or for rent), but it certainly is for the two agricultural crops, as one can see from occasional entries in the questionnaire where the ranges are given instead of the average. Thus at Kennoway, Fife, the answer ran (23.250b):

Meal, in 1838, 19s. per boll; 1839, 24s.; 1840, 22s.; 1841, 17s.; 1842, 15s. Potatoes, in 1838, 10s. per boll; 1839, 6s. 6d.; 1840, 1841, 1842,

about 6s. Coals, 6s. 6d. per ton; driving 2s.: total 8s. 6d.
At Keith, in Banff, it was (23.365b):

> May 1839, meal per stone, 2s. 4d.; 1840, 2s.; 1841, 1s. 9d.; 1842, 1s.
> 7d.; 1843, 1s. 3d.; May 1839, potatoes per bushel, 9d.; 1840, 8d.; 1841,
> 10d.; 1842, 1s.; 1843, 7d.; May 1839, coals, per barrel, 1s. 7d.; 1842,
> 1s. 6d.; peats, 2s. 6d. per load; turf, 1s. 6d.

Nevertheless, there is no reason to believe that most did not make a serious attempt to discover a mean; where they err, they are probably more likely to reflect the prices close to 1843 than those close to 1838. In any case, the main interest is in the regional variation in the price rather than in the absolute levels. There is no reason to believe that biased or eccentric answers should be concentrated more in one district rather than another.

Let us consider the regional pattern of the four prices in detail.

1. Oatmeal

Oatmeal was the commodity of the four in which there was least regional variation of the price, as is evident from Table 3.A and Map 3.1. The average (mean) price of a boll of 140 lb. was given as 17 shillings, with a standard deviation of 1·85 and a response rate of 80 per cent. (729 cases). Variation seems in the north often to be related in a straightforward way to the fertility of the district. Oatmeal was 4 shillings a boll more expensive in Shetland than in Orkney, and generally considerably more expensive down the wild western coast of the Highlands than in the north-east of the country: oatmeal was least important as an item of diet in the west Highlands, and probably most important in the north-east.[3] Perhaps too much should not be made of occasional differences of a shilling or two between adjacent districts given the way the data were compiled, and the entire centre and south of the country varied comparatively little despite a tendency for price to be again a trifle higher in upland districts along the Border.

2. Potatoes

Potatoes showed much more variation than meal: see Table 3.B and Map 3.2. The mean price of a cwt. was 1·81 shillings, with a standard deviation of 0·45 and also an 80 per cent. response rate (723 cases).

The cheapest districts for potatoes were in Orkney, Shetland and the Hebrides, but even on the mainland they were cheap throughout the northern and western Highlands where they were the staff of life. By contrast relatively few seem to have been sold for the market (and fewer eaten as part of the staple working-class diet in the countryside) in parts of the north-east: thus at Clatt, Aberdeenshire, it was said that 'none |are| sold, but raised only for domestic use' and at Kildrummy, 'few potatoes sold' (23.326b, 328b). This shortfall in supply does not appear to have created high prices except in the district containing Aberdeen itself, where (if our calculations are correct) the price of potatoes was about a third higher than in adjacent districts. A similar effect of high prices created by the presence of large towns can be seen to a less marked degree in the Edinburgh area, in Dunbarton and Renfrew district and in North Lanarkshire, though these were not embedded, like Aberdeen in regions where the potato was an unpopular commercial crop. One area of few towns where potatoes were expensive, however, was the south-east, perhaps because the arable land there was of such high quality that it was preferred for wheat and other grain crops. Being bulky in relation to their selling price, potatoes were so much more expensive to transport than meal that a greater regional variation in their price is to be expected.

3. *Coal*

Not surprisingly, coal prices varied even more than those of potatoes: see Table 3.C and Map 3.3. The mean selling price of a ton of coal was 14·6 shillings, with a standard deviation of 6·26 and a 69 per cent. response rate (624 cases). The main causes of regional variation in price were the location of the coalfields and transport costs. The only railways in Scotland in 1843 were the Edinburgh–Glasgow trunk route (opened in February, 1842) and a handful of branch lines linking the coalfields of the central belt with those cities, so most coal moved about southern Scotland by road, and elsewhere had a sea journey before further redistribution by road.

Coal was under 10 shillings a ton only in those districts in Lanarkshire, Ayrshire, Fife, the Lothians and Stirlingshire where it was actually mined and where industry used it. It rose to about double this level in the south-east after a journey of twenty or thirty miles from the nearest mines. Some of the parishes along the Border found it cheaper to be supplied by Northumberland – this was the case, according to the *NSA*, for Jedburgh and Kelso (for example) while Melrose and Hawick drew equally on Scottish and English supplies. Despite the lack of railways, costs had come down in recent years even here: an interesting entry in the *NSA* for Maxton (Roxburghshire), dated 1834, comments that the price of 10d. per cwt. was half the price of twenty years before (*NSA*, III, Roxburgh, 125). Similarly in the south-west there was a division between Scottish and English suppliers. The mines at Sanquhar supplied parts of inland Dumfriesshire and Kirkcudbright from the north, but the coast of the Solway firth was supplied by sea-borne coal from the mines in Cumberland.

North of the Crinan Canal and Fife Ness, coal had to face a longer sea journey and became distinctly more expensive than in the central belt. It did not vary a great deal along the coast – even in remote locations like Shetland or Skye it was well under £1 a ton – but in inland districts in the central Highlands it quickly rose to about twice what it was along the coast. Perhaps generally in the north transport costs doubled or tripled the pit-head price, but in inland districts they could be six or seven times the pit-head price. (This calculation assumes a pit-head price of 5 to 7 shillings, and that even in the coal districts the average price included an element of cartage – as at Kennoway in Fife in the quotation cited above.) Much of the coal sold beyond the Tay was English: the Forth field was a high-cost producer and seemed unable to compete extensively with the well-organised mines and collier fleets of Newcastle-upon-Tyne.

The expense of coal beyond the central industrial belt meant that many consumers preferred to use other fuels where they were available – peat, turf or occasionally firewood. Even in Angus there was a difference of over 5 shillings a ton for coal between the coastal district and the inner district, and the poor round Forfar were said to be 'very ill off in point of fuel, particularly in the country, where they depend very much upon the materials they may be able to collect, such as whins and broom' (22.77). At Inverness and in Roxburghshire the poor were said to 'plunder' the neighbouring plantations by breaking down the fences and stealing the wood (21.501; 22.672). 137 parishes reported that other fuels were used in addition to coal: 61 others (almost all in the north) reported that these fuels were used instead of coal. These figures understate the true extent to which peat was used in the north and west: since it was often available at no other cost than the labour of cutting and carting, it did not always have a 'price' in the sense meant by the questionnaire, and would often be neglected in the answer. Map 3.5 shows the districts where more than one parish in eight reported using non-coal fuels as an indication of where supplementary supplies were important, viz., everywhere except in the central belt and in the south-east; the latter region so far from the coalfields and without native peat, must have found fuel of any kind impossible to obtain cheaply. There was extensive use of peat in Dumfriesshire and Galloway (more than a third of the parishes reported its use, though only four used nothing else). Throughout the Highlands, the north-east and the far north peat was very heavily used, often to the virtual exclusion of coal. In Shetland, for instance, 9 parishes reported using peats or turf, only 2 using coal, and in both cases coal was of minor importance: there were 37 parishes in Aberdeenshire using non-coal fuels, including 11 that used nothing else. Generally beyond the Highland fault between a third and three-quarters of all parishes in the different districts reported the use of peats, and the real total would have been a good deal higher. Nevertheless there were communities even here that had no native fuel and relied on imported coal – like Rosemarkie in Easter Ross which reported 'coals, 1s. and 1s. 2d. per English barrel; no other fuel used' (23.388b).

4. Rent

Question 20 on the rent paid by a labourer for his cottage had certain problems of its own. It was clearly framed with a Lowland farm-worker in mind. The cottage in question would be a one- or (less often) a two-roomed home of a very humble kind, no doubt often like those described to the Royal Commission by an Angus landowner who clearly did not have to live in one: '... good enough houses. Some of them are of clay and turf – but they are good enough houses' (22.5). A Roxburghshire observer described a hind's cottage as 'of one apartment with a little porch inside', divided by the box beds into two areas, one for living in and one for storing lumber: it had no ceiling but matting laid over the rafters – 'while the furniture is all standing the cottage looks very snug' (22.672). In many parts of the Highlands and Islands, however, there were few such wage labourers and no such cottages.

The homes of the crofters were 'black houses' shared with livestock like those on Lewis, or perhaps mere huts and hovels often regarded as having no value at all by the rating assessors, and the rent for them was inseparable from that for the croft. Some of the scanty replies from this region must be regarded as representing notional rents for the dwelling, the respondents guessing what such a home would be worth if it was separately let. At the opposite extreme, in the towns, there were labourers but there were few or no cottages. Replies from urban parishes are therefore generally in terms of the rent for a one- or two-roomed house (usually the former), perhaps part of a tenement. How variable they could be was shown again and again in the pages of the Royal Commission Report: in Dundee, for example, Margaret Kay (aged 80) paid 24s. a year for 'one small low damp room', Janet Duncan a shilling more for a 'neat clean small house', Ann Robertson and Elizabeth Howie (both in their 70s) 35s. for a but-and-ben, Widow Davidson (aged 45) and her three children paid 55s. for 'one large room dirty with work' (22.169–71). Where one can check the replies to the questionnaire against the detailed particulars of individual cases given in the body of the Royal Commission Report there is, however, a close correspondence between the two.

The mean rent of a labourer's home, then, was 37·5 shillings a year, with a standard deviation of 12·2 and an 83 per cent. response rate (749 cases). Table 3.D and Map 3.4 give the particulars.

Rents clearly tended to be much lower in the north and north-west, even allowing for the vagaries of the data. The north-east provided abundant information and was clearly a region of low rent despite contemporary complaints (always from middle class observers) of 'shortage of cottages':[4] as many farm-labourers were unmarried here, and lived in the farmhouse 'chaumer', perhaps demand was not really as great as was often made out. In the Lowlands from Kincardineshire to Wigtownshire, rents were almost always at or above the mean. The similarity in rent levels along the Border conceals, however, important differences in the quality of rural housing between east and west. In Galloway labourers paid rents as high as or higher than those in Roxburgh-shire or Fife, but the cottages were much inferior, and not merely because some of the Irish settlers in Wigtownshire chose to live with their pigs (22.522, 528). There appears to have been a serious shortage, and rent payments were a higher proportion of average labourer's income than in most places.

In absolute terms, though, rents were highest in industrial areas, especially in the western central belt. The consequences of industrialisation in creating relative pressure on housing can clearly be seen in the contrast between industrial North Lanarkshire and agricultural South Lanarkshire, the rents in the former being some 40 per cent. above those in the latter.

The questionnaire asked, of course, only about labourers' housing. Rents in industrial areas for superior artizans' dwellings were often greatly above the 40- to 50-shilling level normal for unskilled workers. The mean rent paid by seven unemployed skilled workers (five of them iron founders) visited in their homes by the Commissioners at Greenock was £5 a year (22.485), which corresponds with the £5–£6 paid for a house by an affluent calico-printer at Alexandria in Dunbartonshire.

Prices and economic structure

Several observations made so far on the regional pattern of prices suggest
a relationship with economic structure. We can carry the analysis a little
further by examining (Table 3.E) how prices varied in six different types of
parish ranging from large towns to crofting communities. For oatmeal there
turns out to be no correlation between price and the degree of urbanisation
and industrialisation: the highest price for meal is in the crofting parishes, and
in those small manufacturing towns and mining or factory villages that make
up category 1.2. Potatoes, however, are distinctly more expensive in urban-
industrial areas than elsewhere. Both these staples of life happen to be cheapest in small country towns, perhaps because they had on the one hand ready
access to supplies and on the other active markets that ensured a degree of
effective competition between outlets. Conversely, the rather high cost of food
in small manufacturing and mining communities may reflect the undeveloped
retailing and wholesaling sectors of such localities, the *locus classicus* of the
truck system. Coal was, broadly speaking, cheapest where there was most
industrialisation (or rather, industry concentrated where coal was cheapest).
House rents were plainly correlated with the degree of urbanisation, which
was probably a function both of a housing shortage and of the fact that (even
among labourers) many workers in these communities could afford slightly
better housing than the average farm-worker or crofter. As we shall see in the
subsequent chapters, high prices of essentials often went hand-in-hand with
high money wages, with effects on the level of real wages that need to be carefully considered.

REFERENCES

1. Ian Levitt and Christopher Smout, 'Some Weights and Measures in Scotland, 1843',
   Scottish Historical Review, vol. LVI (1977), pp. 146–52.
2. The problem of the scope and extent of payments in kind is dealt with in Chapter 4 below,
   especially pp. 72–5.
3. For local variation in the consumption of foodstuffs, see Chapter 2 above, especially
   pp. 23–5.
4. T. C. Smout, 'Aspects of Sexual Behaviour in Nineteenth-century Scotland', in A. A.
   MacLaren (ed.), *Social Class in Scotland: Past and Present* (Edinburgh, 1976), p. 66.

TABLE 3.A: OATMEAL PRICE
per Boll, by District

	Shillings	S.D.	N	% of Scottish mean
1. Shetland	19·3	3·80	10	114
2. Orkney	15·0	1·99	19	88
3. Caithness	16·0	1·74	12	94
4. East Sutherland	19·4	1·08	10	114
5. East Ross	18·0	0·98	12	106
6. N.-E. Inverness	17·3	1·30	14	102
7. North-west coast	19·0	2·04	10	112
8. Skye and Outer Hebrides	18·2	2·22	12	107
9. West Argyll	19·4	1·64	13	114
10. North Argyll	19·6	1·85	9	115
11. South Argyll	17·2	1·58	18	101
12. Highland Inverness, Banff, Moray	18·2	1·95	11	107
13. Highland Perth, Aberdeenshire	16·4	1·20	10	97
14. N.-W. Perth	16·8	2·05	13	99
15. Nairn, Lowland Moray	18·0	0·76	16	106
16. Lowland Banff	15·4	1·02	22	91
17. Buchan	15·8	1·00	22	93
18. S.-E. Aberdeenshire	15·7	0·99	26	92
19. Inner Aberdeenshire	15·9	0·84	19	93
20. Kincardine	16·7	1·60	16	98
21. Inner Angus	17·2	1·22	30	101
22. Coastal Angus	17·0	1·19	23	100
23. East Perthshire	15·9	1·18	16	93
24. South Perthshire	16·3	1·44	18	96
25. East Fife	17·0	1·35	28	100
26. West Fife	17·4	1·56	24	103
27. North Stirling-Clackmannan	16·6	1·76	16	98
28. West Lothian, East Stirling	18·0	2·39	17	106
29. Edinburgh area	17·3	3·66	18	102
30. Dunbarton, Renfrewshire	17·2	1·69	17	101
31. North Ayrshire	17·2	1·84	21	101
32. South Ayrshire	16·9	2·00	15	100
33. North Lanarks.	17·3	1·17	19	102
34. South Lanarks.	17·6	1·50	15	103
35. Peeblesshire	16·3	1·10	15	96
36. Dunbar area	16·7	1·45	13	98
37. South Berwick	18·1	1·28	26	107
38. Kelso area	18·3	1·52	18	108
39. Hawick area	16·5	1·97	8	97
40. Inner Dumfries, Kirkcudbright	16·6	1·39	19	98
41. South Dumfries	18·2	2·14	23	107
42. South Kirkcudbright	16·4	1·29	20	96
43. Wigtown and south tip of Ayr	16·5	1·66	16	97
SCOTLAND	17·0	1·85	729	

TABLE 3.B: POTATO PRICE
per Cwt, by District

	Shillings	S.D.	N	% of Scottish mean
1. Shetland	1·16	0·65	11	67
2. Orkney	1·15	0·22	19	66
3. Caithness	1·56	0·27	11	90
4. East Sutherland	1·54	0·31	9	89
5. East Ross	1·43	0·14	10	82
6. N.-E. Inverness	1·63	0·27	14	94
7. North-west coast	1·44	0·18	10	82
8. Skye and Outer Hebrides	1·20	0·15	14	69
9. West Argyll	1·64	0·26	13	94
10. North Argyll	1·87	0·21	10	107
11. South Argyll	1·87	0·29	17	108
12. Highland Inverness, Banff, Moray	1·57	0·16	10	90
13. Highland Perth, Aberdeenshire	1·88	1·01	10	108
14. N.-W. Perth	1·57	0·22	14	90
15. Nairn, Lowland Moray	1·63	0·25	16	94
16. Lowland Banff	1·88	0·43	21	108
17. Buchan	1·80	0·49	22	103
18. S.-E. Aberdeenshire	2·53	0·30	23	146
19. Inner Aberdeenshire	1·95	0·42	16	112
20. Kincardine	1·93	0·59	15	111
21. Inner Angus	1·72	0·22	30	99
22. Coastal Angus	1·78	0·19	23	102
23. East Perthshire	1·76	0·24	16	101
24. South Perthshire	1·69	0·18	19	97
25. East Fife	1·64	0·18	29	94
26. West Fife	1·69	0·22	24	97
27. North Stirling-Clackmannan	1·87	0·21	17	107
28. West Lothian, East Stirling	2·01	0·28	20	115
29. Edinburgh area	2·38	0·21	19	137
30. Dunbarton, Renfrewshire	2·16	0·34	17	124
31. North Ayrshire	1·94	0·35	19	111
32. South Ayrshire	1·70	0·36	15	98
33. North Lanarks.	2·25	0·30	17	129
34. South Lanarks.	1·82	0·39	16	104
35. Peeblesshire	2·20	0·28	15	127
36. Dunbar area	2·20	0·22	15	127
37. South Berwick	2·20	0·38	25	127
38. Kelso area	2·40	0·52	18	138
39. Hawick area	2·05	0·28	6	118
40. Inner Dumfries, Kirkcudbright	1·53	0·28	19	88
41. South Dumfries	1·78	0·30	23	102
42. South Kirkcudbright	1·68	0·40	20	96
43. Wigtown and south tip of Ayr	1·50	0·15	16	87
SCOTLAND	1·81	0·45	723	

TABLE 3.C: COAL PRICE
per Ton, by District

	Shillings	S.D.	N	% of Scottish mean
1. Shetland	18·0	0·00	2	*
2. Orkney	17·1	2·03	10	119
3. Caithness	15·8	0·29	3	*
4. East Sutherland	17·2	0·24	4	119
5. East Ross	16·5	2·20	9	114
6. N.-E. Inverness	14·8	0·91	14	103
7. North-west coast	18·6	1·73	9	129
8. Skye and Outer Hebrides	18·8	1·77	2	*
9. West Argyll	14·3	1·16	8	99
10. North Argyll	13·6	0·89	5	94
11. South Argyll	12·9	1·66	15	89
12. Highland Inverness, Banff, Moray	38·3	3·34	4	265
13. Highland Perth, Aberdeenshire	27·5	7·29	5	190
14. N.-W. Perth	23·3	6·17	12	161
15. Nairn, Lowland Moray	18·3	2·45	14	127
16. Lowland Banff	18·4	4·96	20	128
17. Buchan	19·8	4·98	16	137
18. S.-E. Aberdeenshire	21·9	5·53	24	152
19. Inner Aberdeenshire	26·1	4·77	13	181
20. Kincardine	16·5	3·98	14	114
21. Inner Angus	20·3	3·78	26	140
22. Coastal Angus	14·9	1·37	23	103
23. East Perthshire	16·0	3·34	16	111
24. South Perthshire	16·5	4·91	19	114
25. East Fife	11·1	3·09	24	77
26. West Fife	7·3	2·71	25	51
27. North Stirling-Clackmannan	10·4	5·21	16	72
28. West Lothian, East Stirling	8·5	2·06	19	59
29. Edinburgh area	8·4	2·25	19	59
30. Dunbarton, Renfrewshire	9·99	4·63	18	69
31. North Ayrshire	6·89	1·92	18	48
32. South Ayrshire	7·00	3·35	13	49
33. North Lanarks.	5·57	1·50	18	39
34. South Lanarks.	9·42	3·47	17	65
35. Peeblesshire	16·42	3·87	16	114
36. Dunbar area	12·38	3·04	16	86
37. South Berwick	13·88	3·43	24	96
38. Kelso area	16·76	4·06	19	116
39. Hawick area	19·75	4·57	9	137
40. Inner Dumfries, Kirkcudbright	14·38	2·57	16	98
41. South Dumfries	13·85	2·78	16	96
42. South Kirkcudbright	14·22	2·86	20	99
43. Wigtown and south tip of Ayr	13·84	1·35	14	96
SCOTLAND	14·6	6·26	624	

TABLE 3.D: COTTAGE RENT
per Year, by District

	Shillings	S.D.	N	% of Scottish mean
1. Shetland	17·5	3·5	2	*
2. Orkney	19·9	10·4	12	53
3. Caithness	22·8	11·7	10	61
4. East Sutherland	12·5	10·6	2	*
5. East Ross	30·6	10·5	8	82
6. N.-E. Inverness	25·6	11·4	13	68
7. North-west coast	30·0	10·0	3	*
8. Skye and Outer Hebrides	17·5	17·7	2	*
9. West Argyll	21·8	7·7	10	58
10. North Argyll	24·8	5·0	9	66
11. South Argyll	37·7	12·5	13	101
12. Highland Inverness, Banff, Moray	19·3	7·1	11	51
13. Highland Perth, Aberdeenshire	35·0	13·9	9	93
14. N. W. Perth	30·5	13·9	12	81
15. Nairn, Lowland Moray	31·7	10·5	21	84
16. Lowland Banff	25·2	9·0	23	67
17. Buchan	27·5	9·1	22	73
18. S. E. Aberdeenshire	35·0	11·6	25	93
19. Inner Aberdeenshire	30·5	12·1	18	81
20. Kincardine	40·4	6·0	18	108
21. Inner Angus	40·0	8·0	35	107
22. Coastal Angus	43·2	8·1	26	115
23. East Perthshire	42·9	10·0	18	114
24. South Perthshire	37·0	8·0	22	99
25. East Fife	40·6	7·2	33	108
26. West Fife	38·6	8·6	26	103
27. North Stirling-Clackmannan	49·9	13·4	18	133
28. West Lothian, East Stirling	37·8	7·8	22	101
29. Edinburgh area	39·6	8·2	22	106
30. Dunbarton, Renfrewshire	58·1	15·3	20	155
31. North Ayrshire	48·5	10·1	26	129
32. South Ayrshire	42·5	6·0	17	114
33. North Lanarks.	50·5	12·9	20	134
34. South Lanarks.	36·0	10·9	20	95
35. Peeblesshire	38·1	6·2	16	101
36. Dunbar area	34·5	6·6	19	92
37. South Berwick	41·1	4·1	29	109
38. Kelso area	37·4	10·3	23	100
39. Hawick area	43·3	5·5	10	116
40. Inner Dumfries, Kirkcudbright	36·2	7·8	21	97
41. South Dumfries	42·5	10·1	24	113
42. South Kirkcudbright	41·6	5·4	21	111
43. Wigtown and south tip of Ayr	39·0	4·4	18	104
SCOTLAND	37·5	12·2	749	

TABLE 3.E

Prices of Oatmeal, Potato, Coal and Rent, by Economic Type of Community

	Oatmeal (shillings per boll)			Potatoes (shillings per cwt.)			Coal (shillings per ton)			Rent (shillings per year)		
	Mean	S.D.	N	Mean	S.D.	N	Mean	S.D.	N	Mean	S.D.	N
1.1. Urban-industrial: large towns	16·93	1·57	29	1·98	0·37	26	11·04	4·08	28	49·4	12·2	27
1.2. Urban-industrial: smaller towns, etc.	17·32	1·52	102	1·91	0·38	102	10·44	5·58	100	45·3	12·7	115
2.1. Mixed economy: rural parishes	16·94	1·72	165	1·85	0·37	167	13·74	5·97	152	40·0	10·2	192
2.2. Mixed economy: country towns	16·78	1·44	39	1·78	0·38	39	14·63	4·21	41	39·5	9·0	42
3.1. Agricultural: farming parishes	16·95	1·76	306	1·89	0·47	300	16·78	6·43	266	34·1	10·4	331
3.2. Agricultural: crofting parishes	17·71	2·70	88	1·39	0·39	89	16·58	2·32	37	21·8	9·7	42

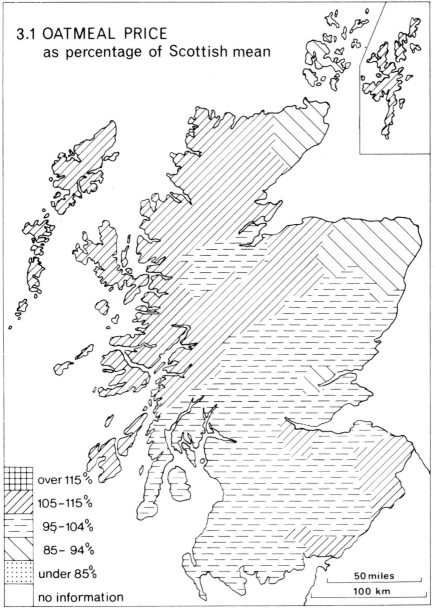

3.1 OATMEAL PRICE
as percentage of Scottish mean

over 115%
105–115%
95–104%
85–94%
under 85%
no information

50 miles
100 km

See Table 3.A (p. 60) and discussion on p. 55.

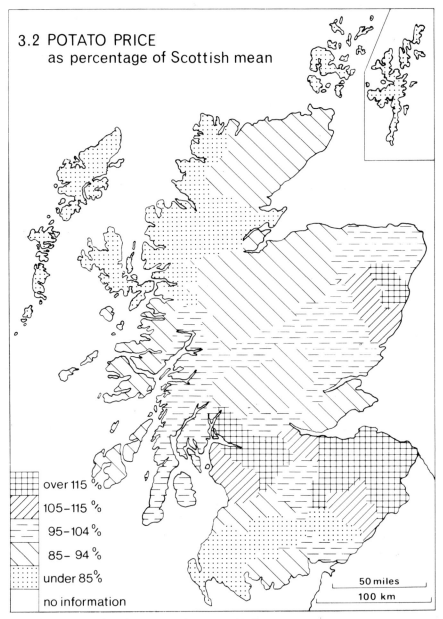

3.2 POTATO PRICE
as percentage of Scottish mean

over 115 %
105–115 %
95–104 %
85– 94 %
under 85%
no information

50 miles
100 km

See Table 3.B (p. 61) and discussion on pp. 55–6.

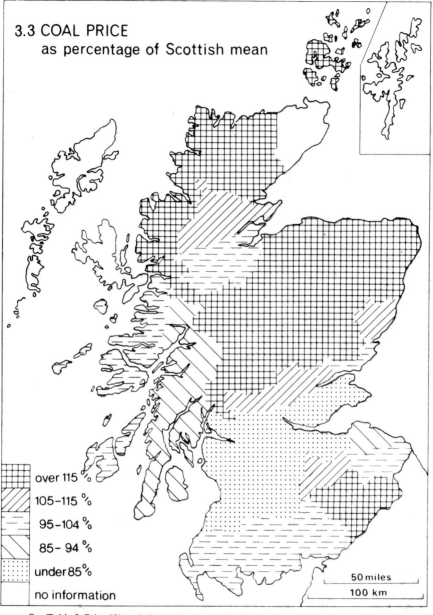

3.3 COAL PRICE
as percentage of Scottish mean

over 115 %
105–115 %
95–104 %
85– 94 %
under 85%
no information

50 miles
100 km

See Table 3.C (p. 62) and discussion on pp. 56–7.

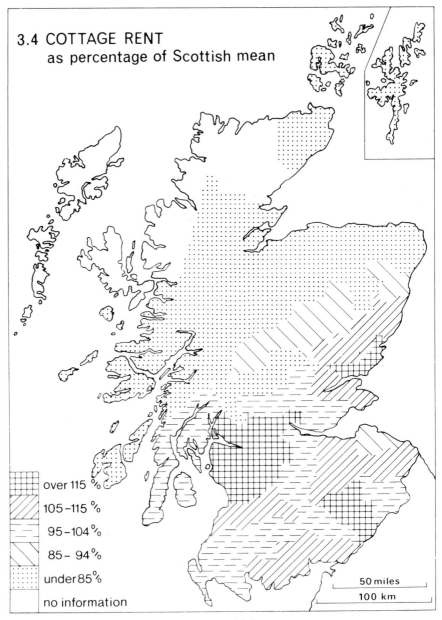

3.4 COTTAGE RENT
as percentage of Scottish mean

over 115 %
105–115 %
95–104%
85– 94%
under85%
no information

50 miles
100 km

See Table 3.D (p. 63) and discussion on pp. 57–9.

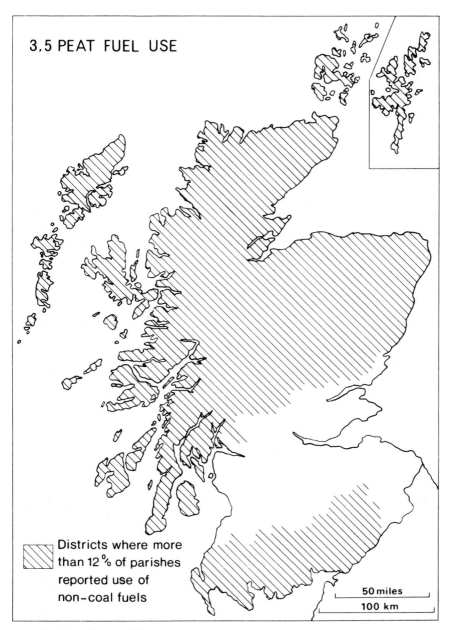

3,5 PEAT FUEL USE

Districts where more than 12 % of parishes reported use of non-coal fuels

50 miles

100 km

See discussion on p. 57.

Chapter 4

FARM-WORKERS AND FARM WAGES

1. *Male farm servants hired by the year*

The wages of nineteenth-century Scottish farm-workers are difficult to estimate, partly because they were paid to a considerable, but variable, extent in
kind, and partly because several different types of worker were involved. In
the first part of this chapter we shall concentrate on the male farm servant
hired by the year (or by the half-year in some cases). We are not for the
moment concerned with day-labourers, or with women and children on the
land. Characteristically such a farm servant was a ploughman, called a hind
in the south-east of Scotland. He was the subject of Question 9 in the questionnaire:

> Q. 9. What are the average allowances, and average wages of
> hinds or servants, hired for farming work by the year, in
> your parish?

There were, however, three distinct categories of worker subsumed even
in this question. One was a cottager, who lived in a rented cottage. The second
was a bothy-man, who lived in a purpose-built bothy, or barrack for farm-
workers. The third was a living-in servant, who lived within the farmer's own
household, eating in the kitchens and sleeping in an attic or outhouse of the
farm itself. The cottager was married: the other two generally were not. The
balance between the numbers of married and unmarried farm servants varied
enormously from district to district; another question in the inquiry sought
to throw light on this:

> Q. 24. Is any preference shown to unmarried labourers over
> married labourers, as farm servants in your parish, or
> the reverse?

Before we consider the level of wages we should first consider the replies to
this inquiry. There were 814 responses (89 per cent. of parishes) divided into
263 (32 per cent.) that declared married servants were preferred, 315 (39 per
cent.) that declared unmarried servants were preferred and 236 (29 per cent.)
that could find no preference. Table 4.A and Maps 4.1 and 4.2 show how this
varied by district.

There was a strong preference for married servants or cottagers in the
grain-producing districts of the south-east of Scotland, especially in East
Lothian and the eastern Borders. This was the traditional area of the hind who

70

served with his wife and children as a family work unit, the wife being called the 'bondager' — she had to perform a set number of days free labour at harvest time (often 20 days) in order to pay the rent of the cottage, and she was expected to be available on other days (often 4 a week) to do paid labour as required (22.790). The same socio-economic pattern was found in Northumberland, which suggests a very ancient origin, perhaps even from the seventh century when a single Anglian kingdom of Northumbria stretched from the Humber to the Forth. Some preference for married servants was also evident in parts of the south-west, though it was less strong: here they were known as 'cottars' or 'benefit men', and there was no formal obligation on their wives to work though no doubt they often did so.

The replies to Question 24 show that there was also a strong preference for married men in Fife and that this also stretched north (though in a weaker form) into Angus and lowland Perthshire. At first sight this is extremely surprising, as this area (especially beyond the Tay) was the heartland of the bothy system for unmarried farm servants. Perhaps married cottagers would indeed have been 'preferred' on economic grounds (as well as on social and moral ones) if they could have been obtained. One Angus farmer said that he did not approve of the bothy system 'where it can be avoided', as married men were steadier 'and he, besides, gets the labour of their families . . . and they are absolutely necessary to him' (22.94). This was a region of labour-intensive arable and root husbandry competing for labour with a widespread linen industry which was particularly suited to female and to family employment. So sharp was the competition that there were even reports of married women and their children remaining as weavers in Forfar and living apart from their husbands, who became ploughmen in bothies outside the town (22.69). Plainly this was exceptional, but it is reasonable to suppose that the bothy system for single men was effectively forced on the farmer when he could no longer obtain family labour. It was new in the nineteenth century and declined again at much the same period as employment in rural textiles began to dry up.

Outside these areas married men were not widely preferred, except in certain northern arable pockets like Easter Ross. The unmarried were strongly preferred throughout most of the Highlands, but this has little significance in the crofting areas where there was seldom wage employment for farm-hands of any kind. In the north-eastern counties there was also a strong and important (but not a total) preference for the unmarried. A system of boarding single men in a 'chaumer' in the farmhouse prevailed in this region, though here, too, married ploughmen sometimes lived in 'chaumers' and visited their wives and families in villages several miles from the farm. Less well known is the tendency also to avoid married farm servants throughout west-central Scotland — cottagers were scarce in Lanarkshire, parts of Stirling, Dunbarton and Renfrew. This may again be connected both with the small size of farms in this area and the structure of the labour market in heavily industrialised districts: families could earn more in industry than in farming. As these counties (like the others that clearly preferred unmarried labour) depended more on pastoral than on arable farming, they were also less thirsty for labour than

Perthshire and Angus and had less need to try to marshal a force in a bothy. The ratio of family labour to employed labour in East Lothian in 1861 was 1 : 8·3. In Aberdeenshire it was 1 : 0·7.[1]

It is striking that so many areas should, for whatever reason, employ few married farm servants: it implies that in a majority of parishes the ploughman's job was likely to be a phase in a life cycle rather than a whole-time career. What did farm servants do when they got married? Many, particularly in pastoral counties where the farms tended to be smaller, may have been the children of other farmers and returned to inherit their fathers' farms. In the north-eastern counties at least, as Malcolm Gray has conclusively demonstrated,[2] they might become crofters occupying poor-quality smallholdings on the fringe of the main farming areas, supplying occasional help as day-labourers when required. Alternatively they might become whole-time agricultural day-labourers, living in a rented house; they might become involved in mining or textile industry within the parish; or they might migrate into the towns. Carters were often former farm servants putting their expertise with horses to a new use.

The pattern in pastoral areas was nowhere simple or uniform, but it was undoubtedly often determined by the wish of farm servants ultimately to own a little land, or at least to have some independence. That in the dairy county of Ayrshire was described by an experienced factor for several large estates. Most farm servants, he explained, were unmarried and lived as boarders in the farmhouse, but a number married and lived in rented cottages. It was common for the unmarried to 'look forward to having farms of about twenty acres. I could point out a dozen instances of farmers who were originally merely ploughmen. And these, after having been for a time in the small farms generally feel inclined to have larger farms.' They achieved their ambition by carefully saving enough wages to begin stocking a farm, and then marrying a female farm servant who had been equally thrifty. On their marriage both left paid employment and set up as farmers with their joint capital. If they could not attain this the couple might marry, the man remain a farm servant and his wife rent a certain number of cows from the farmer: 'the farmer supplies (the) food ... the produce becomes her own ... instead of farming his land, she farms the cows' (22.498).

Information on the wage of married farm servants is summarised in Table 4.B.[3] From 201 replies where it is either explicitly stated or is implicit in the context that a married worker is involved it appears that the mean total value of the wage was around £24 a year. From 139 replies that state the money component, however, it appears that the average for this in Scotland was only around £10 a year. About 60 per cent. of the wage was paid in kind.

Such an overall mean, however, conceals remarkable variations from district to district in the nature and value of the payments in kind. The following account depends on a scrutiny of over 200 statements in the questionnaire and all entries under farm servants' wages in the NSA – a formidable body of data that can, nevertheless, only give a sketch of the complexity of regional practices.[4]

In the heart of the eastern Borders there were three districts, the Dunbar area, South Berwick and the Kelso area, roughly coterminous with the counties of East Lothian, Berwickshire and Roxburghshire, where the most valuable item in the hinds' wages was an allowance of unground grain – generally 10 or 12 bolls of oats, 3 of barley and 1 or 2 of peas or beans, their total value at current 1843 prices being about £12. In addition they were often allowed free carriage of up to four tons of coal, free manured potato ground (between 600 and 1200 yards in linear extent), the keep of a cow (worth £5) and a cottage paid for by 18 to 20 days' labour by the wife, the 'bondager'. The most valuable things a hind could possess, according to an East Lothian farmer, was 'a good wife, a good cow and a good razor' (22.803). The hind's traditional right to enough ground to sow a capful of lint (flax seed) was generally commuted to £1 in cash; in Berwickshire and Roxburghshire a traditional right to keep sheep was commuted to £3 'sheep siller'; in Roxburghshire there was a right to keep chickens or 10 shillings in lieu. In fact in the Dunbar district cash wages were often as little as £1, in South Berwick were under £5 and in the Kelso district under £4 – in other words the only money items in the wage were generally fixed and identifiable commutations of traditional allowances in kind. Between 80 and 95 per cent. of the hinds' wages were thus in kind (for a detailed example see 22.732–3). Yet unquestionably these areas were among the most advanced in Scotland in terms of their agricultural practice: it was the region of the largest farms and the most sophisticated capitalist farmers. Why was the cash component of their most skilled workers' wage so extremely small?

Part of the answer must be that it was fixed by tradition, evidently one of extraordinary antiquity since, again, it spanned each side of the Anglo-Scottish border.[5] But such a tradition probably would not have continued unless it had been satisfactory to both employer and employee. For the farmer payment in kind was payment out of his own barns – it was simple, fixed and easily calculable. For the worker it represented a comfortable subsistence in good harvests and in bad; so much food was as much as a large family might want, and the south-east corner of Scotland was consequently well fed. If there was a surplus the ploughmen sold or exchanged the grain with others in the community – you could buy your shoes with oats from the village cobbler.

Such an economy presupposes, however, firstly, that there was no great shortage of labour that would begin to bid up the wage dramatically. It was true that allowances in kind were increased from time to time, but it would have been foolish to increase them if they had lost all relation to a family's subsistence needs – paying a cash bonus would then become a simpler and more acceptable solution. Secondly (and more relevantly in 1843, since this corner actually already had the highest value of hinds' wages in Scotland) payment in kind presupposed no great local demand for urban consumer goods that would have to be paid for in cash. For all their advanced nature these were deeply rural districts, far from the main manufacturing and retailing centres. The fact that payment in kind persisted here more strongly than elsewhere in Scotland, while at the same time the wage was more valuable, suggests the Border hind ate better but spent less on clothes, small luxuries and general town wares than other ploughmen.

Outside this area there was a crescent of east-coast districts where cottagers were common, reaching from Fife, through West Lothian, the Edinburgh area, Peeblesshire and the Hawick area. The basis of the hinds' allowances here was payment in ground oatmeal, usually $6\frac{1}{2}$ bolls (worth nearly £6), together with enough potato ground to raise between 3 and 6 bolls (a privilege worth about £2), free house rent and often coals driven. In the southern districts here it was customary to allow the keep of a cow, and the value of the wage in kind would be at least 55–60 per cent. of the total wage. In Fife, an allowance of a Scotch pint of sweet milk a day generally replaced the cow – as that was worth only about £2 or £3 in place of £5, the cottager's money wage was proportionately higher, and often 50 per cent. of the total wage. In the Edinburgh area and West Lothian there were no allowances of milk or cow's keep at all: here, oatmeal, potato ground, house rent and driven coals were together worth £10 or £11, but the money wage rose to £14 or £15 – so the value of the allowance was only 40 to 45 per cent. of the total wage. Evidently over this whole area the nearer the hind was to the urban centres and to industry the smaller the proportion of his wage was paid in kind.

Married farm servants in the south-west, the 'benefit men' as they were called locally, were again paid allowances of $6\frac{1}{2}$ bolls of oatmeal, ground for at least 6 bolls of potatoes, house rent and carriage of coals, but generally nothing for milk or cows. Because the carriage of coals was rather expensive and the potatoes plentiful, allowances in Wigtown were worth around £13, or 60 per cent. of the total wage. Further north in Ayrshire such cottagers as there were had rather fewer potatoes but a little extra in cash – the money element again slightly exceeded the kind element as the industrial heartland was approached.

Outside these areas there were only pockets in which cottagers were found. Such as there were in Angus, Kincardine and Perth were paid like those in Fife, with $6\frac{1}{2}$ bolls of oatmeal, 1 to $1\frac{1}{2}$ Scotch pints of milk, potato ground, house rent and sometimes coals driven. In Argyll the system was the same, with a cow's keep replacing the milk allowance. In Aberdeenshire married farm servants were less common, but where they occurred they had peats driven instead of coals driven, and sometimes no potato ground – another indication of the singular aversion of the north-east to potatoes. Cottagers in the strip between Orkney and Inverness were given the traditional $6\frac{1}{2}$ bolls of meal, a quantity of potatoes, house rent, generally pasture for a cow, or a certain quantity of milk. The privilege of keeping a cow was less valuable in the north than in the south. South of Caithness they also often had 6–10 barrels of coal. The total value of allowances came to about £11 to which £6–£8 was added in cash – again approximately 60 or 65 per cent. of the wage was in kind. In such deeply rural and relatively undeveloped areas one would expect kind to be a high proportion, but it is remarkable that even here it never came near to approaching the figure for south-eastern Scotland.

From 553 replies in the questionnaire it is possible to calculate the money wages of unmarried farm servants (see Table 4.C). To arrive at a total wage that would be comparable with that of the cottagers, however, we must add their payments in kind. For some reason evidence on this for living-in servants and bothy-men is unusual in the 1843 report, but there is a certain amount in the *NSA*. To derive the second column in Table 4.C we have added £8 to the money wage in the far north and the northern and western Highlands, £9 in the central Highlands and the north-east, £10 in the bothy districts of the Tay area and £11 elsewhere.

Except in the bothy areas, unmarried servants living in were simply given board and lodging. In the south of Scotland the value of 'victuals' was often quoted at 6d. a day, but in the well-fed districts some were given slightly more – £10 a year for food plus £1 for lodging (half the rent of a cottage) seems a fair average. In the north-east, victuals were certainly worth less: £8 a year was the estimate for Drumblade in Aberdeenshire (*NSA*, XII, 306) to which something must be added for lodging. Further north and west it is likely that living would be slightly inferior again. The bothy-workers enjoyed in their districts an allowance system not unlike that of the cottagers: each got $6\frac{1}{2}$ bolls of oatmeal, a Scotch pint of milk and often some potatoes. They could not possibly consume so much (the allowances were the same as a married couple would get to stay alive on) and often sold half (21.35). It was estimated, e.g. at Panbride in Angus (*NSA*, XI, Forfar, 70), that the meal was worth £6 and the milk £3: a little extra must be added for the potatoes and their very poor lodging in the bothy. These figures are necessarily rough guesses and the gradations are no doubt more subtle between districts than we can indicate on the evidence available. Overall, unmarried servants were paid roughly 15 per cent. less than married ones, no doubt because the married brought with them wives and children who could be employed at cheap rates, or be made to labour for the rent of the cottage at harvest time in the case of the Border bondager. They were also likely to have been younger and therefore less skilled.

An overall picture of how the farm servant was remunerated is presented by Table 4.D, which puts the data on both married and unmarried servants together to arrive at a mean wage for each district irrespective of marital status. Its most interesting feature is the degree of regional variation, from the extremely poor pay in the north where most districts had less than 80 per cent. of the Scottish mean, to the relatively high pay of the industrial areas and the rural south-east, which hovered some 20 per cent. above the mean. It needs to be stressed again, however, that there would be few farm servants employed in the far north and on the west Highland coast where most people were crofters; the overwhelming majority elsewhere would receive a wage within the range of £20–£26 per annum.

2. *Agricultural day-labourers*

In addition to the farm servants, hired on annual contracts and provided with free accommodation, there were also varying numbers and types of agricultural labourers, generally less skilled, hired on a short-term basis and finding their own places to live. Question 10 asked about them in the following terms:

> Q. 10 What are the average wages of able-bodied agricultural
>   day labourers in your parish?

There were 807 replies covering 89 per cent. of parishes, divided in an interesting way between three-quarters that quoted rates per day and one quarter that quoted rates per week. The latter type suggests more regular and stable employment. Map 4.6 shows that such parishes were commonest in two areas, the central industrial belt where there was most competition for general labour, and the south-east where the high wages of hinds already noted suggests a strong market for specifically agricultural labour. In North Lanarkshire 75 per cent. of the parishes quoted agricultural labourers' wages by the week, although there were scarcely any quotations here of farm servants' wages: it looks like a district where small farmers and their families did most of their own work but hired outsiders on a regular basis, perhaps for the less skilled tasks. In most of the districts of the eastern Borders four-fifths of the quotations were also for weekly wages, though here many of the labourers were probably the unmarried sons of hinds, work being regular partly because whole families were employed to cultivate large farms where the farmer was essentially a manager.

In Fife also there were many agricultural labourers who depended entirely on day wages. Such men were described at Leuchars (as also at Inveresk in Midlothian) to be past the age when they could hold down a job on yearly contract as farm servants, and as single or without families; but at Kingsbarns some, at least, were family men (22.282, 295, 300, 304, 768). In Wigtownshire the labourers were often Irish immigrants working for Scottish farmers: their influx was said to have brought the rate of wages down heavily for the native Scots, but they certainly had large families: 'a labourer in this county gaining 8s. a week in summer, and 7s. in winter, will support a family of at least six or seven children, and keep them all decently dressed and make a very respectable appearance at church' (22.535). Probably in most arable districts south of the Tay there were a good many who were agricultural labourers by profession.

In the Highlands and the north, however, where there were scarcely any wage quotations by the week, few were labourers by profession except in Easter Ross. Most day-labour was needed for a specific task – like digging a drainage ditch – or was seasonal – like harvesting and hay-making: small tenants and crofters worked for farmers in this way to supplement their income, but did not try to live off such employment alone. Thus in Orkney 'there are scarcely any persons who come within the class of what would be called day labourers in Scotland or England, (but) those who have very small bits of land sometimes come and work as day labourers' (21.229). There was a similar situation in the Hebrides, except that there a crofter would often have been fortunate even to get casual employment. In Aberdeenshire and the surrounding counties most work of this kind was also supplied by crofters, perhaps with three or four acres and a cow or two, as at Tough: 'the circumstances of this class of persons, when they are provident and careful, are on the whole comfortable. In the few instances in which our labourers have not bits of land, they have not the same abundance of supply' (21.676). In the Black Isle of Easter Ross, however, there were a good many without cows or holdings, just as in Fife (21.31): this northern patch of good arable land reproduced in many respects the social relationships of the south.

Agricultural labourers everywhere, like farm servants, were often paid partly in kind, though in this case it was simply an allowance of victuals worth (at least in 27 out of the 38 cases in which their value was quoted) 6d. a day – scarcely more than one third of their average weekly wage. Wages also varied to a marked extent between the lows of winter and the highs of summer. Over Scotland as a whole it appears the labourer's wage rates tended to be about 12 per cent. below the mean in winter and 10 per cent. above it in summer, though, interestingly in the Highlands and the north the range was greater – from about 20 per cent. below to about 20 per cent. above. This reflects the more severe climate: in winter little could be done and labour was in gross oversupply; in the brief summer it was needed quickly to perform the essential tasks of gathering the crop before the weather failed again.

Naturally, the mere quotation of a daily or weekly wage rate can tell us nothing in detail of the real annual earnings of agricultural labourers. Jobs were not only less well paid in the winter, they were harder to come by; day-labourers in Easter Ross worked only nine or ten months in the year (21.31, 480), and in Fife winter destitution through unemployment was often severe (22.295, 300).

Table 4.E and Map 4.7 show the regional variation in agricultural day-labourers' wage rates, including the value of victual allowances. In order to standardise the data the median was taken wherever a range was given for summer and winter work in the same parish, and a six-day week was assumed where day rates alone were given: but such a table cannot so closely reflect earnings throughout the year as those on the farm servants do, for the reasons just stated.

If the wage rates of the farm servants are compared with those of the day-labourers, by dividing the yearly wage of the former by 52 to arrive at a weekly rate, it appears that, despite the greater skill assumed to be needed by the farm servant, the day-labourer has a better rate. The last column in Table 4.D shows the pattern: generally the differential is greater in the north and least in the south, especially where married farm servants are preferred. But as pay was not earnings, the yearly contract was everywhere preferred by the worker because of the certainty of income which it implied. Agricultural day-labour should perhaps be considered as a topping-up process as far as the employer was concerned, a way of supplementing the work of his own family and his yearly hired servants: as such it was an extra for a special task, paid over the odds. In many parts of the country a day-labourer was called the 'orra-man' or 'owrie' – the extra man (22.295). This incremental nature of day-labour was particularly true in Shetland or the western Highlands where a crofter had to be tempted into special employment for a short period. It was less true in Berwickshire, where a day-labourer (or, more strictly, a weekly paid labourer) could expect a job for more of the year and would be paid less on a *pro rata* basis, not absolutely, but relatively: in the south-east the wage rates of farm servants and labourers were virtually identical in real terms, though of course the former was paid mainly in kind and the latter mainly in cash.

3. *Women and children in agriculture*

In the middle decades of the nineteenth century women worked on the land almost everywhere, and children over the age of 8 or 9 also worked in farming in many places: these features of rural life only began to disappear after 1870 when males began to earn sufficient to be able to withdraw their dependants from back-breaking toil in the fields. The commissioners asked about this type of employment in these terms:

Q. 13   Are women and children usually employed in field labour,
and at what rate of wages?

There were 825 replies (from 91 per cent. of all parishes) of which 793 (96 per cent. of responding parishes) were positive; of these 57 per cent. implied that women were employed but not children; 40 per cent. that children as well as women were involved; 3 per cent. gave an ambiguous reply. A fifth of the responses were, however, qualified by the remark that female and juvenile labour was only used seasonally or irregularly, although the question had not been framed to elicit this information. This suggests that their employment was often more spasmodic even than that of the male day-labourers.

In arable districts women and children probably only had jobs for about one half of the year at best. In Easter Ross they were used for cleaning the land of couch-grass and rubbish when it was to be prepared for a turnip crop, for manure spreading, for putting bone-meal in the turnip drills, for hoeing and cleaning the crop subsequently, for hay-making and for harvest work (21.56). Certainly more parishes reported the employment of children in the south-east and other arable districts than elsewhere. The later phases of the agricultural revolution with the spread of turnip and potato husbandry must have created many more family jobs in agriculture (even if only seasonal ones) than had been available in the eighteenth century, and augmented total family earnings accordingly.

In pastoral districts, however, the pattern of employment had changed less: there were jobs for women as dairy hands throughout the year, and also some jobs for children as herds tending the animals especially where there was rough grazing. Of course, everyone also worked at harvest who could wield a sickle or tie a sheaf. Some women were hired by the year, mostly in the pastoral districts of the west, the south-west and the north-east, as living-in farm servants. 82 parishes reported these in their replies to Question 9: presumably they were mainly dairy maids.

How well were the women paid? The quotations for day-labour were generally given in pence and inclusive of the value of victual payments which are less common than with men. 8d.–9d. was the mean day wage: to facilitate comparison with male labourers, however, we have reduced the figure to a notional weekly wage on the basis of a six-day week (see Table 4.F). Generally a women was paid about half the man's wage for labour over the same period, though it fell to as little as 35 per cent. in parts of the western Highlands and rose to 57 per cent. in Dunbarton and Renfrew district where there was a great deal of alternative employment for women (see also Map 4.8).

Industrial work for women was usually better paid than agricultural: even in these years when handloom weaving was falling on hard times a woman at Girvan in Ayrshire was said to be able to earn 1s. or 1s.4d. a day at the loom compared to 8d. for outdoor work (22.442). Overall the differential was not so great, however. Quotations from 127 parishes that were urban-industrial or rural parishes with a mixed economy (1.1, 1.2 and 2.1 of our classification by economic type of community) suggest that women in industry obtained only 10 per cent. more than women on the farm, measured as a day wage rate; in 16 parishes of farming or crofting character they were actually paid a quarter or a third less than those working on the land – but 'industrial' employment in such deeply rural locations was often only knitting stockings or plaiting straw on a very casual basis. Such calculations perhaps aggregate too much. It can hardly be doubted that a girl in a cotton factory working six days a week winter and summer would bring home much more than an outdoor farm girl in the same district who could only find a job for a few months of the year.

Those women farm servants hired by the year who lived in, had (from 82 reports) a mean cash wage of £5, taking the country overall: again, this is about half the male equivalent.

For children, the position is shown in Table 4.G and Map 4.9. A wage of a little under 6d. put them at 30 per cent. of the rate earned by adult males for a day's field labour: and, again, the overall differential in areas where there was much industry put children in industrial employment 10 per cent. above the wage rate for those in farm work. The most highly paid children in farm-work were, however, those in the western industrial districts where there was most juvenile employment in manufactures. Weeding was better paid than herding: in the Black Isle (where squads of 8 or 9 children would work a field) they were paid 6d. a day for the former but only 4d. for the latter (21.56, 60).

The narrowness of the overall differentials between industrial and agricultural rates for women and children's labour, combined with the clear way in which the agricultural rates rise in the vicinity of towns, suggests an active labour market in the Lowlands, with ready mobility from one type of occupation to another. Indeed, it was a great advantage to live within reach of the magic pull of industry, even if you did not choose to work in industry yourself. Conversely, the farm-worker and his family in the north were deprived of high wages, of such constant employment and of the possibility of shifting to other jobs. It would have been better for everyone if the jam of the industrial revolution could have been spread over a wider area than it actually was.

4. *Long-term wage changes and regional inequality*

How does our picture of agricultural wages compare with that of other scholars investigating different periods of Scottish history? Valerie Morgan[6] considered the wage data in the first *Statistical Account* of the 1790s, concentrating mainly on male farm servants paid by the year: she studied only the cash element of the wage and disregarded the extraordinary variations in the proportion paid in kind, a weakness that obviated some of the value of her findings and misled her into thinking that Fife, the Lothians and the southeast generally was a low wage area. Otherwise, however, there is an interesting general resemblance between her maps of the distribution of wages and ours. On both, the Clyde appears as a 'high-wage region'; wages north of a line from south Argyll to the Angus–Kincardine border are lower than those south of that line, and very much lower in the islands and in the northern and western Highlands. It is interesting that these features should have appeared so early in the history of Scottish industrialisation.

Comparing the overall national picture from the 1790s with that from 1843 in detail, it seems that yearly cash wages for male farm servants increased from £6·8 to about £11·0, and for female farm servants from £2·9 to about £5·0, an increase of 62 per cent. and 72 per cent. respectively. For day-labourers the weekly wage rate rose from 6·0s. to 9·1s., an increase of 52 per cent. It is hard to say much about the cost of living, but the biggest single item in it – the cost of oatmeal – was almost identical at the two dates. Such a comparison of benchmark dates scarcely throws light on trends in the standard of living between the two, but agricultural workers were clearly better off by a substantial margin at the second date than at the first.

Perhaps even more significant than the overall national picture for Scotland is the question as to whether the prosperity of the different regions grew at the same rate – whether there was divergence or convergence. Many regional economists believe that the first effects of sustained economic growth in a capitalist society will be to increase the gap between incomes in different regions of the developing nation, since wages and salaries in those areas that first experience growth will rise most rapidly.[7] Some, however, hold that it is likely that regional differentials will narrow again as labour moves to where it is best rewarded and capital to where labour costs are lower: if there is perfect competition, factor mobility will restore equilibrium. Others object that the advantages which initially favoured the growth points may prove cumulative, and institutional factors arise to impede a free factor market: in this case the 'backwash' effects of development at the centre will perpetuate if not exacerbate the regional imbalance.

Valerie Morgan's work appears, indeed, to confirm the first part of the thesis: variation in agricultural wages increased very substantially between the earlier eighteenth century and the 1790s, 'an indication perhaps that there was rather less contrast in the type and level of economic development in different parts of Scotland' before 1745 than at the end of the century.[8]

It is not easy to use a comparison between Valerie Morgan's work and ours to measure the degree to which convergence or divergence took place between the 1790s and the time of the Poor Law Inquiry in 1843 because of the different geographical bases on which the data were collected. There is, however, another way into the problem. A. J. Bowley gathered agricultural wage rates on a simple county basis for a series of years between 1790 and 1890–2.[9] Table 4.H shows the results of applying a measure of inequality based on the coefficient of variation (adapted from J. G. Williamson's work in another context[10]). Wages are not income, of course: yet the trend of the day-labourer's wage in particular may indicate at least the general direction of working-class living standards, especially as unskilled labour in farming was relatively free to switch to industry if higher incomes were available there. The drop in the coefficient by a quarter between 1810 and c. 1840, and by a further half between c. 1840 and 1892 (though apparently not evident between 1790 and 1810 or between 1860 and 1880) is fairly impressive, and supports to a certain extent the views of the 'convergence' school. Ultimately economic growth did bring wages closer together, but it took a long time to do it. Progress was twice as rapid in the second part of the century as in the first.

If there is a single reason for the prevalence of regional inequalities in the 1840s it must be sought in the immobilities of the north. Highlanders did not leave the Highlands, nor Shetlanders the Shetlands, and so on, in sufficient quantity to bring the price of labour into closer line with what it was in the south. Nor did capital determinedly pursue labour into the wilder fastnesses — transport costs and the absence of a commercial superstructure in many parts made it unlikely that it would.

In a real sense, Scotland in the 1840s was a dual economy, not unlike similar economies in Latin-America today.[11] The south was economically sophisticated, capitalist, oriented around growth in textiles and heavy industry; the north was a world of traditional values, oriented round the peasant desire to cling to a holding of land despite intolerable demographic pressures. It would take the shock of famine and clearance after 1846 combined with the slower erosion of local values by greater familiarity with the south (in which railways, boats, migrant labour and schools played a part) to alter this situation in any basic way: and that was a story belonging more to the second half of the nineteenth century than to the first.

REFERENCES

1. Ian Carter, 'Oral History and Agrarian History – the North East', *Oral History*, vol. 2 (1974), pp. 35–6.
2. Malcolm Gray, 'North-East Agriculture and the Labour Force, 1790–1875', in A. A. MacLaren (ed.), *Social Class in Scotland: Past and Present* (Edinburgh, 1976).
3. Throughout the tables on wages, we have chosen the mean rather than the median for representational purposes. This was largely the result of the SPSS package which produces means and associated statistics, rather than medians in its tabulations. In order to satisfy ourselves that the representation of data would not be distorted (i.e., its distribution), we also computed medians for a certain number of wages and found very little

difference in scores. These results, plus the fact that we were dealing with parish scores of distinct sets of wages and not the wages of individuals, gave us a reasonable confidence in the use of the mean as an average of wages.

4. We are also grateful to Professor George Houston for allowing us to consult his unpublished Oxford University D.Phil. thesis, 'A History of the Scottish Farm Workers, 1800–1850'. See also M. Gray, 'Scottish Emigration: the Social Impact of Agrarian Change in the Rural Lowlands 1775–1875', in *Perspectives in American History*, vol. VII (1973).

5. For the practice in Northumberland see W. S. Gilly, *The Peasantry of the Border* (1842, reprinted with an introduction by R. H. Campbell, Edinburgh, 1973), Appendix, pp. 2–4.

6. Valerie Morgan, 'Agricultural Wage Rates in Late Eighteenth-Century Scotland', *Economic History Review*, second series, vol. 24 (1971), pp. 181–201.

7. The problem is discussed in H. W. Richardson, *Regional Economics: Location Theory, Urban Structure and Regional Change* (Penguin, Harmondsworth, 1969), and in J. G. Williamson, 'Regional Inequality and the Process of National Development: A Description of the Patterns', *Economic Development and Cultural Change*, vol. 13 (1965), pp. 3–45.

8. Morgan, *loc. cit.*, p. 190.

9. A. J. Bowley, 'The Statistics of Wages in the United Kingdom during the Last Hundred Years. Part II, Agricultural Wages, Scotland', *Journal of the Royal Statistical Society*, vol. 62 (1899).

10. Williamson, *loc. cit.*

11. Alan Gilbert, *Latin American Development: a Geographical Perspective* (Penguin, Harmondsworth, 1974), chapter 7.

TABLE 4.A

Percentages of Parishes clearly Preferring (a) Married or (b) Unmarried
Farm Servants by District

	(a)	(b)	N
1. Shetland	44	56	9
2. Orkney	17	72	18
3. Caithness	0	92	12
4. East Sutherland	36	36	11
5. East Ross	58	8	12
6. N.-E. Inverness	0	62	16
7. North-west coast	18	82	11
8. Skye and Outer Hebrides	18	92	12
9. West Argyll	33	47	15
10. North Argyll	0	80	10
11. South Argyll	11	67	18
12. Highland Inverness, Banff, Moray	17	67	12
13. Highland Perth, Aberdeenshire	30	60	10
14. N.-W. Perth	21	64	14
15. Nairn, Lowland Moray	0	67	21
16. Lowland Banff	19	39	26
17. Buchan	8	56	25
18. S.-E. Aberdeenshire	4	73	26
19. Inner Aberdeenshire	15	50	20
20. Kincardine	17	50	18
21. Inner Angus	31	40	35
22. Coastal Angus	42	27	26
23. East Perthshire	35	50	20
24. South Perthshire	18	59	22
25. East Fife	62	15	34
26. West Fife	59	4	27
27. North Stirling-Clackmannan	29	53	17
28. West Lothian, East Stirling	38	10	21
29. Edinburgh area	80	0	19
30. Dunbarton, Renfrewshire	5	85	20
31. North Ayrshire	25	42	24
32. South Ayrshire	50	31	16
33. North Lanarks.	15	50	20
34. South Lanarks.	11	42	19
35. Peeblesshire	47	23	17
36. Dunbar area	83	0	18
37. South Berwick	63	0	30
38. Kelso area	100	0	22
39. Hawick area	30	0	10
40. Inner Dumfries, Kirkcudbright	43	5	21
41. South Dumfries	30	13	23
42. South Kirkcudbright	29	24	21
43. Wigtown and south tip of Ayr	38	6	16
SCOTLAND	32	39	814

TABLE 4.B

Married Farm Servants' Wage Rates, by District

	Mean value of money wage (£ p.a.)	N	Mean value of total wage (£ p.a.)	N	Total wage as % of Scottish mean
1. Shetland	—	0	—	0	*
2. Orkney	6·0	1	14·0	1	*
3. Caithness	7·5	2	16·0	3	*
4. East Sutherland	8·3	3	18·0	1	*
5. East Ross	6·9	7	18·3	4	76
6. N.-E. Inverness	8·2	8	19·0	1	*
7. North-west coast	7·7	3	—	0	*
8. Skye and Outer Hebrides	—	0	—	0	*
9. West Argyll	7·7	3	20·0	1	*
10. North Argyll	9·5	2	—	0	*
11. South Argyll	11·3	3	—	0	*
12. Highland Inverness, Banff, Moray	—	0	—	0	*
13. Highland Perth, Aberdeenshire	—	0	—	0	*
14. N.-W. Perth	12·0	2	—	0	*
15. Nairn, Lowland Moray	—	0	—	0	*
16. Lowland Banff	—	0	—	0	*
17. Buchan	9·0	2	22·0	2	*
18. S.-E. Aberdeenshire	5·0	2	—	0	*
19. Inner Aberdeenshire	13·0	1	—	0	*
20. Kincardine	9·9	7	25·0	1	*
21. Inner Angus	9·8	5	24·0	2	*
22. Coastal Angus	11·3	6	23·0	3	*
23. East Perthshire	11·3	3	—	0	*
24. South Perthshire	12·0	1	—	0	*
25. East Fife	10·2	16	22·2	13	93
26. West Fife	11·9	10	23·6	9	98
27. North Stirling-Clackmannan	13·7	3	23·0	2	*
28. West Lothian, East Stirling	15·3	6	25·0	9	104
29. Edinburgh area	14·8	8	25·5	21	106
30. Dunbarton, Renfrewshire	—	0	24·0	2	*
31. North Ayrshire	14·0	1	24·2	6	101
32. South Ayrshire	12·0	3	23·0	5	95
33. North Lanarks.	—	0	—	0	*
34. South Lanarks.	11·0	3	24·0	2	*
35. Peeblesshire	11·1	8	23·5	11	98
36. Dunbar area	9·0	1	25·5	17	107
37. South Berwick	4·7	6	26·5	24	111
38. Kelso area	3·7	3	26·2	19	109
39. Hawick area	10·0	3	25·5	6	106
40. Inner Dumfries, Kirkcudbright	12·5	2	22·3	3	*
41. South Dumfries	10·0	3	22·6	9	94
42. South Kirkcudbright	—	0	22·3	11	93
43. Wigtown and south tip of Ayr	9·0	2	21·7	13	90
SCOTLAND	10·2	139	24·0	201	

TABLE 4.C
Unmarried Farm Servants' Wage Rates, by District

	Mean value of money wage (£ p.a.)	S.D.	N	Mean value of total wage (£ p.a.)	Total wage as % of Scottish mean
1. Shetland	3·33	0·82	6	11·33	55
2. Orkney	6·24	0·83	17	14·24	69
3. Caithness	8·44	2·24	9	16·44	80
4. East Sutherland	6·60	2·30	5	14·60	71
5. East Ross	7·00	0	1	15·00	*
6. N.-E. Inverness	7·89	1·17	9	15·89	77
7. North-west coast	6·43	1·90	7	14·43	70
8. Skye and Outer Hebrides	6·00	1·28	12	14·00	68
9. West Argyll	8·00	1·29	7	16·00	78
10. North Argyll	9·70	1·16	10	17·70	86
11. South Argyll	12·21	2·04	19	20·21	98
12. Highland Inverness, Banff, Moray	9·50	1·09	12	18·50	90
13. Highland Perth, Aberdeenshire	11·70	1·42	10	20·70	100
14. N.-W. Perth	11·42	1·08	12	20·42	99
15. Nairn, Lowland Moray	10·58	1·64	19	19·58	95
16. Lowland Banff	11·27	0·96	26	20·27	98
17. Buchan	11·85	1·09	20	20·85	101
18. S.-E. Aberdeenshire	10·71	1·49	24	19·71	96
19. Inner Aberdeenshire	11·75	1·29	20	20·75	101
20. Kincardine	11·13	1·85	15	20·13	98
21. Inner Angus	11·10	1·60	31	21·10	102
22. Coastal Angus	10·84	1·12	19	20·84	101
23. East Perthshire	11·90	1·10	19	21·90	106
24. South Perthshire	12·18	1·71	22	22·18	108
25. East Fife	10·69	0·75	13	20·69	100
26. West Fife	12·54	2·47	13	22·54	109
27. North Stirling-Clackmannan	13·55	1·44	11	24·55	119
28. West Lothian, East Stirling	14·00	2·79	10	25·00	121
29. Edinburgh area	14·00	2·83	2	25·00	*
30. Dunbarton, Renfrewshire	14·36	1·69	11	25·36	123
31. North Ayrshire	13·75	2·18	16	24·75	120
32. South Ayrshire	12·64	1·29	11	23·64	114
33. North Lanarks.	14·64	2·37	14	25·64	124
34. South Lanarks.	12·13	1·78	16	23·13	112
35. Peeblesshire	11·00	0·74	12	22·00	107
36. Dunbar area	10·00	0	1	21·00	*
37. South Berwick	10·00	0	3	21·00	*
38. Kelso area	11·00	1·41	2	22·00	*
39. Hawick area	11·40	0·55	5	22·40	109
40. Inner Dumfries, Kirkcudbright	11·67	0·97	18	22·67	110
41. South Dumfries	10·94	1·71	17	21·94	106
42. South Kirkcudbright	10·47	1·33	17	21·47	104
43. Wigtown and south tip of Ayr	10·00	1·05	10	21·00	102
SCOTLAND	10·99	2·55	553	20·65	

TABLE 4.D
Married plus Unmarried Farm Servants' Wage Rates, by District

	Mean value of total wage (£ p.a.)	N	Total wage as % of Scottish mean	Farm servants wage rate as % of agricultural day labourers wage rate
1. Shetland	11·3	6	53	76
2. Orkney	14·2	18	66	81
3. Caithness	16·3	12	76	75
4. East Sutherland	15·2	6	71	76
5. East Ross	17·6	5	82	95
6. N.-E. Inverness	16·2	10	74	77
7. North-west coast	14·4	7	67	67
8. Skye and Outer Hebrides	14·0	12	65	83
9. West Argyll	16·5	8	77	86
10. North Argyll	17·7	10	82	77
11. South Argyll	20·2	19	94	86
12. Highland Inverness, Banff, Moray	18·5	12	86	84
13. Highland Perth, Aberdeenshire	20·7	10	96	89
14. N.-W. Perth	20·4	12	95	89
15. Nairn, Lowland Moray	19·6	19	91	84
16. Lowland Banff	20·3	26	95	90
17. Buchan	21·0	22	98	88
18. S.-E. Aberdeenshire	19·7	24	92	80
19. Inner Aberdeenshire	20·8	20	97	85
20. Kincardine	20·4	16	95	86
21. Inner Angus	21·3	33	99	91
22. Coastal Angus	21·1	22	98	86
23. East Perthshire	21·9	19	102	91
24. South Perthshire	22·2	22	103	92
25. East Fife	21·4	26	100	92
26. West Fife	24·0	22	112	98
27. North Stirling-Clackmannan	24·4	13	113	96
28. West Lothian, East Stirling	25·0	19	116	96
29. Edinburgh area	25·5	23	119	100
30. Dunbarton, Renfrewshire	25·2	13	117	93
31. North Ayrshire	24·6	22	114	92
32. South Ayrshire	23·4	16	109	98
33. North Lanarks.	25·6	14	119	90
34. South Lanarks.	23·2	18	108	93
35. Peeblesshire	22·7	23	106	89
36. Dunbar area	25·3	18	117	100
37. South Berwick	25·9	27	120	102
38. Kelso area	25·8	21	120	95
39. Hawick area	24·1	11	112	89
40. Inner Dumfries, Kirkcudbright	22·6	21	105	97
41. South Dumfries	22·2	26	103	98
42. South Kirkcudbright	21·8	28	101	101
43. Wigtown and south tip of Ayr	21·4	23	100	104
SCOTLAND	21·5	754		91

TABLE 4.E
Agricultural Day-labourers' Wage Rates, by District

	Shillings per week	S.D.	N	% of Scottish mean
1. Shetland	5.70	0.26	10	62.4
2. Orkney	6.78	1.32	15	74.5
3. Caithness	8.33	0.97	12	91.4
4. East Sutherland	7.68	1.08	10	84.2
5. East Ross	7.11	0.82	11	77.9
6. N.-E. Inverness	8.11	0.75	14	88.9
7. North-west coast	8.22	1.37	9	90.3
8. Skye and Outer Hebrides	6.52	1.42	11	71.6
9. West Argyll	7.35	1.04	12	80.7
10. North Argyll	8.81	1.33	11	96.8
11. South Argyll	9.04	1.21	20	99.3
12. Highland Inverness, Banff, Moray	8.50	1.24	12	93.5
13. Highland Perth, Aberdeenshire	8.98	1.82	10	98.4
14. N.-W. Perth	8.80	0.86	13	96.7
15. Nairn, Lowland Moray	9.01	1.09	21	98.9
16. Lowland Banff	8.73	1.59	26	95.8
17. Buchan	9.17	1.18	22	100.7
18. S.-E. Aberdeenshire	9.51	1.36	26	104.3
19. Inner Aberdeenshire	9.41	1.21	20	103.3
20. Kincardine	9.12	1.17	18	100.2
21. Inner Angus	8.98	0.93	34	98.6
22. Coastal Angus	9.48	0.89	26	104.1
23. East Perthshire	9.21	0.48	19	101.2
24. South Perthshire	9.27	0.83	22	101.8
25. East Fife	8.92	0.70	33	97.9
26. West Fife	9.43	0.84	27	103.5
27. North Stirling-Clackmannan	9.81	0.94	18	107.6
28. West Lothian, East Stirling	10.02	0.82	22	110.1
29. Edinburgh area	9.81	0.61	22	107.8
30. Dunbarton, Renfrewshire	10.45	1.26	19	114.9
31. North Ayrshire	10.35	1.02	26	113.7
32. South Ayrshire	9.18	0.73	17	100.8
33. North Lanarks.	10.95	1.65	20	120.3
34. South Lanarks.	9.62	0.78	20	105.7
35. Peeblesshire	9.84	0.87	16	108.1
36. Dunbar area	9.71	0.35	19	106.6
37. South Berwick	9.79	0.66	29	107.5
38. Kelso area	10.51	0.95	22	115.5
39. Hawick area	10.48	0.93	10	115.1
40. Inner Dumfries, Kirkcudbright	8.95	0.75	21	98.3
41. South Dumfries	8.73	1.21	23	95.8
42. South Kirkcudbright	8.27	1.06	21	90.9
43. Wigtown and south tip of Ayr	7.94	0.95	18	87.1
SCOTLAND	9.12	1.39	807	100.1

TABLE 4.F

Women Field Workers' Wage Rates, by District

	Shillings per week	S.D.	N	% of Scottish mean
1. Shetland	3·27	0·66	11	78·1
2. Orkney	3·31	0·47	11	79·1
3. Caithness	3·27	0·39	12	77·9
4. East Sutherland	3·21	0·56	7	77·0
5. East Ross	2·89	0·20	12	69·5
6. N.-E. Inverness	3·06	0·21	13	73·3
7. North-west coast	2·25	0·42	6	66·0
8. Skye and Outer Hebrides	2·94	0·13	4	70·5
9. West Argyll	4·00	0·70	10	95·2
10. North Argyll	4·62	0·64	8	110·0
11. South Argyll	4·85	0·76	15	115·4
12. Highland Inverness, Banff, Moray	3·60	0·90	10	85·8
13. Highland Perth, Aberdeenshire	4·06	0·53	9	96·4
14. N.-W. Perth	3·92	1·28	12	103·1
15. Nairn, Lowland Moray	3·60	0·49	21	85·6
16. Lowland Banff	4·00	0·71	21	95·2
17. Buchan	4·39	0·97	19	104·7
18. S.-E. Aberdeenshire	4·33	1·15	24	107·8
19. Inner Aberdeenshire	3·95	1·04	20	99·3
20. Kincardine	3·61	0·42	16	85·8
21. Inner Angus	3·94	0·47	35	93·7
22. Coastal Angus	4·11	0·46	26	97·8
23. East Perthshire	4·26	0·59	19	101·3
24. South Perthshire	4·25	0·60	22	101·0
25. East Fife	4·00	0·25	33	94·7
26. West Fife	4·17	0·71	26	102·2
27. North Stirling-Clackmannan	5·21	0·74	18	124·0
28. West Lothian, East Stirling	4·91	0·53	22	116·9
29. Edinburgh area	4·42	0·38	22	105·1
30. Dunbarton, Renfrewshire	5·81	0·71	17	138·4
31. North Ayrshire	5·47	0·81	19	130·4
32. South Ayrshire	4·60	0·76	15	109·4
33. North Lanarks.	5·59	0·69	19	133·2
34. South Lanarks.	4·83	0·81	20	114·9
35. Peeblesshire	4·72	0·81	16	112·4
36. Dunbar area	4·76	0·29	19	113·3
37. South Berwick	5·09	0·43	29	121·1
38. Kelso area	4·98	0·42	22	118·5
39. Hawick area	5·13	0·43	10	122·0
40. Inner Dumfries, Kirkcudbright	4·64	0·61	20	110·3
41. South Dumfries	4·31	0·43	21	102·5
42. South Kirkcudbright	4·35	0·46	20	103·5
43. Wigtown and south tip of Ayr	3·84	0·57	17	91·2
SCOTLAND	4·32	0·91	749	

TABLE 4.G

Child Field Workers' Wage Rates, by District

	Shillings per week	S.D.	N	% of Scottish mean
1. Shetland	3·00	0	1	*
2. Orkney	1·97	0·24	7	70·8
3. Caithness	2·00	0	1	*
4. East Sutherland	2·13	0·25	4	76·3
5. East Ross	2·00	0·55	6	71·8
6. N.-E. Inverness	3·00	0	1	*
7. North-west coast	*	*	0	*
8. Skye and Outer Hebrides	3·00	0	1	*
9. West Argyll	2·75	0·50	4	98·7
10. North Argyll	2·70	0·67	5	96·9
11. South Argyll	3·10	0·65	5	111·3
12. Highland Inverness, Banff, Moray	2·40	0·90	5	86·2
13. Highland Perth, Aberdeenshire	1·75	0	1	*
14. N.-W. Perth	2·81	0·38	4	100·9
15. Nairn, Lowland Moray	2·75	0·50	4	98·7
16. Lowland Banff	2·50	0·71	2	*
17. Buchan	2·00	0	1	*
18. S.-E. Aberdeenshire	2·50	0·50	3	*
19. Inner Aberdeenshire	3·00	0	2	*
20. Kincardine	2·40	0·55	5	86·2
21. Inner Angus	2·64	0·55	11	94·7
22. Coastal Angus	2·67	0·54	12	95·8
23. East Perthshire	2·25	0	1	*
24. South Perthshire	2·89	0·68	6	101·7
25. East Fife	2·82	0·34	11	101·2
26. West Fife	2·72	0·61	9	97·7
27. North Stirling-Clackmannan	3·25	0·38	8	116·7
28. West Lothian, East Stirling	2·95	0·39	9	105·7
29. Edinburgh area	2·92	0·49	13	104·9
30. Dunbarton, Renfrewshire	3·25	0·74	6	116·7
31. North Ayrshire	3·50	0·89	6	125·7
32. South Ayrshire	2·78	0·39	7	100·0
33. North Lanarks.	3·46	0·89	7	124·4
34. South Lanarks.	4·00	0	1	*
35. Peeblesshire	3·17	0·76	3	*
36. Dunbar area	2·73	0·43	14	98·1
37. South Berwick	2·83	0·46	21	101·7
38. Kelso area	2·79	0·52	13	100·1
39. Hawick area	3·25	1·06	2	*
40. Inner Dumfries, Kirkcudbright	2·79	0·35	9	100·3
41. South Dumfries	2·61	0·60	9	93·8
42. South Kirkcudbright	2·87	0·33	11	102·8
43. Wigtown and south tip of Ayr	2·80	0·59	10	100·5
SCOTLAND	2·78	0·59	261	

TABLE 4.H

Co-efficients of Inequality in Agricultural Wage Rates in Scottish Counties, 1790–1892

	Married farm servants	Day-labourers
1790	—	0·17
1794	0·16	0·17
1810	—	0·16
1834–45	0·13	0·12
1860	—	0·09
1867–70	—	0·10[1]
1880–1	—	0·09
1892	0·10	0·06

[1] This is arrived at by excluding one eccentric report, Argyll: if it is included it becomes 0.12.
Source: see reference 9, p. 82.

The co-efficient of variation is Williamson's measure Vuw.

$$\text{Vuw} = \frac{\sqrt{\sum_i (yi - \bar{y})^2 / \text{N}}}{\bar{y}}$$

Where N = number of counties
yi = wage rate of the ith county
$\bar{y}$ = mean wage rate for Scotland.

See reference 11, p. 82.

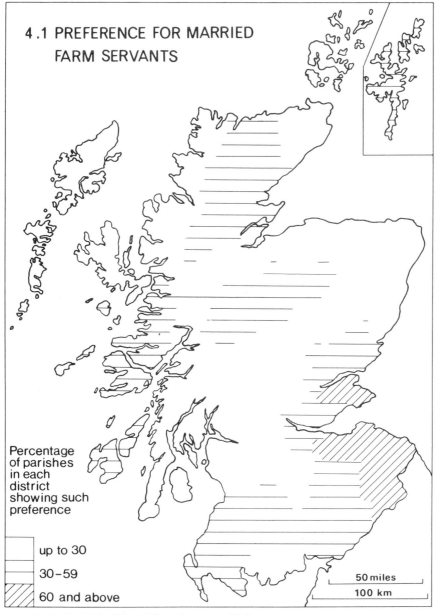

4.1 PREFERENCE FOR MARRIED FARM SERVANTS

Percentage
of parishes
in each
district
showing such
preference

up to 30

30–59

60 and above

50 miles

100 km

See Table 4.A (p. 83) and discussion on pp. 70–2.

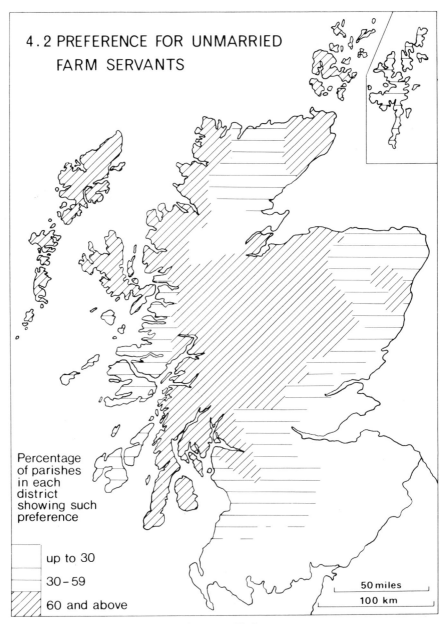

4.2 PREFERENCE FOR UNMARRIED
FARM SERVANTS

Percentage
of parishes
in each
district
showing such
preference

up to 30

30 – 59

60 and above

50 miles

100 km

See Table 4.A (p. 83) and discussion on pp. 70–2.

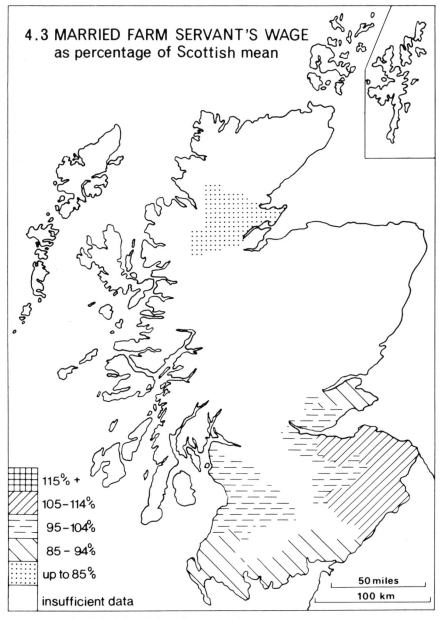

4.3 MARRIED FARM SERVANT'S WAGE
as percentage of Scottish mean

115% +
105–114%
95–104%
85–94%
up to 85%

insufficient data

50 miles
100 km

See Table 4.B (p. 84) and discussion on pp. 72–4.

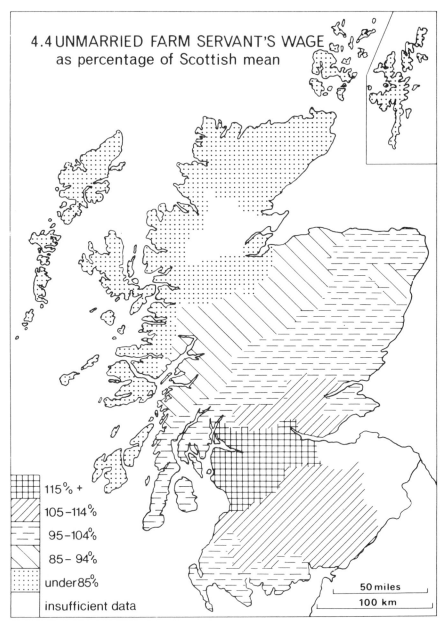

4.4 UNMARRIED FARM SERVANT'S WAGE as percentage of Scottish mean

115% +

105–114%

95–104%

85–94%

under 85%

insufficient data

50 miles
100 km

See Table 4.C (p. 85) and discussion on pp. 74–5.

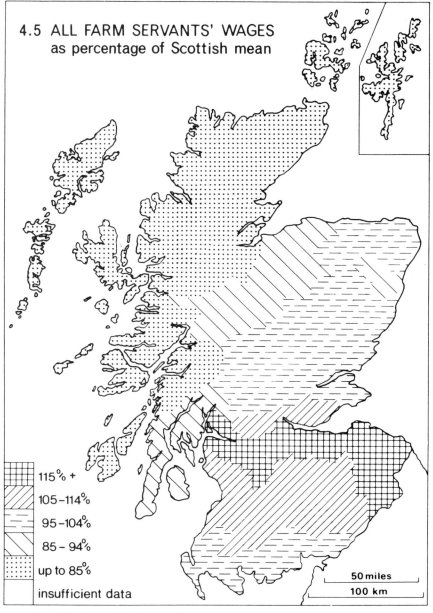

4.5 ALL FARM SERVANTS' WAGES
as percentage of Scottish mean

115% +

105 – 114%

95 – 104%

85 – 94%

up to 85%

insufficient data

50 miles

100 km

See Table 4.D (p. 86) and discussion on p. 75.

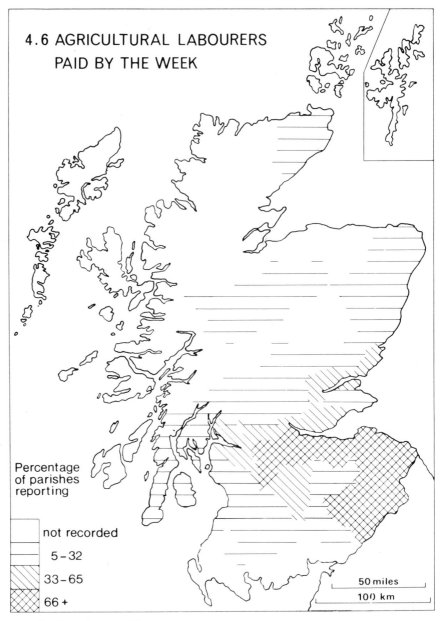

4.6 AGRICULTURAL LABOURERS
PAID BY THE WEEK

Percentage
of parishes
reporting

not recorded

5 – 32

33 – 65

66 +

50 miles

100 km

See discussion on p. 76.

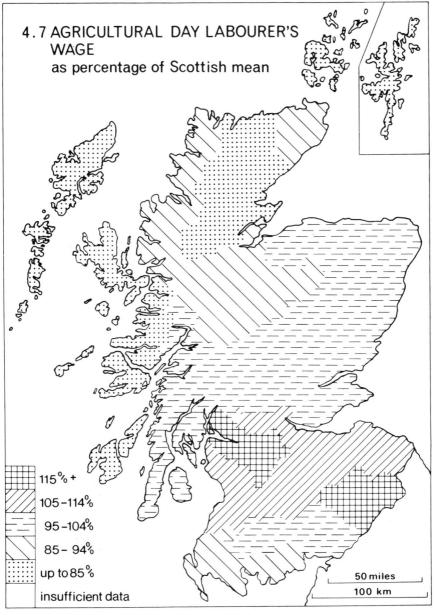

4.7 AGRICULTURAL DAY LABOURER'S
WAGE
as percentage of Scottish mean

115% +
105–114%
95–104%
85– 94%
up to 85%
insufficient data

50 miles
100 km

See Table 4.E (p. 87) and discussion on pp. 77–8.

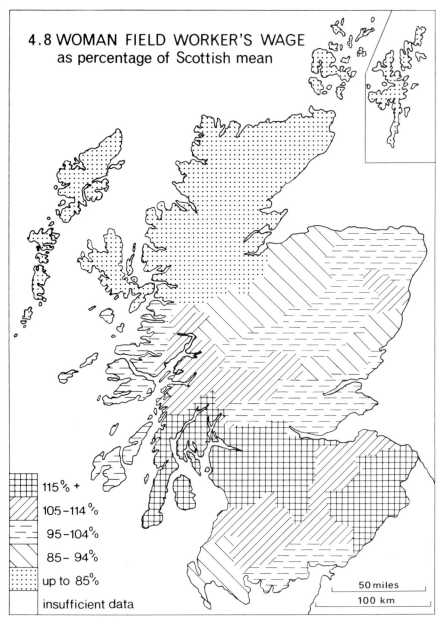

4.8 WOMAN FIELD WORKER'S WAGE
as percentage of Scottish mean

115% +

105–114%

95–104%

85– 94%

up to 85%

insufficient data

50 miles

100 km

See Table 4.F (p. 88) and discussion on pp. 78–9.

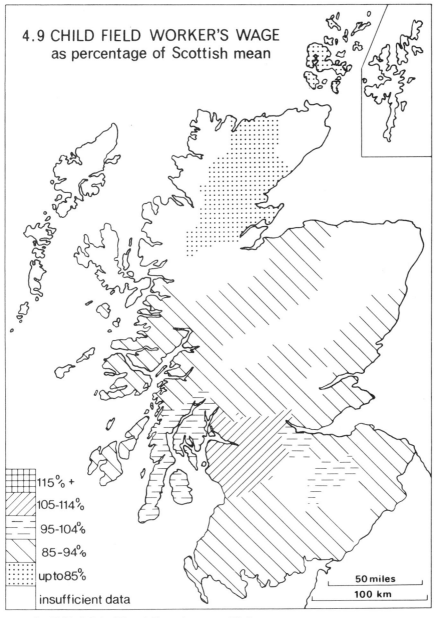

4.9 CHILD FIELD WORKER'S WAGE
as percentage of Scottish mean

115% +
105-114%
95-104%
85-94%
up to 85%
insufficient data

50 miles
100 km

See Table 4.G (p. 89) and discussion on pp. 78–9.

Chapter 5

INDUSTRIAL WAGES AND THE
WORKING-CLASS BUDGET

1. *The skilled worker's wage*

Information on male wage rates outside the agricultural sector is provided in the answers to two questions in the 1843 questionnaire:

Q. 11. What are the average wages of artizans, and colliers and miners, in your parish?

Q. 12. What are the weekly wages of the lowest class of labourers, or artizans in your parish, who have no parochial relief?

The answers provide the raw materials for tables 5.A–C. There are data in the replies to Question 11 for 'artizans' wages' in general terms (561 cases cited), and more specifically for masons (90 cases), wrights (107 cases), colliers (62 cases), shoemakers (25 cases) and smiths (30 cases).

In the replies to Question 12 there are data for 'the lowest class of labourers' and for handloom weavers (452 and 68 cases respectively). The term 'artizan' in early Victorian Britain implied a skilled worker pursuing a trade for which an apprenticeship was normally necessary, though it was realised that trades varied in skill and that in some cases the custom of apprenticeship may have died out: normally artizans were well paid, but the outstanding exception was the craft of the handloom weaver, hopelessly over-supplied with cheap labour and now threatened by competition from factory looms. They had become as poor as the lowest class of unskilled labourer – hence the phrasing of Question 12.

Table 5.A and Map 5.1, then, can be regarded as demonstrating the 'average' skilled workers' wage rates. At 13s. a week they were about 45 per cent. above that of agricultural day-labourers, taking Scotland as a whole. But as the last column of the table shows, there was much variation from place to place. Curiously enough, the 8 districts where artizans were paid 60 per cent. or more than unskilled farm labourers comprised the Edinburgh area and 7 poor rural districts – 5 in the Highlands and 2 in the south-west. That skilled workers should be particularly well paid near Edinburgh is to be explained in terms of demand: the capital was famous for the craft traditions of its consumer industries and its pull was bound to have an effect on the parishes around. That they should be relatively well paid in the north and the south-west is perhaps to be explained in terms of supply; not very many craftsmen were needed in the Highlands, in absolute terms they could get better pay by going south, and Dr. Lobban's work on Highland migrants into Greenock[1] suggests they were probably more mobile than crofters and cottars without a skill. Consequently those who did stay were fairly well paid by local standards, though that is not, perhaps, saying very much: an analysis of how artizans were paid in the different economic categories of parish shows that in urban-industrial parishes they could attain over 2s. a week more than in crofting parishes (see Table 5.G). It is also notable that the six districts where artizans were paid less than 30 per cent. above unskilled farm labourers lay with one exception (South Ayr) in the shires of Perth, Angus and Kincardine where farm-work was fairly well paid but the average for skilled industrial work perhaps brought down by the large numbers in the village linen trades.

None of the individual artizan trades mentioned in the replies to Question 11 occurs in enough parishes to justify drawing many conclusions from a breakdown by districts but Tables 5.B and C compare what data there are. Colliers and masons were the best-paid artizans of all, averaging over 15s. a week: the wages of colliers, however, were subject to deductions for their tools, lights and powder which might amount to 1s. or more a week (22.439), bringing them down in reality to the level of wrights or smiths at 13–14s. Shoemakers at 10· 7s. were barely better off than unskilled farm labour except, perhaps, for greater seasonal regularity in their employment.

With masons and wrights there are enough cases to demonstrate how the wage varied according to the economic categories of parishes (Table 5.G). Masons were paid very much better in the large towns and very much worse in crofting parishes than elsewhere – apparently a differential of 7s. a week, which goes far to explain the migration of men like Hugh Miller, who had moved from the Highlands to Edinburgh to work at the construction of the New Town a generation earlier.[2] Perhaps the big towns, with their large and elaborate buildings, also attracted the masons with the best skill. With wrights, however, the differential appears much less: the pay was lowest in crofting parishes, but outside them there was scarcely a shilling a week's difference in whatever economic category of parish they were working. It is hard to see why there should be so much difference in the pattern of remuneration for these two categories of building workers: and it is possible that the low number of cases at the extremes has in fact exaggerated differences between the two occupations.

The text of the Poor Law Inquiry also provides information on the wages of some other skilled workers, though not in any systematic way. One learns, however, that the wages of engineers in Glasgow were '22s. to 28s. and as high as 30s. weekly' (20.375) and that founders in Greenock were earning 18s. to 23s. a week (22.485); 'ordinary skilled workmen' in the foundries in Kirkcaldy earned 16s. a week (22.321). All these were high wages for characteristic trades of the industrial revolution in comparison with the more traditional crafts of the mason or wright. In textiles, however, such high earnings for men may be less typical, even in factories. Males in a cotton factory at Rothesay, Bute, were earning between 22s. a week (working 69 hours) and 11s. (21.72). Near Hawick, stocking weavers (not in a factory) earned 12–15s. a week (22.660).

One of the most interesting pieces of evidence on wages presented to the commissioners was a return from a textile printing works at Bonhill, in the Vale of Leven, Dunbartonshire, employing nearly a thousand hands, of whom a minority, 416, were adult males (22.458). Of these, only 5 per cent. earned more than 20s. a week – the best paid were the engravers, who averaged 39s. 6d. However, 41 per cent. of the adult male workers earned exactly 20s. a week: the majority of these were block printers, who clearly regarded themselves as well off in the hierarchy of Scottish labour (22.466–7). Below them were a further 20 per cent. who earned 15s. to 18s., including mechanics, carpenters and mill-wrights – these appear to obtain about the norm for artizans in our returns from Dunbarton and Renfrew district. Finally there were 33 per cent. of the workers who were more or less unskilled, like scourers, carters and labourers, who earned from 14s. down to 10s. The really cheap labour at the print works, however, was female and juvenile. Adult women comprised 22 per cent. of the total work force: none earned more than 9s. (less than the lowest paid male labourer here), and 80 per cent. earned 6s. or less. Juveniles comprised 36 per cent. of the work force: 90 per cent. of the boys earned 4s. 6d. or less; the same proportion of the girls 3s. 6d. or less. In this context the man's wage of £1 a week does indeed seem an achievement of which he would be proud.

2. *The general labourer's wage*

The 'lowest labourers' wages of Question 12, shown in Table 5.D and Map 5.2, represent the opposite end of the earnings spectrum to the skilled artizans: with wages of under 6s. a week they were earning a third less than the agricultural day-labourers and only about 46 per cent. of the artizans' weekly wage. They are, however, the '*lowest* class of labourers', not the average labourers (indeed, we have disregarded a number of cases where the respondent appears to have misunderstood this and entered the same figure as for agricultural day-labourers). There was a sense in which the 'lowest class of labourer' was regarded as the bottom of the social pile, perhaps already old, or broken by sickness or bad habits of drink. Evidence before the commissioners occasionally stated the wages of industrial labourers other than those of the 'lowest class'. Those at Bonhill textile printing works earned 10–12s., and those in Greenock in 'ordinary times' earned 12s. (22.458; 20.533): this compares to a district mean of 6·5s. for the 'lowest class'. At Kirkcaldy on the other side of Scotland labourers in the foundries also earned 12s. a week, compared here to a district mean of 6·2s. for the 'lowest class' (22.321). This suggests a range for labourers which was at least as large as the differential between skilled and unskilled occupations. It is seldom appreciated just how much the return for general labouring work depended on the fitness and competence of the individual.

Our statistics in Table 5.D relate, therefore, to those least able to provide for themselves and their dependants in the struggle for subsistence. There are few quotations for the north, where there was little industrial work in any case. The wages of such labourers as there were both in the Highlands and in the south-western and north-eastern rural districts were usually low: the highest paid were in the industrial west, and in the arable south-east where farm-work was also well rewarded. But wherever they were to be found they were extremely badly off, especially if they were married with a wife or child who did not earn. To support two or more individuals on less than 6s. a week, with food and fuel to find and rent to pay, must have been to live on the edge of purgatory.

3. *The handloom weavers*

The last column in Table 5.C lists the weekly wages of the depressed handloom weavers, for whom there were 68 replies, mainly under the heading 'lowest class of . . . artizans' in Question 12. They appear generally to have been only a trifle better off than the 'lowest class of labourers', with a wage slightly over 6s. a week. The weavers were the cause of much social anxiety and several government investigations in the 1830s and 1840s, which gave ample illustrations of their suffering and sense of degradation that stemmed partly from having been, a generation earlier, the most prosperous group in the working class.

The Poor Law Inquiry added to this volume of evidence, and many reports stressed the weavers' particular plight in the depression of 1841–2. At Auchtermuchty in Fife, for instance, there had been more than 200 families on charitable relief, obtaining up to 10d. a day for which they had to perform a 'labour test' of breaking stones: but for the previous two or three years even their average wages in employment had only been 10d. or 1s. a day: 'we have more weavers than there is work for at remunerative wages' (22.263). At Irvine in Ayrshire wages were a little better ('of late . . . from 1s. to 2s. a day') but the depression had ruined many families who had pawned their clothing and furniture: 'the distress lasted so long that the savings of those who had been provident were exhausted' (22.497). Not that it was easy even by working excessive hours in prosperous years to put anything by for hard times, as comments from a flax-mill owner at Kirkcaldy showed: handloom weaving was not, he said, 'sufficiently remunerated to enable the workmen to save money' at wages ranging from 5s. a week to a ceiling of 11s.; 'Some few able-bodied weavers may earn as much as 11s. a week for a few years of their lives, by working twelve hours a day; but the ordinary hours for weavers working are longer' (22.337).

No community suffered more terribly from this kind of under-pay with alternating overwork and unemployment than the burgh of Paisley, home of the hand-made fancy shawl trade. The story of the depression of 1841–3 is told in Chapter 7 below: at its worst, in the spring of 1842, there were 14,000 individuals subsisting on public relief valued at 2d. per head per day. A year later, when trade had revived, Dr. Burns the minister of the principal kirk counted the cost (20.565):

There is a large body of respectable operatives dunning us daily for
means to emigrate. I have said to them, 'Are you not all employed?' –
'Yes.' 'What makes you think of going away?' 'We dread the winter.'
They have been left perfectly bare. Their clothes are pawned, and
anything they can make goes to redeem the things they have pawned.
If they are not redeemed before winter, they will be as they were last
winter, in the most distressing state. Had they no drawbacks – no
pawns to redeem, no rent to pay, no children to educate, no delicate
wives to provide necessaries for, they might live; but with these,
accompanied by a long period of periodical depression, they are
incapable of living as working classes in the community ought to live,
or as they did live in my remembrance.

He went on to contrast attendance at funerals in prosperous times and
now. Formerly large numbers of weavers would leave their work and 'dress
themselves like gentlemen, in black' to follow the corpse of a deceased
acquaintance; now scarcely a quarter of the numbers appeared, and when he
asked the weavers why this was so they replied that their clothes were worn
out, or in pawn, or that 'time was precious, and they could not spare it'. He
concluded, 'it is degrading to make such men paupers'; but he had no remedy,
except to propose free trade in the manner of the Anti-Corn Law League.

Middle-class contemporaries, indeed, were puzzled by the tenacity of the
weavers. Even around 1840 new communities were appearing, like a village
for 300 inhabitants recently constructed in the parish of Kettle in Fife
(22.281–2). Children were still entering the trade, from the age of 12 at Irvine
(22.496–7). A typical comment came from J. H. Burton, the Edinburgh
advocate and historian, who blamed the weavers for hanging on 'in this
hopeless trade' despite the literacy which should have given them the means
to understand their plight and their crying need to learn new jobs. He proposed teaching them political economy so that they would understand that
their predicament was due to the unalterable laws of supply and demand on
the labour market, not to the 'avarice of others – the employers' (20.791). It
was a remedy more inappropriate even than the abolition of the corn laws,
but clearly prompted by the fact that the weaving villages and towns were the
main strongholds of Chartism.[3]

It may fairly be asked, however, whether the weavers could have behaved
in a more rational way, economically or intellectually. What jobs could they
have learned? Unskilled industrial workers had a similar range of earnings,
from somewhat under 6s. a week for the 'lowest class' to 10–12s. at the top
end: it was unlikely that a raw recruit from the sedentary life of a weaver
would earn at the top unless he was exceptionally fit, young, strong and able
to learn. Furthermore, a mature weaver could hardly hope to enter a factory
as a skilled worker without having worked his way up the shop floor as a
juvenile, or to enter a traditional craft like a mason or a wright without having
served an apprenticeship in his teens. The mobility of the next generation was
hindered by the weaver's need for a juvenile to help him operate the harness
looms on which the most skilled and best paid work was made; to send his

child to the factory was to put his own earning power immediately at risk. Besides, as is demonstrated below, not all factory children were able to earn as much to begin with as a child at a handloom, derisory though the sum might appear to a well-paid worker.

The job mobility of which Burton spoke, therefore, was a delusion. The weavers could only stay put hoping for better days to return, or emigrate: a third alternative, minimum wage legislation, had been repeatedly suggested by the weavers in the past and as frequently rejected by a Parliament working in the name of *laisser-faire* and political economy. The Chartists, however, proposed a democracy where workers would be in a majority and such thoughts not automatically ruled out of court. Weavers showed more common sense in following that creed than anything their middle-class friends dreamed up for them.

4. *Women and children in industry*

The Poor Law Commissioners also investigated the problem of the industrial remuneration of women and children. Following up a prior question about the type of manufactures located in the parish, they asked:

Q. 15. Do women find any employment in such manufactures, and of what description, and at what rate of wages?

Q. 16. Do children find employment in such manufactures, and of what description, and from what age and at what rate of wages?

As to whether or not women and children found industrial employment there was in each case a 92 per cent. response rate. Of the responding parishes, 241 or 29 per cent. said there was such employment for women, 208 or 25 per cent. for children. Maps 5.3 and 5.4 show the distribution of female and juvenile work by district – heavily concentrated, as one would expect, in the textile manufacturing areas: about 80 per cent. of the jobs mentioned fell into that sector. The description of what work women and children actually performed is not usually very specific, but more parishes reported handloom weaving than cotton-spinning (for women, 46 parishes as compared with 22; for children, 24 as compared with 19). More localities, indeed, reported women employed in linen and woollen textiles than in cotton (62 for the first two, 45 for the last); the same was again true in respect of children (45 and 51 as against 33). On the other hand, the cotton industry was more concentrated in its main centres and no doubt in absolute terms employed far more people of both sexes. This pattern nevertheless emphasises the way gains from the other textiles could supplement family earnings over a very wide area of Scotland. Indeed the linen and woollen industries were made viable in Scotland, in the absence of sophisticated mechanisation, largely by the manufacturer's ability to exploit these pools of cheap family labour.

It is also true, of course (as we shall see in more detail in the next section) that many families could themselves hardly have subsisted without earnings from the labour of women and children because the adult male was himself paid too little. Handloom weavers were again the extreme case, but the dilemma they found themselves in was well put by a Kirkintilloch weaver in his late forties with 11 children who gave evidence before the commissioners (22.381–2). He recalled how as a lad of 13 he could earn a guinea a week for 9 hours' labour a day, but said that children now could not earn 5s. a week (or 4s. net after expenses were deducted) for working less than 12 hours a day: yet necessity drove families to make them work – 'It is a distressing thing for a father to be obliged to put a boy to the loom at nine years of age; but the thing must be done, or he must starve.' His evidence was corroborated by a surgeon at Kilsyth (22.389). He said that weavers set their children (both boys and girls) to work at the loom because their own wages were so very low – 'A man earning only from 5s. to 8s. a week, having, perhaps, a wife, with two or three children, is naturally anxious to derive profit from his children's labour, at the earliest possible age.'

How typical was it to start work so young? In 132 parishes the age of the first employment of children was given: the mean was 11·2 years, but in a quarter of the parishes they had indeed begun before they were aged 10, and in 92 per cent. of cases they were at work when they were aged 13. Working 10 to 14 hours a day at such a tender age produced what the doctor at Kilsyth called 'debility and general exhaustion' among the weavers' children, as well as making it impossible for them to attend school. In the factories efforts were made at some works to provide evening classes for juveniles: it did not work successfully at Neilston in Renfrewshire because 'the children are so exhausted that they feel more inclined to fall asleep than to receive instruction: hence they grow up ignorant of their duty to God and man' (22.416). Another minister, speaking of similar classes at the print-fields at Tibbermore in Perthshire, said that the children 'after standing ten hours on their feet are quite unfit' for education: 'I have gone again and again and found half of them sleeping' (22.228). Print-fields had a reputation for accepting very young children: they were working at the age of 7 or 8 for 2s. a week at New Kilpatrick (22.455).

What was the labour of women and children usually paid? Unfortunately there are far fewer quotations of wage rates than there are bald statements that such employment was available. Only 165 parishes gave such information for women, and 134 for children – too few to provide satisfactory data on the different wage rates in the different trades but enough, perhaps, to show the general variation in earnings opportunity from district to district. Table 5.E and 5.F and Maps 5.5 and 5.6 present the results: the overall mean for Scotland suggests a female wage of 4s. 6d., and a juvenile wage of about 3s. On average, then, children were paid two-thirds of what a woman could obtain, though in some places, e.g., North Lanarkshire, the juvenile wage was as high as 84 per cent. of the female wage. Even women, however, were on average paid less than 'the lowest class of labourer', and received only half the rate of agricultural day-labourers or a third the wage of artizans. Their weekly wage rates were scarcely better than those of their sisters in agricultural labour, but their annual earnings must have been higher as the strong seasonal element was less marked in industrial employment.

It is, of course, an oversimplification to imagine that agricultural and industrial employment were always mutually exclusive. In many country areas this was not so. Thus at Dryfesdale in Dumfriesshire women could make £2 in a month's harvest work, £2.7s. at field labour over 3 or 4 months in the summer and £2–£2.10s. by spinning or knitting in winter (22.612). On the other hand by the 1840s there was a strong tendency for such domestic industrial work to die out, or to become much less well paid due to competition from the factories. There were many comments like that of the session clerk of Brechin who said how hard it was for an old woman to obtain light tasks – she 'can now with difficulty get 1s. 6d. a week, and she formerly might have maintained herself pretty well by spinning and knitting stockings' (22.39). In the west of Scotland tambouring and flowering muslins had been a traditional task: the doctor at Kilsyth reported (again typically) heavy falls of wages – from 2s. to 2s. 6d. a day 'about twenty-five or thirty years ago' to 4d. to 6d. a day now – with similar hardships for old people (22.389). In the opinion of a Fife farmer the greatest drawback in the comfort of his labourers was that 'the factories have put it out of the power of female members of the family to add anything to the general stock of earnings, except by out-door labour, which is only to be obtained from April to the end of harvest. They can now only earn the merest trifle by spinning and knitting' (22.283).

Factory work seems after all to have been quite well paid compared to this: the fact that all the 223 women at Bonhill print-field in Dunbartonshire obtained 5s. a week or more and that the usual rate for similar workers at Paisley print-fields was 6–7s. must have seemed very enviable to tambourers in the same areas (22.458). This no doubt helps to explain why the best-paid women in industrial employment were found near Edinburgh, in Dunbarton and Renfrewshire, and in the Hawick area: the best-paid children were in the Edinburgh area and in Lanarkshire. Table 5.G, analysing the data by economic type of community, shows that women in industry obtained almost double the pay in urban communities of that in deep rural ones. The same tendency to pay more in urban areas is much less marked for children, perhaps because towns found more jobs for very young children who were paid very little: 42 per cent. of the 350 Bonhill print-field children were paid 2s. and 2s. 6d.

Some difference may also have been made, especially for women's wages, in the Edinburgh area by competition between manufacturing industry and domestic service for the urban middle class. Unfortunately we know nothing of the actual rates of pay for female domestic service in Scotland in the 1840s.

5. *The Dryfesdale budget*

What did the wages we have examined so far mean in real terms? What could working people buy with them? Our understanding of this is greatly helped by one of the witnesses before the Royal Commission, Mr. David Stuart, Distributor of Stamps at Dumfries in 1843, but before that a resident in the rural parish of Dryfesdale in that county. For his own interest, he had worked out the budget of a local man, 'a hired servant with a yearly income of

£26 and having a wife and four children under twelve years of age'. He admitted 'the yearly income ... is somewhat above the average of ordinary labourers, which may not exceed £20 to £22', but 'to counterbalance this ... there are four children under twelve which is more than the average number; and therefore, the style of living here represented may be considered as the common standard, or nearly so.' The mother was too busy looking after her four small children to be able to work, so the father's income was everything. The expenditure in one year amounted to virtually the same sum, being made up as follows:

Rent—£2·00,
Fuel—£2·00,
Food—£13·13,
Tobacco and whisky—£0·75,
Clothes—£6·00,
Soap, candle, school and doctors fees—£2·10.

The exact particulars of this (and another budget for a single woman) are given with information on the quantities involved in Appendix II – suffice to say that 85 per cent. of the food bill went on meal, potatoes and milk, with twice as much spent on meal as on potatoes. It was a typical diet for a family of this income, but not the cheapest diet, which 'is of course sometimes effected by substituting potatoes entirely for oatmeal, potatoes being generally more than one-half cheaper as an article of food', and presumably by omitting the small quantities of meat, fish, tea and sugar that were in the residual expenditure on food.

Stuart's Dryfesdale budget was by no means the only estimate in the Inquiry of the cost of living, though it was by far the most detailed. Others calculated what it cost to keep an adult alive in good health on his or her food alone: estimates varied from 1s. a week (a labourer at Urquhart, Inverness-shire) to 1s. 5½d. (Longformacus, Berwickshire), 1s. 6d. (North Uist and Kilmarnock) and 1s. 9d. (for print-field girls at Paisley). Those who tried to calculate an 'all-in' allowance put it at about 3s. a week (Paisley, Aberdeen and Inverness) (20.676,708,758; 21.39,467,592; 22.736). They therefore broadly agree with Stuart that about half the income would go on food. The yearly expenses for one individual at 3s. a week would be £7·8 a year, for a married couple say £15. In the Dryfesdale family there would be another £9 left to support four young children. All the other calculations seem roughly compatible with Stuart's on this reckoning.

Using this Dryfesdale family budget as a standard, we have therefore constructed Table 5.H to show how four other families of the same size would fare in eight different districts of Scotland, depending on whether the man alone was working, or if he was joined by his wife, or by his wife and two children. We have assumed that everyone wished to buy exactly the same goods as the Dryfesdale family, and the aim is to see how far they exceeded or fell short of achieving this expenditure pattern, 'the common standard or nearly so'. By using district price data on rent, fuel, meal and potatoes we can accurately estimate the local variation in the cost of one half of the budget:

the other half is necessarily assumed not to vary, which is perhaps not un-reasonable as the principal items are clothing, school fees, doctor's bills, etc. The only variation in consumption we have assumed is substituting free peats for coal in Orkney and Skye and the Hebrides, and in the latter district, we have also assumed that the accommodation had no value (see above p. 9).

We have also made certain assumptions about the four families:

1. *Artizan's family*. The man obtains the average artizans' wage for his district: his wife and children have industrial employment. They all work throughout the year.

2. *Lowest labourer's family*. The man obtains $10\frac{1}{2}$ months work as one of 'the lowest class of labourers' in the districts, suffering a spell of winter unemployment characteristic of this type of worker. His wife and children, however, have industrial employment throughout the year (as they were likely to work indoors unlike the man, this is realistic).

3. *Farm servant's family*. The man is hired by the year as a married farm servant; his wife (when working) is a field labourer for one half of the year; the children (when working) have field employment for half of the year as well. These are generous assumptions as regards the regularity of the female and juvenile labour, but as no account is taken of supplementary industrial earnings from knitting, spinning etc. we feel justified in making them.

4. *Agricultural day-labourer's family*. The man is hired on a day basis for $10\frac{1}{2}$ months of the year, suffering a short spell of winter unemployment. His wife and children work under the same conditions as the farm servants.

In every case we have omitted a family or the earnings of a member of the family if it seems improbable that they could get employment at all in the district – e.g., there is no entry of the farm servant's family for Lanarkshire because married hinds of this type were seldom employed; and as there is no regular employment in agriculture for children in Skye and the Hebrides it is assumed the family has no choice but to forgo the chance of juvenile earnings in that district. Where there are payments in kind the cash value is included in the wage.

Of the four model families, the only one which could attain and surpass the 'Dryfesdale standard' consistently on the man's wage alone was the artizan's – this was true wherever he was in Scotland. Given full employment, a skilled worker, taking Scotland as a whole, would have 22 per cent. of his wage left when he had satisfied these fairly comfortable basic needs, a figure that exceeded 30 per cent. in the Edinburgh area and North Lanarkshire. Some of this surplus he would have to spend buying his own tools: the collier's pick and powder or the mason's trowel which employers did not normally supply. For some groups of artizans the assumption that they would evade seasonal unemployment was unrealistic, too. Hugh Miller explained that masons 'of the north country . . . have very little employment during the winter'; in Coldstream, Berwickshire, they had been out of work for 16 or 17 weeks due to severe weather in the winter of 1842–3 and in 'great distress' (understandably, as such a spell without work would reduce an artizan's earnings there from 32 per cent. above the Dryfesdale standard to 11 per cent. below it). However, said Miller, masons in the south were normally employed in sheds in the winter, and thus escaped the hardship of the northern counties: he was probably thinking of conditions in Edinburgh, where he had himself migrated as a working mason from Cromarty (20.209; 22.711).

Despite qualifications, however, it is likely that the artizan would normally accumulate an appreciable surplus which he might save through a subscription to a friendly society or a deposit in a savings bank, or spend on drink, or on renting a better house, eating better food or buying good furniture. 'Decent work people', said Alexander Watt in Glasgow, 'have generally a tolerably furnished house ... a carpet, a mahogany chest of drawers, an eight-day clock, good blankets and bedding' (20.365). The fact that the surplus appeared in all eight districts makes comprehensible remarks about how well the 'tradesmen' lived even in remote parishes like Golspie in Sutherland (see above p. 31). It also makes plausible the comments of censorious observers on well-paid groups like the miners, whom the minister of Newton in Midlothian described as 'not only dissolute in their habits, but ... expensive in a way which is unknown to the agriculturalists. The colliers are exceedingly well dressed.' He also averred that mining families 'have £3 or £4 or £5 a week coming in, and I do not know how they contrive to spent it' (22.782).

Miners were perhaps exceptional in having (at least in the eastern coalfields) their womenfolk working. It is likely that most skilled artizans would not in fact allow their wives to work while they were in good health themselves; the family would forgo the chance of incremental earnings for the sake of the better comfort won by the wife staying at home. This can be seen in the calico-printing industry where the block printers earned £1 a week and enjoyed a high standard of living, exemplified by the Bonhill printer who ate splendid breakfasts of ham (see above p. 34): but the women in such print-fields (as at Paisley) were often not their own wives and daughters but Highlanders, earning a small wage which they no doubt sent home to the croft (20.676,708). The children of these well-paid artizans, too, would be more likely to stay on at school for a longer period to gain the advantages of literacy which, in turn, would reinforce their chance of obtaining a good position in industrial society.

These calculations, indeed, help to make sense of the concept of a labour aristocracy removed in prosperous times from the cold edge of poverty, unaware of and unsympathetic towards the realities of life for the unskilled poor. The short-term threat to the artizan's position lay in the down-turn of a trade cycle that would stop the factories or halt the construction industry. If the stoppage was not prolonged, he could sit it out on his cushion of savings or even use his capital to buy a little shop from which he could live until industrial employment returned again, as George Patterson, an Aberdeen blacksmith who gave evidence before the Inquiry, did in 1843 (21.657). If it was prolonged, however, there was a danger of the artizan exhausting his savings and falling into the pit of total destitution from which he could never climb out again. The problem of the degradation of the 'decent working man' much exercised the Poor Law Commissioners, as we shall see in later chapters; it was a threat not only to the individual but to the stability of society itself, and the deep and long depression centred on 1842 naturally stoked the Chartism of those years.

The artizan could also, of course, face a long-term threat – that his trade would be destroyed either by dilution from incomers attracted by its initial high wages or by a changing technology that would replace human skill with a mechanised process. The fate of the handloom weavers stood as an example to all, and the artizans were, wherever possible, devoted to the maintenance of apprenticeship as a way of limiting entrance to the craft and to restrictive practices as a way of limiting the march of the machine. It is not fanciful to see that in this respect (as in others) the twentieth century still suffers from attitudes engendered by nineteenth-century capitalism.

In contrast to the relative security of the artizan and his family we must consider the hopeless position of the 'lowest labourer' in industry. The very phrase suggests someone barely able to cope, and perhaps such men were not often encumbered with families of four young children since they were often elderly when their earnings fell to this level. On the other hand some were social casualties in early life, and in any case their position is so similar to that of the handloom weaver that the calculations can serve as proxy for the latter group as well – and among the weavers there were many with small families.

In the 'lowest labourer's' (or weaver's) family the father, on $10\frac{1}{2}$ months work, could barely reach half the sum required in the Dryfesdale budget, and even if he found work for the entire year he would (taking Scotland as a whole) only reach 54 per cent. of the necessary earnings, or about enough to cover the food bill for the six mouths he had to feed. Such families could and did cut all possible corners, replacing meal by potatoes, giving up meat and all in-essentials (except perhaps drink), living in the worst and cheapest slums, spending as little as possible on clothes and fuel and not sending their children to school at all. Thus at Kinnell in Angus the minister remarked that 'the labourers and weavers are, many of them, not very able to pay for the education of their children' (22.48), and the city-missionary of Dundee reported that 'many little children are kept in the house, literally from want of clothes to go out with' (22.168). Statements of this sort were commonplace in the towns and industrial villages as soon as a trade depression struck.

Whatever economies they made, however, a 'lowest labourer's' family with four children could hardly have stayed alive unless the mother also worked. If she did, and if she kept her job for a full year, on average they would attain 93 per cent. of the income needed for the Dryfesdale standard, which would be a viable sum. If two of the children were old enough to work as well the family would actually be quite well off, earning an amount in excess of an artizan's income from the pooled earnings of four breadwinners. This illustrates the imperative need for the poor to have the dependent members of the family employed in the factories for as long and as fully as possible. Such considerations applied to those well above the status of the 'lowest class' of labourer: thus at Inverness, in a district where the 'lowest class' of labourer earned about 5s. a week, a sacking manufacturer explained how 'the average wages of able-bodied men' in his works were 8s. or 9s. a week, which was below the sum necessary for his family to support themselves properly, but 'his wife spins, and some of the children weave, and their earnings together may amount to 15s. or 16s. a week. Some few families can make 30s. a week' (21.504).

There was also, obviously, a cycle of poverty dependent on the children's age as well as on their employment opportunities: when the children are tiny and need their mother's care most the family is in desperate straits; when two are working they are better off than any other family on the table except if an artizan also sends his wife and children out to work. Alexander Guthrie, surgeon in Brechin, remarked that many young couples fell deeply into debt when the family was small − 'it is only when they can carry on till their children become fit to go into the spinning mills that they can recover from their embarrassments', perhaps 'at the distance of twenty years from the time of their marriage, through the aid afforded them from the wages of their children' (22.30). Others also found that the earnings of their children in a time of economic recession saved them from pauperism: the minister of Neilston parish in Renfrewshire explained that in the depression of 1841−2 his parish was better off than many in the county because cotton factories, print-fields and bleach-fields 'still afforded employment to a certain number of the children whose wages were applied to keep their parents in better circumstances than would otherwise have been the case' (22.416).

The data in Table 5.H help, indeed, to explain several aspects of working-class life that puzzled contemporary observers who did not have to live in the same way. It shows why many poor people married young: children were the best form of insurance against old age and family ill-health in a world without a welfare state. Such alliances were, in their own way, thrifty and functional rather than premature and profligate as their critics assumed. It also shows why remarriage for a widow with a large family could be an attractive proposition for both parties. Sheriff Alison alleged, indeed, that 'children, so far from being felt as a burden, are found to be a benefit . . . often if a man can only get a widow with eight children, he can give over working, and drink the rest of his life' (20.473). It becomes clear why very poor, unskilled families would immigrate into industrial districts with the men earning extremely low wages: under some circumstances they had much better expectations than if they had stayed outside.

Such a dependency on children as wage earners in the family also had very serious general implications for society. If children had to earn bread, they could not be at school; if they were not at school they had small chances of bettering the condition of the next generation; a vicious circle of poverty begetting ignorance and ignorance begetting poverty was established, and the brutality of the lives of the poor perpetuated.

The two agricultural families also fail to attain the Dryfesdale standard on the men's wages alone, though the married farm servant's wage comes on average within 90 per cent. of the target, and, if the day-labourer had been employed for a full year instead of for the $10\frac{1}{2}$ months assumed, he would have reached 83 per cent. The fact that they nevertheless fall short shows, however, that the economic need for women to work was as general on the land as in the towns. The decline in female field labour at the end of the nineteenth century came about when agricultural earnings for men at last rose decisively over the subsistence threshold: agricultural families followed the lead of the artizans and improved their standard of comfort by keeping the wife at home.

Table 5.H also shows that in some rural districts there was no way in which some families with four children could survive except under the most difficult conditions. The 'lowest labourer' in South Kirkcudbright was unlikely to be able to find industrial employment for his wife and children, yet he could only make 45 per cent. of the Dryfesdale target by his own efforts. For this reason, of course, such men almost always made for the towns where the other members of the family could get gainful employment. Again, if a man tried to live as an agricultural day-labourer on some big estate farm on Skye even with the help of his wife he could only make three-quarters of the required sum. Such men therefore almost invariably had crofts from which they tried to eke out a living.

It is poverty like this which underlies what can be too easily interpreted as a 'preference' of certain districts for inferior foods (like potatoes and herring), and their high levels of illiteracy – they could not afford even the Dryfesdale standard. It reinforces E. H. Hunt's conclusion on 'the plight of the rural labourer of southern England and parts of Wales and Northern Scotland': there is 'no major occupational group more worthy of compassion'.[4] Interestingly enough, the table also shows that an agricultural worker could improve his standard of living simply by moving towards an industrial or urban area and remaining as an agricultural worker. The buoyant effects of industrialisation on the rate of common labourers' wages had been noted at a very early date by Adam Smith when he wrote 'the wages of labour in a great town and its neighbourhood are frequently . . . twenty or five-and-twenty per cent. higher than at a few miles distance'.[5] The market for labour was no doubt more perfect in 1843 than in 1775, but the principle was the same.

REFERENCES

1. R. D. Lobban, 'The Migration of Highlanders into Lowland Scotland, 1750–1890' (unpublished Edinburgh University Ph.D. thesis, 1969).
2. Hugh Miller, *My Schools and Schoolmasters* (Edinburgh, 1907 edn.), chapter 14.
3. A. Wilson, *The Chartist Movement in Scotland* (Manchester, 1970). See especially the map on page 84.
4. E. H. Hunt, *Regional Wage Variations in Britain, 1850–1914* (Oxford, 1973), p. 356.
5. Adam Smith, *The Wealth of Nations* (Everyman edn., 1957), vol. I, p. 66.

TABLE 5.A
Artizans' Wage Rates

	Shillings per week	S.D.	N	% of Scottish mean	Artizan's wage as % of agricultural day-labourers' wage
1. Shetland	10·00	—	1	*	*
2. Orkney	9·28	1·77	9	72·4	153
3. Caithness	11·33	1·39	9	88·7	137
4. East Sutherland	12·00	1·64	6	94·0	160
5. East Ross	11·63	2·37	8	90·1	166
6. N.-E. Inverness	12·15	1·65	10	95·1	151
7. North-west coast	12·17	2·05	9	95·1	151
8. Skye and Outer Hebrides	12·11	2·89	9	94·8	184
9. West Argyll	12·12	1·78	13	94·8	170
10. North Argyll	13·67	2·31	9	106·8	162
11. South Argyll	12·70	2·39	10	99·3	140
12. Highland Inverness, Banff, Moray	11·86	1·68	7	92·7	141
13. Highland Perth, Aberdeenshire	11·81	2·59	8	92·3	128
14. N.-W. Perth	11·78	1·00	9	92·2	133
15. Nairn, Lowland Moray	13·46	2·00	14	105·4	144
16. Lowland Banff	12·02	1·90	21	94·1	138
17. Buchan	12·21	1·80	12	95·6	138
18. S.-E. Aberdeenshire	13·06	1·94	16	102·2	140
19. Inner Aberdeenshire	13·03	1·67	16	101·9	137
20. Kincardine	11·93	1·53	13	93·3	127
21. Inner Angus	11·52	1·66	24	90·1	128
22. Coastal Angus	12·03	1·33	19	94·2	128
23. East Perthshire	13·15	1·86	13	103·0	142
24. South Perthshire	11·53	1·57	16	90·2	123
25. East Fife	12·32	1·52	19	96·4	137
26. West Fife	13·09	1·70	17	102·5	140
27. North Stirling-Clackmannan	14·92	2·84	12	116·7	152
28. West Lothian, East Stirling	15·13	2·69	15	118·4	152
29. Edinburgh area	15·93	2·46	15	124·7	160
30. Dunbarton, Renfrewshire	15·07	2·36	15	117·8	142
31. North Ayrshire	14·22	3·07	18	111·2	137
32. South Ayrshire	11·96	2·43	12	93·6	129
33. North Lanarks.	15·39	2·06	14	120·5	140
34. South Lanarks.	14·50	1·12	7	113·1	150
35. Peeblesshire	14·41	1·91	16	112·8	149
36. Dunbar area	14·90	1·49	15	116·5	155
37. South Berwick	14·37	1·55	19	112·4	146
38. Kelso area	14·65	1·51	17	114·4	142
39. Hawick area	15·00	1·92	6	117·5	143
40. Inner Dumfries, Kirkcudbright	13·38	2·06	15	108·3	157
41. South Dumfries	13·11	2·01	19	102·4	155
42. South Kirkcudbright	14·42	1·89	13	112·7	177
43. Wigtown and south tip of Ayr	13·97	1·62	16	109·2	173
SCOTLAND	13·2	2·35	561		

TABLE 5.B
Specific Artizans' Wage Rates, Shillings per Week

	Masons (=N)		Colliers (=N)		Wrights (=N)	
1. Shetland	11·70	(5)	—		12·75	(4)
2. Orkney	11·00	(2)	—		10·25	(2)
3. Caithness	15·00	(1)	—		16·50	(1)
4. East Sutherland	—		—		—	
5. East Ross	—		—		—	
6. N.-E. Inverness	15·00	(1)	—		15·00	(1)
7. North-west coast	—		—		—	
8. Skye and Outer Hebrides	—		—		—	
9. West Argyll	—		—		—	
10. North Argyll	13·50	(1)	—		13·50	(1)
11. South Argyll	18·20	(5)	12·50	(1)	15·70	(5)
12. Highland Inverness, Banff, Moray	15·72	(2)	—		12·00	(2)
13. Highland Perth, Aberdeenshire	—		—		—	
14. N.-W. Perth	12·50	(2)	—		11·00	(2)
15. Nairn, Lowland Moray	12·00	(1)	—		12·00	(1)
16. Lowland Banff	16·00	(2)	—		15·50	(2)
17. Buchan	15·56	(8)	—		12·25	(6)
18. S.-E. Aberdeenshire	18·00	(1)	—		15·75	(2)
19. Inner Aberdeenshire	—		—		13·83	(3)
20. Kincardine	12·00	(2)	—		13·00	(2)
21. Inner Angus	12·00	(2)	—		11·67	(3)
22. Coastal Angus	15·00	(1)	—		13·67	(3)
23. East Perthshire	—		—		14·00	(1)
24. South Perthshire	14·00	(1)	—		12·00	(1)
25. East Fife	13·50	(4)	12·75	(2)	12·60	(5)
26. West Fife	15·43	(7)	15·55	(10)	13·61	(9)
27. North Stirling-Clackmannan	17·00	(3)	18·50	(3)	17·00	(3)
28. West Lothian, East Stirling	20·00	(3)	16·61	(9)	18·00	(3)
29. Edinburgh area	18·00	(1)	16·88	(4)	14·00	(1)
30. Dunbarton, Renfrewshire	18·00	(1)	12·50	(3)	18·00	(3)
31. North Ayrshire	19·00	(2)	14·94	(8)	16·25	(4)
32. South Ayrshire	15·00	(2)	17·00	(5)	15·00	(1)
33. North Lanarks.	21·00	(1)	15·56	(9)	14·33	(3)
34. South Lanarks.	16·83	(6)	15·20	(5)	16·19	(8)
35. Peeblesshire	14·00	(1)	18·00	(1)	12·00	(2)
36. Dunbar area	18·50	(2)	—		—	
37. South Berwick	17·17	(6)	—		14·13	(8)
38. Kelso area	15·00	(1)	—		—	
39. Hawick area	19·50	(2)	—		11·33	(3)
40. Inner Dumfries, Kirkcudbright	17·25	(2)	—		14·17	(3)
41. South Dumfries	15·00	(2)	13·50	(1)	13·50	(2)
42. South Kirkcudbright	15·00	(4)	—		13·13	(4)
43. Wigtown and south tip of Ayr	13·50	(3)	—		12·00	(3)
SCOTLAND	15·63	(90)	15·51	(62)	14·00	(107)

TABLE 5.C
Specific Artizans' Wage Rates, Shillings per Week

	Smiths (=N)		Shoemakers (=N)		Weavers (=N)	
1. Shetland	—		—		—	
2. Orkney	10·50	(1)	—		—	
3. Caithness	16·50	(1)	8·50	(1)	—	
4. East Sutherland	—		—		—	
5. East Ross	—		—			
6. N.-E. Inverness	—		—		—	
7. North-west coast	—		—		—	
8. Skye and Outer Hebrides	—		—		—	
9. West Argyll	—		9·00	(1)	—	
10. North Argyll	—		—		—	
11. South Argyll	14·00	(1)	11·00	(3)	—	
12. Highland Inverness, Banff, Moray	12·00	(1)	—		—	
13. Highland Perth, Aberdeenshire	—		—		—	
14. N.-W. Perth	—		10·00	(1)	10·00	(1)
15. Nairn, Lowland Moray	—		—		—	
16. Lowland Banff	10·00	(1)	10·00	(1)	—	
17. Buchan	—		9·00	(1)	7·50	(1)
18. S.-E. Aberdeenshire	16·00	(3)	15·00	(1)	—	
19. Inner Aberdeenshire	14·25	(2)	15·00	(1)	—	
20. Kincardine	11·83	(3)	11·00	(2)	6·17	(3)
21. Inner Angus	14·00	(1)	12·00	(1)	5·18	(8)
22. Coastal Angus	13·00	(3)	—		8·00	(1)
23. East Perthshire	12·50	(1)	—		5·00	(1)
24. South Perthshire	—		—		6·00	(2)
25. East Fife	—		—		6·57	(7)
26. West Fife	—		9·50	(1)	6·00	(8)
27. North Stirling-Clackmannan	—		—		6·50	(2)
28. West Lothian, East Stirling	15·00	(1)	12·00	(1)	6·00	(2)
29. Edinburgh area	14·50	(1)	—		—	
30. Dunbarton, Renfrewshire	18·00	(1)	12·00	(1)	6·25	(4)
31. North Ayrshire	12·00	(1)	10·25	(4)	7·08	(6)
32. South Ayrshire	9·00	(1)	15·00	(1)	7·00	(2)
33. North Lanarks.	—		10·00	(1)	6·81	(8)
34. South Lanarks.	—		—		6·43	(7)
35. Peeblesshire	13·67	(3)	—		—	
36. Dunbar area	—		—		—	
37. South Berwick	13·00	(1)	—		5·00	(1)
38. Kelso area	15·00	(1)	—		—	
39. Hawick area	—		—		12·00	(1)
40. Inner Dumfries, Kirkcudbright	—		—		—	
41. South Dumfries	—		7·50	(1)	7·50	(1)
42. South Kirkcudbright	9·00	(1)	8·00	(1)	8·00	(1)
43. Wigtown and south tip of Ayr	12·00	(1)	9·00	(1)	7·50	(1)
SCOTLAND	13·30 (30)		10·70 (25)		6·50 (68)	

TABLE 5.D
'Lowest Class of Labourer's' Wage Rates

	Shillings per week	S.D.	N	% of Scottish mean
1. Shetland	2·25	0·35	2	*
2. Orkney	4·50	2·12	2	*
3. Caithness	5·56	1·18	9	97·9
4. East Sutherland	4·25	2·48	2	*
5. East Ross	4·00	1·73	3	*
6. N.-E. Inverness	5·08	1·28	6	89·7
7. North-west coast	4·50	1·06	5	79·4
8. Skye and Outer Hebrides	3·00	0·00	2	*
9. West Argyll	5·25	0·96	4	92·5
10. North Argyll	6·25	0·87	4	110·3
11. South Argyll	5·75	1·26	4	101·3
12. Highland Inverness, Banff, Moray	5·29	1·60	7	93·3
13. Highland Perth, Aberdeenshire	6·40	0·55	5	112·8
14. N.-W. Perth	4·70	0·91	5	82·3
15. Nairn, Lowland Moray	5·87	1·03	15	103·4
16. Lowland Banff	5·54	0·99	14	97·6
17. Buchan	5·32	1·10	14	93·8
18. S.-E. Aberdeenshire	5·89	1·10	13	103·7
19. Inner Aberdeenshire	5·46	1·28	13	96·3
20. Kincardine	5·32	0·93	11	93·8
21. Inner Angus	5·53	1·36	17	97·4
22. Coastal Angus	6·36	0·98	18	112·1
23. East Perthshire	6·19	0·90	13	109·2
24. South Perthshire	6·16	0·77	16	108·6
25. East Fife	5·56	0·99	25	99·0
26. West Fife	6·20	1·25	15	109·3
27. North Stirling-Clackmannan	6·15	0·75	13	108·5
28. West Lothian, East Stirling	6·46	1·15	13	113·9
29. Edinburgh area	6·38	1·30	16	112·3
30. Dunbarton, Renfrewshire	6·54	1.22	12	115·3
31. North Ayrshire	6·17	1·46	18	108·8
32. South Ayrshire	5·92	1·59	13	104·3
33. North Lanarks.	6·50	1·62	13	114·7
34. South Lanarks.	5·29	1·16	14	93·2
35. Peeblesshire	5·31	1·31	8	93·6
36. Dunbar area	5·93	0·73	14	104·5
37. South Berwick	6·32	1·82	11	111·4
38. Kelso area	6·71	1·25	12	118·3
39. Hawick area	6·44	1·70	8	113·6
40. Inner Dumfries, Kirkcudbright	5·25	0·86	10	92·5
41. South Dumfries	5·19	1·09	13	91·6
42. South Kirkcudbright	5·29	1·14	12	93·3
43. Wigtown and south tip of Ayr	6·00	0·71	8	105·9
SCOTLAND	5·79	1·28	452	

TABLE 5.E

Woman Industrial Worker's Wage Rates

	Shillings per week	S.D.	N	% of Scottish mean
1. Shetland	—	—	—	*
2. Orkney	1·75	1·66	6	36·7
3. Caithness	1·25	—	1	*
4. East Sutherland	—	—	—	*
5. East Ross	—	—	—	*
6. N.-E. Inverness	4·06	1·68	2	*
7. North-west coast	—	—	—	*
8. Skye and Outer Hebrides	3·00	—	1	*
9. West Argyll	4·00	—	1	*
10. North Argyll	—	—	—	*
11. South Argyll	—	—	—	*
12. Highland Inverness, Banff, Moray	—	—	—	*
13. Highland Perth, Aberdeenshire	—	—	—	*
14. N.-W. Perth	6·00	—	1	*
15. Nairn, Lowland Moray	3·75	0·35	2	*
16. Lowland Banff	—	—	—	*
17. Buchan	3·13	2·32	4	65·5
18. S.-E. Aberdeenshire	4·44	2·08	8	93·0
19. Inner Aberdeenshire	1·35	0·60	4	28·3
20. Kincardine	4·46	0·86	9	93·6
21. Inner Angus	4·80	0·77	15	102·3
22. Coastal Angus	5·03	0·38	10	104·3
23. East Perthshire	5·50	0·71	2	*
24. South Perthshire	4·93	0·84	7	103·1
25. East Fife	4·38	0·94	12	90·8
26. West Fife	5·07	0·44	10	106·2
27. North Stirling-Clackmannan	5·39	0·75	11	113·0
28. West Lothian, East Stirling	1·25	—	1	*
29. Edinburgh area	6·00	2·03	7	123·6
30. Dunbarton, Renfrewshire	5·75	0·42	6	120·7
31. North Ayrshire	4·65	1·41	13	97·2
32. South Ayrshire	3·80	0·84	5	75·6
33. North Lanarks.	4·25	1·60	5	88·0
34. South Lanarks.	4·75	1·77	2	*
35. Peeblesshire	4·00	—	1	*
36. Dunbar area	—	—	—	*
37. South Berwick	4·83	2·02	3	*
38. Kelso area	5·00	—	1	*
39. Hawick area	5·63	1·11	4	118·0
40. Inner Dumfries, Kirkcudbright	3·38	—	2	*
41. South Dumfries	5·16	2·00	4	115·3
42. South Kirkcudbright	3·50	0·87	3	*
43. Wigtown and south tip of Ayr	3·00	1·41	2	*
SCOTLAND	4·49	1·52	165	

TABLE 5.F
Child Industrial Worker's Wage Rates

	Shillings per week	S.D.	N	% of Scottish mean
1. Shetland	—	—	—	*
2. Orkney	0·50	0	3	*
3. Caithness	0·75	—	1	*
4. East Sutherland	—	—	—	*
5. East Ross	—	—	—	*
6. N.-E. Inverness	1·75	—	1	*
7. North-west coast	—	—	—	*
8. Skye and Outer Hebrides	—	—	—	*
9. West Argyll	—	—	—	*
10. North Argyll	—	—	—	*
11. South Argyll	6·00	—	1	*
12. Highland Inverness, Banff, Moray	4·00	—	1	*
13. Highland Perth, Aberdeenshire	—	—	—	*
14. N.-W. Perth	2·42	0·38	3	*
15. Nairn, Lowland Moray	3·13	0·18	2	*
16. Lowland Banff	2·00	—	1	*
17. Buchan	2·33	0·29	3	*
18. S.-E. Aberdeenshire	3·42	0·80	3	*
19. Inner Aberdeenshire	—	—	—	*
20. Kincardine	2·88	0·65	6	102·5
21. Inner Angus	2·73	1·17	10	97·4
22. Coastal Angus	3·02	0·70	7	107·9
23. East Perthshire	2·75	—	1	*
24. South Perthshire	2·81	0·77	9	100·1
25. East Fife	2·50	0·50	7	89·1
26. West Fife	2·85	0·99	10	101·7
27. North Stirling-Clackmannan	2·95	0·77	10	105·4
28. West Lothian, East Stirling	—	—	—	*
29. Edinburgh area	3·88	1·13	4	131·8
30. Dunbarton, Renfrewshire	2·85	0·60	5	101·6
31. North Ayrshire	2·90	0·73	12	103·3
32. South Ayrshire	3·83	1·89	3	*
33. North Lanarks.	3·59	1·46	8	122·5
34. South Lanarks.	3·63	0·95	4	129·5
35. Peeblesshire	4·38	1·59	2	*
36. Dunbar area	5·50	—	1	*
37. South Berwick	3·67	0·58	3	*
38. Kelso area	3·00	—	1	*
39. Hawick area	3·13	0·48	4	111·5
40. Inner Dumfries, Kirkcudbright	2·75	—	1	*
41. South Dumfries	3·63	0·18	2	*
42. South Kirkcudbright	2·33	0·58	3	*
43. Wigtown and south tip of Ayr	2·88	0·18	2	*
SCOTLAND	2·97	1·05	134	

TABLE 5.G

Wage Rates, by Economic Type of Community

	Artizans			Masons		
	Shillings per week	S.D.	N	Shillings per week	S.D.	N
1.1 Urban-industrial: large towns	13·6	2·28	22	18·5	2·89	4
1.2 Urban-industrial: small towns, etc.	13·9	2·74	83	15·2	2·85	17
2.1 Mixed economy: rural parishes	13·3	2·40	124	15·5	2·61	19
2.2 Mixed economy: country towns	13·3	2·04	27	16·8	2·64	6
3.1 Agricultural: farming parishes	13·2	2·01	248	16·2	2·28	36
3.2 Agricultural: crofting parishes	11·5	2·16	57	11·9	1·69	8
SCOTLAND	13·2	2·35	561	15·6	2·76	90

TABLE 5.H

Model Expenditure and Incomes for Families with Four Children,

		Artizan's yearly earnings (£s)		
	Cost of 'Dryfesdale standard' expenditure	Father only working	Father and mother working	Father, mother and two children working
Orkney	21·7	24·1	28·7	*
Skye and Outer Hebrides	22·1	31·5	*	*
Buchan	26·4	31·7	39·8	*
Inner Angus	27·4	30·0	42·5	56·7
Edinburgh area	27·6	41·4	57·0	77·2
North Lanarks.	27·6	40·0	51·0	69·7
South Berwick	28·4	37·4	*	*
South Kirkcudbright	26·3	37·5	*	*
Scottish mean	26·8	34·3	46·0	61·4

TABLE 5.G *continued*

Wrights			Women in industry			Children in industry			'Lowest Labourers'		
Shillings per week	S.D.	N	Shillings per week	S.D.	N	Shillings per week	S.D.	N	Shillings per week	S.D.	N
13·6	1·08	5	4·94	1·73	20	3·09	1·15	19	6·38	1·53	17
14·3	2·87	22	5·09	1·01	56	3·09	0·99	55	6·06	1·34	74
14·5	2·58	22	4·60	1·09	59	2·95	0·73	41	5·85	1·18	123
14·0	2·07	6	3·78	1·77	9	2·79	1·45	7	5·94	1·00	26
13·9	2·49	45	2·70	1·74	13	2·80	1·3	9	5·74	1·21	188
12·6	2·35	7	2·19	1·65	8	*	*	*	4·58	1·51	24
14·0	2·50	107	4·49	1·52	165	2·97	1·05	131	5·79	1·28	452

TABLE 5.H *continued*

by Selected Districts

'Lowest labourer's' yearly earnings (£s)			Farm servant's yearly earnings (£s)			Agricultural day-labourer's earnings (£s)		
Father only working	Father and mother working	Father, mother and two children working	Father only working	Father and mother working	Father, mother and two children working	Father only working	Father and mother working	Father, mother and two children working
*	*	*	*	*	*	15·4	19·7	24·8
*	*	*	*	*	*	14·8	18·6	*
12·1	20·2	*	22·0	26·7	*	17·9	23·6	*
12·6	25·1	39·2	24·0	29·1	36·0	20·8	25·9	32·8
14·5	29·9	50·3	25·5	31·2	38·8	22·2	27·9	35·5
14·8	25·9	44·6	*	*	*	24·9	32·2	41·2
14·3	*	*	26·5	33·1	40·5	22·3	28·9	36·3
11·9	*	·*	22·3	27·9	35·4	18·8	24·3	31·8
13·2	24·8	41·4	24·0	29·6	36·8	20·7	26·3	33·5

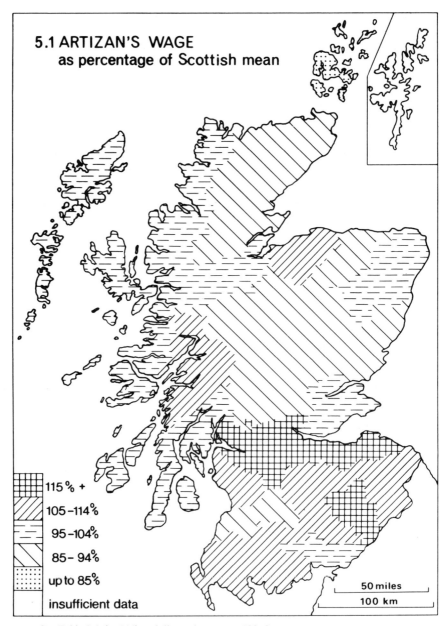

5.1 ARTIZAN'S WAGE
as percentage of Scottish mean

115 % +
105 –114%
95 –104%
85 – 94%
up to 85%
insufficient data

50 miles
100 km

See Table 5.A (p. 114) and discussion on pp. 100–2.

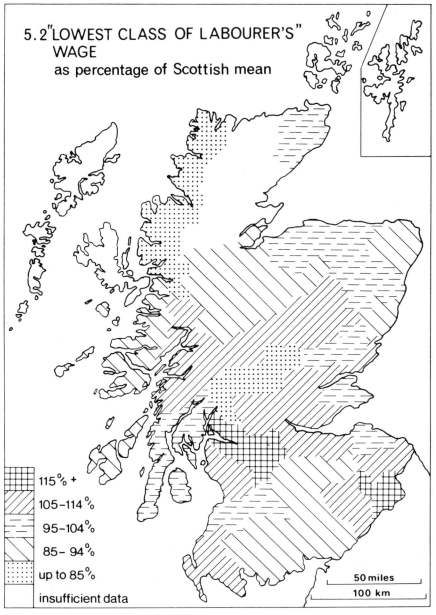

5.2"LOWEST CLASS OF LABOURER'S"
WAGE
as percentage of Scottish mean

115% +
105–114%
95–104%
85– 94%
up to 85%
insufficient data

50 miles
100 km

See Table 5.D (p. 117) and discussion on pp. 102–3

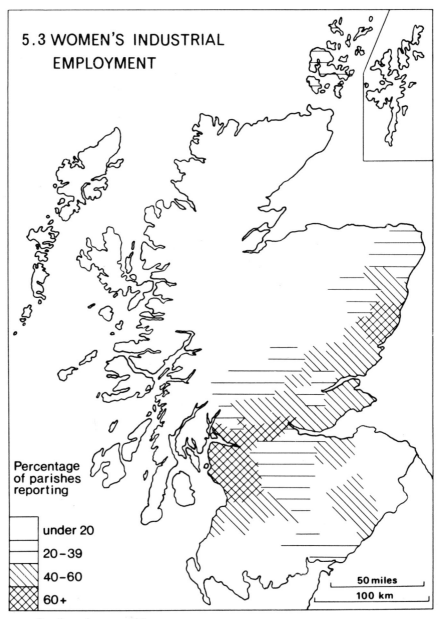

5.3 WOMEN'S INDUSTRIAL
    EMPLOYMENT

Percentage
of parishes
reporting

under 20
20–39
40–60
60+

50 miles
100 km

See discussion on p. 105.

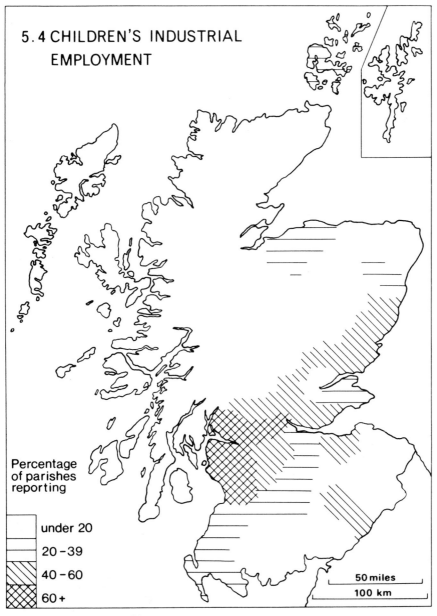

5.4 CHILDREN'S INDUSTRIAL EMPLOYMENT

Percentage of parishes reporting

under 20

20 – 39

40 – 60

60 +

50 miles

100 km

See discussion on p. 105.

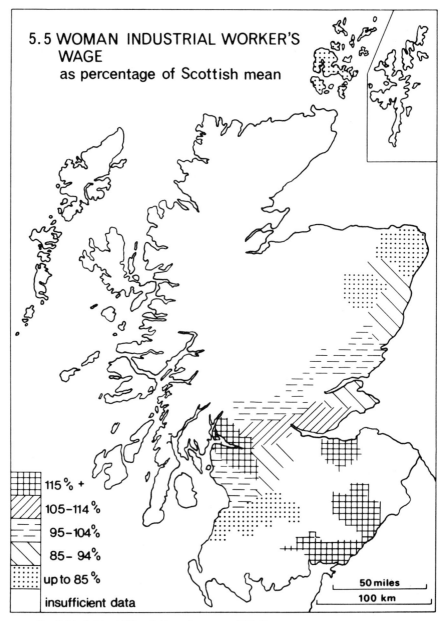

5.5 WOMAN INDUSTRIAL WORKER'S WAGE
as percentage of Scottish mean

115% +
105–114%
95–104%
85– 94%
up to 85%
insufficient data

50 miles
100 km

See Table 5.E (p. 118) and discussion on pp. 106–7.

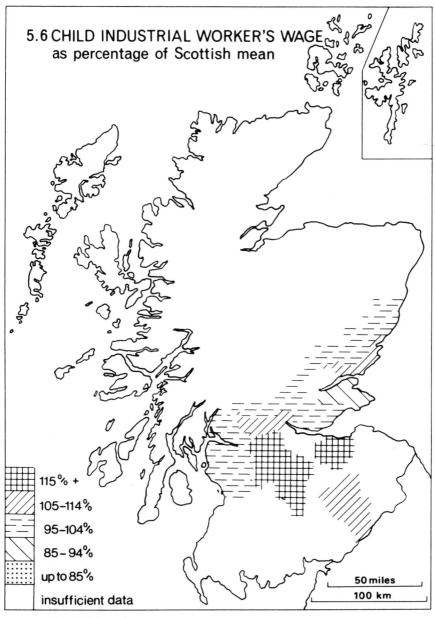

5.6 CHILD INDUSTRIAL WORKER'S WAGE
as percentage of Scottish mean

115% +
105–114%
95–104%
85–94%
up to 85%
insufficient data

50 miles
100 km

See Table 5.F (p. 119) and discussion on pp. 106–7.

Chapter 6

THRIFT AND DISSIPATION

If a worker had a surplus after meeting the subsistence needs of his family, what would he do with it? Invest it in a subscription to a friendly society or (better still) deposit it in a savings bank was the advice of middle-class commentators, anxious both to produce the virtue of self-help among their employees and to keep down the poor rates: and many held up the Scottish working man to the world as a paragon of thrift, in distinction from the easy-come-easy-go southerner who was supposed to take no thought for the future because of an over-generous English poor law. An artizan or a servant who systematically put a little by every time he or she could afford it was not, however, following the advice of his or her social superiors for the sake of conformity. It was practical, functional working-class self-interest to do so. In a world without a welfare state, in which the existing Scottish poor law would normally provide nothing for the able-bodied man who became destitute through unemployment and precious little even for the sick and elderly, it was important to save. The Poor Law Commission asked two questions about friendly societies and savings banks from which much information on the savings habits of the Scottish working-class can be gleaned.

If the surplus above subsistence was not saved it would be spent. In early Victorian Scotland, however, there was little for a working man to buy once he had fed and clothed himself, and bought what few pieces of furniture his one- or two-roomed home might need. Spending therefore often concentrated on drink, which brought its own problems. Scotland had long had an alcohol culture dedicated to the pleasures of escapism from a drab life in a drab climate; with the onset of industrialisation working-class drinking seemed to become more intense, and was perceived as more of a social problem.[1] Middle-class moralists deplored dissipation no less fervently than they praised thrift, but in this case they believed the Scottish worker had a more disgraceful reputation than the Englishman – possibly a consequence of drinking whisky rather than beer. The temperance movement had been formed by bourgeois leaders like William Collins, the Glasgow publisher and churchman. Significantly, however, the leadership of the movement in the 1840s began to pass to working men themselves – many of the Scottish Chartists were temperance men, and expected abstinence and democracy to arrive together. Again they perceived temperance as useful, if addiction to drink was to mean inability to save or to avoid the pit of destitution. The Poor Law Commission asked questions about licensed outlets, and also inquired about the pawn-shops where many in the towns raised the wherewithal either to drink or to survive in the absence of saving.

1. *Friendly Societies*

The questionnaire asked about friendly societies in these terms:

Q. 29. Are there any friendly societies which have their place
of meeting in your parish? If yes, state the number of
such societies, and the number of members in each
respectively.

817 parishes replied, a 90 per cent. response rate, of which 288 (35 per cent. of responding parishes) replied that they did have friendly societies meeting within their bounds. These parishes contained no fewer than 748 individual friendly societies or their branches. Table 6.A and Map 6.1 show the distribution of these societies: they are thin on the ground in most rural districts, but plentiful in the central belt where there were towns, mines or factories.

In nearly half the cases the type of friendly society in the parish was specified – and they were very various. Table 6.B shows that the most popular were those of the simplest type, general burial clubs providing a funeral benefit, and 'yearly' societies which divided up most of what funds remained at the end of the year as dividends for the subscribers. 37 per cent. of members belonged to these two types. A further 15 per cent. belonged to societies with a specific occupational allegiance; most of these provided both burial and sickness benefits articulated to the risks of the job in question – a few endeavoured to cover unemployment as well. 9 per cent. were 'masons' or 'freemasons'. 14 per cent. belonged to one of the large 'affiliated orders' – the Oddfellows, Gardeners, Foresters and Rechabites (the last was restricted to members of the temperance persuasion). These 'affiliated orders' were much the strongest type of friendly society, as they were based on a network of lodges or branches covering the whole of the United Kingdom, and were also able by virtue of their size to call upon a range of actuarial expertise beyond that of the local burial clubs. In 1848 the House of Lords Committee on Friendly Societies observed that 'While the small bodies are decaying or sinking into neglect, the affiliated bodies are growing rapidly in strength, and extending their branches into every part of the kingdom.'[2] To judge from the 1843 returns, however, this process had not gone far in Scotland yet.

The remaining friendly societies covered a wide range, from 'female' societies, taking advantage of the differential in the life expectancy of women, and 'youth societies', which accepted only young men as entrants, to 'cow clubs', for hinds in East Lothian and Berwickshire, and 'whipmen societies' (both Peebles and Torphichen had one, with 200 members in each), besides curiosities like the Innerwick 'Society for Protecting the Dead by Deep Burying' – against body-snatchers.

A town might have several different friendly societies providing different levels of benefit depending on the subscription the workers could afford. Thus at Hawick (24.65c):

> There are five different societies, viz. No. 1, and also No. 2, which pay
> 2d. per week, and in case of sickness, receives 6s. per week, both these
> societies yearly dissolved; No. 1 consists of 150, and No. 2 of 139
> members. There are also three other societies, viz. Rechabites, consisting
> of 150 members, and pay 3d. per week – in case of sickness they receive
> 7s. 6d. per week; Foresters, consisting of 114 members, and pay 4d. per
> week – in case of sickness, they receive 10s. per week; and, Oddfellows,
> consisting of 120 members, and pay 4d. per week – in case of sickness
> they receive 10s. per week also.

Different types of society served different functions and had different
advantages, not all pecuniary. Councillor John Wright, of Edinburgh, explained to the Commission that he dated 'the first movement I ever made to
get out of the working classes from the time I became a member of the youth's
friendly society', at the age of 12 (20.180). The purpose of this society was, at
one level, to provide sickness and funeral benefit: but it was also a social
organisation, a genuine *friendly* society. If a member died, up to 400 of his
comrades would follow the coffin to burial as a mark of respect. It also
organised cheerier processions, first to mark the anniversary of the landing of
George IV in Edinburgh, later (in more nationalist mood) to mark Bannock-
burn day – this may have been to counteract the appeal of a rival society, the
Wallace Youths. It also had debates, from which the members would return
at one or two in the morning, and Councillor Wright believed that it was this
side of its activities which gave him the impetus to become an organiser and
to perfect his own education. Another member of the Caledonian Youths'
Friendly Society, Alexander Allan, a cabinet-maker, agreed that it had also
led him to 'mental improvement', but he denied that other similar organis-
ations necessarily conferred the same benefits (20.240). The masonic lodges,
he said, only led to drinking 'and alienate men from home'; the teetotal Rechabites were no better – 'they plunge into processions, soirees and other species
of sober excitement, get involved in squabbling and debating; and the result is,
alienation from home'. One man's meat was another man's poison.

The 'yearly societies' (alternatively called 'menage', 'manage' or 'dividing'
societies) also came in for much criticism, mainly because of their ephemeral
nature, though they had equally vigorous defenders. These societies were not
protected by Act of Parliament like the more permanent bodies who registered
with the Registrar of Friendly Societies. They were essentially saving's clubs
or provident associations, 'like a little joint-stock company' (20.409), formed
and dissolved annually between a few score members. Typically (20.180) a
man would pay 1s. a week and receive 52s. at the end of the year, and also
pay 2d. a week towards a sickness and funeral fund, receiving from the latter
(if he was ill) 5s. a week benefit for the first three weeks' sickness and 3s. for
the next three weeks. It was, however, possible to borrow the 52s. as soon as
the first deposit of 1s. had been made (the societies charged interest at 5 per
cent.): a man, or a married couple making separate applications, could
obtain a loan covering a year's rent for a house in this manner, or borrow

during a period of unemployment, which was one of the attractions. Critics of the institution called them *improvident* societies, encouraging workers to anticipate their incomes rather than to save (20.237), but that was a narrow view taking no account of real working-class budgeting needs.

Some of the largest firms in Scotland established their own factory friendly society, which had neither the recreational element of an institution like the Caledonian Youths or the Rechabites, nor the instability of the yearly societies. New Lanark cotton works made its workers pay one-sixtieth of their pay (up to 1s. a week) into a fund providing both sick pay and superannuation (22.405); Carron iron works had a similar arrangement, dating back as far as 1762 (20.837). Such societies were useful but not popular, as they smacked too much of employers' paternalism.

To get adequate coverage, a thrifty working man might attempt to belong to several societies. A brass-founder and his wife, said Councillor Wright (20.181), might belong to three or four yearly societies ('there are a couple of hundreds [of such societies] in Edinburgh'). A doctor in Brechin (22.30) said he recalled the days when weavers belonging to three or four societies 'had a greater income if they were confined to bed than what they could make when working'. A weaver in Kirkintilloch explained to the Commissioners (22.383) that he belonged to the Oddfellows, the Rechabites and the local youth's society, which would together give him sickness benefit, an old age pension and funeral provision. A calico printer in Alexandria (22.468) belonged to the Foresters, who paid 10s. a week sickness benefit indefinitely, 'even in an incurable disease', plus £10 at death; he also belonged to the Calico Printers Society, which paid a shilling or two in unemployment benefit. Few societies, however, attempted to cover loss of earnings caused by able-bodied unemployment; fewer still gave a pension to widows, though the Glasgow Oddfellows (20.458) and a local society in the Angus fishing village of Ferryden (21.22) apparently did.

There is no doubt, however, that there was a substantial risk of failure for many societies apart from those supported by firms and outside the large affiliated orders. The Vale of Leven calico printers, for example (22.467), had had 2500 members in 13 societies, 8 of which were dissolved in the depression of 1841–2. In Paisley where there were 23 societies, all but one were ruined in the same depression (20.638). Generally their vulnerability in depression was due to the unemployed being unable to keep up payments, but the catastrophe in Paisley was also due to 10 out of the 23 having loaned money to the town, which itself went bankrupt. The almost total collapse of the friendly societies added immensely to the misery of the working population in that town. The other main source of the weakness of friendly societies lay in their actuarial inexperience – there was a strong plea from the Edinburgh Compositors' Benefit Society to make available better life assurance tables through government initiative (22.968f).

How many friendly society members were there? Altogether 528 societies out of 748 gave their numbers, and the mean membership was 123 per society: if the remainder were of equal size there would have been 92,000 members in the responding parishes, which had a population of 1·731 million: 5·3 per cent. of the population would be friendly society members. However, it is clear that a higher percentage of the population belonged to friendly societies in the urban areas than in rural areas: an analysis of parishes by economic structure suggests that in the large towns as many as 8·2 per cent. of the population would belong, and even in small country towns it would be 7·8 per cent.; but it fell to 3·5 per cent. in farming parishes and 1 per cent. in crofting ones. As most of the population missing from the 1843 survey was urban, the overall proportion of the population belonging to friendly societies in Scotland might be around 6 per cent. This, however, allows for no over-lapping memberships (one man belonging to several societies and giving the impression of being several members himself), so perhaps a round figure of 5 per cent. would be more accurate.

In a more speculative view we can carry the analysis a little further. The great majority of members were adult males: men over 18 were about a quarter of the population in 1841. If working-class males were equal to about four-fifths of all adult males, possibly as many as one working man in four or five belonged to a friendly society of one sort or another, the proportion being much lower in the countryside but substantially more in the towns. And that, perhaps, measures the extent of good pay.

2. *Savings banks*

The question on savings banks ran as follows:
   Q. 28.   Is there any saving's bank in your parish? If yes, state
            the number of the depositors in such bank. State the
            increase or decrease, if any, as compared with previous
            years.

To this 821 parishes replied (a 91 per cent. response rate), of which 198 had a bank and another 93 had a substantial number of depositors who used a bank in an adjacent parish — altogether 291 'saving parishes', or 35 per cent. of the responding parishes. Table 6.A and Map 6.2 show how they were distributed across Scotland. While the pattern resembles that of friendly societies in the high densities in many industrial districts in the central belt there are two significant differences. Firstly, some rural districts had generous savings bank facilities — Sutherland, Buchan and South Ayrshire. In Suther-land this was clearly due to the initiative of the local landowner, the Duke of Sutherland, who believed that his tenants should be given the opportunity to put by for a rainy day. Secondly, more east-coast linen districts were well provided with savings banks than they were with friendly societies, though it is unclear why.

Who deposited in savings banks? There was information on this in the body of the report for Edinburgh, Glasgow and Paisley (which did not other-wise make returns), and also for Montrose and some smaller towns. Table 6.C summarises the data for the four large towns — somewhat roughly, as occu-pational definitions differed somewhat from place to place (20.196; 20.408; 20.589; 22.29). The importance of women can be seen at once, both as domestic servants and as housewives. In Edinburgh 61 per cent. of all depositors (with more than 2s. in the bank) were females. It is also clear that savings banks failed to attract factory workers even in Glasgow and Paisley: the situation was much the same as in Manchester in 1842, where only 6 per cent. of depositors were factory operatives.[3] On the other hand they did attract a large number of non-factory artizans and mechanics, especially in Glasgow: and this was noticeably different from England – at Manchester again only 6 per cent. of depositors in 1842 were mechanics or handicraft workers. Very few unskilled urban labourers either in Scotland or in England were interested.

Information from the smaller Scottish towns bears out this pattern. At Fraserburgh out of 51 depositors 35 were minors or female servants (21.707); in the Eyemouth, Ayton and Coldingham bank 30 per cent. of depositors were domestic servants and 24 per cent. mechanics and tradesmen (22.877); at Partick, servants and artizans were the main depositors (20.454); at Cullen, 'many of the depositors are fishermen and small crofters, and servants' (21.704). In purely rural areas there was occasional success in persuading farm labourers to deposit – as at Oathlaw and Auchtertool in Fife (22.81; 22.324) and Turiff in Aberdeenshire where 'it happens very frequently that farm servants accumulate a little money in the savings' bank, and are then able to take small farms' (21.728). At Golspie in Sutherland depositors were 'chiefly domestic and farm servants, including shepherds and some small lotters' (21.288). Most rural workers were too poor to save much, however, and the noble original vision of Rev. Henry Duncan, who had started the first Scottish country savings banks among farm-workers in Dumfriesshire at the start of the century, was never realised.[4]

The disadvantage of a savings bank compared to a friendly society lay, in the eyes of the average male worker, in the former's paternalist nature. A friendly society was usually run by fellow workers: a savings bank was too often run by the upper classes. In Sutherland the Duke encouraged them, in Berwickshire the Earl of Home, on Bute the Marquis of Bute. At Bonhill in Dunbartonshire the operatives withdrew their money after a master manufacturer took an interest in it, believing he would discover the extent of their savings and reduce their wages accordingly (22.457). There was a great deal of suspicion of government motives in calling for a return of savings bank statistics and publishing analyses of the deposits (20.484). Much of it was no doubt misplaced, but in the smaller banks there was a distressing lack of privacy, as the minister of Rothes unconsciously testified when he told the Commissioners (21.547):

A great part of the working population of his parish consists of
mechanics, carpenters and masons, . . . it used to be their custom to
meet each other in the ale-house very frequently, till their savings
were consumed; but now their savings are put into the savings' bank,
from which witness gives them out money when they require it. Their
habits have thus been very much improved.

Such behaviour might work in a small country town, or among domestic servants where deference was normal, but it was unlikely to succeed with a factory population.

How many depositors were there in Scottish savings banks? 167 parishes replying to Question 28 stated the number of depositors, which averaged 244 per parish: if this is extrapolated to cover the remaining 31 parishes with banks, there would prove to be about 48,000 depositors in a population in the responding parishes of 1,920,000. To this we can add 30,000 depositors from a population of 500,000 in Edinburgh, Leith, Glasgow and Paisley, and calculate that 3 per cent. of the total population were depositors in banks. We know independently that in 1844 about £1,000,000 was deposited in Scottish savings banks,[5] and that (from 49 parishes which gave this information in the questionnaire) the average sum deposited was £12. This confirms the suggestion that there may have been some 80,000 depositors in the whole of Scotland, which again amounts to 3 per cent. of the population. The number was much smaller – perhaps barely above one half – of that in friendly societies.

For depositors in Edinburgh, Glasgow and Paisley it is possible to give a more detailed breakdown of the sums which working-class savers had on deposit: the results are presented in Table 6.D, with Manchester added for comparison. Mechanics and artizans had more saved than female domestic servants or factory operatives but not, surprisingly, always more than the few labourers who took the trouble to deposit. The really striking contrast, however, was with the depositors of the Manchester savings bank in 1842. Lancashire domestic servants had about twice the savings of Scottish ones, and the differential with factory operatives and artizans was at least as big.

£12 was nevertheless quite a large sum set against the earnings of Scottish working men: it represents over four months' wages for an artizan, or six months' wage for a married farm servant. Alternatively it can be said to represent the surplus above the 'Dryfesdale standard' of subsistence needs (see above pp. 107–13) gained by an artizan working alone for 19 months, or by a farm servant with his wife and two children employed at field labour working a full year.

Total savings in Scotland appear to be much smaller in per capita terms than in England, and not merely in Lancashire. The average sum saved in 1844 per head of English population was over four times as large as the Scottish figure, which at first sight casts doubt on the idea that the Scots were thriftier than the English. But what it reflects are probably not different moral habits but, firstly, a lower Scottish per capita income (since if less is earned less can be saved whatever the attitudes of the work force) and, secondly, a different use of savings banks. In England, where branch banking was underdeveloped compared to Scotland, the savings bank may have attracted holders of small balances who could not be described as working-class. In Scotland, the savings banks had to compete with a network of joint-stock banks which, while they were not actively very interested in proletarian savings, clearly mopped up some of the savings of small independent men that would have gone to savings banks in England. Although it has been implied that competition between savings banks and other banks in Scotland did not arise until some time later,[6] the answers to the questionnaire suggest otherwise.

Thus at Buchanan in Ayrshire it was said that there was 'No savings' bank in the parish. Some people, however, save a little and put it in a bank.' At Kilconquhar in Fife, 'There is a saving's bank, but hardly any business is done in it, since a branch bank of the Commercial Bank was established in the parish.' And at Banchory-Ternan in Aberdeenshire the savings bank was 'given up about six years ago, at the suggestion of the minister, who was treasurer, because a branch of the Bank of Scotland was established there' (23.169b; 23.269b; 23.318b). Similarly at Leuchars in Fife the farm-servant population used the public banks, at Largs the savings bank and the Paisley Commercial Bank used the same agent, who deflected custom to the Commercial Bank, and at Pollokshaws funds were being shifted to the Western Bank (22.294; 22.484; 20.457).

It is sometimes assumed that savings banks were a failure, either because they attracted those who would have saved in any case but not the 'idle and dissipated, on whose habits they wished chiefly that it should operate', as an observer at Kirriemuir put it (22.77), or because they attracted few devotees compared to the friendly societies. But that is not the whole story. They had unique importance for working-class women who learnt their thrift as young domestic servants saving for their wedding day and maintained the good tradition as housewives. The Edinburgh savings bank treasurer described the category of 'married women' in his returns as 'generally the wives of operatives' (20.197). Without savings banks such women would not have enjoyed even the small degree of financial independence and security that was theirs in early Victorian Britain.

3. Public houses

The two questions relating to sales outlets for alcoholic drink ran as follows:

> Q. 26. How many public houses, or houses having licenses
>   for the sale of spirits, are there in your parish?
> Q. 27. How many shops, not being public houses, are there
>   licensed to sell spirits?

To each there were 829 replies (a 92 per cent. response rate). 89 per cent. of the responding parishes reported that they had public houses – they detailed 8380 pubs, or one for every 222 people living in the responding area. If licensed shops are added, the percentage of parishes with outlets for the sale of alcoholic drink rises to 91 per cent.; the extra 1259 shops reduced the ratio of outlets to one for every 192 people. At the same time we know that Glasgow had 2126 licensed houses and other outlets – one for every 130 inhabitants (it was said one house in 13 was a pub in that city) (20.323; 20.416). If we assume that Edinburgh was as well provided (in 1851 the two cities were virtually identical in this respect), the figure is reduced to one drink outlet for every 177 people.[7] Another return (not broken down by locality) stated that there were 15,003 spirit licences for the whole of Scotland, or one for every 175 people.[8] This is considerably more than would appear from an analysis of the census, where in 1841 only 8588 persons admitted to being tavern-keepers, or one for every 305 Scots. Presumably it was regarded as a somewhat disreputable occupation for which if a respondent could plausibly provide an alternative he would. Temperance propagandists usually worked from census returns, but the situation was in reality far worse than they knew.

The country, then, was plentifully provided with opportunities for dissipation, but as Table 6.E and Maps 6.3 and 6.4 show, these varied in a most interesting way from district to district. At one extreme stood Shetland, with a public house for every 3195 of her inhabitants − a figure mercifully reduced to a drink outlet for every 983 people by the provision of licensed shops. Most of the western Highlands and Islands were no better off, and it cannot be assumed that the gap was being filled by illicit distilling − evidence from within the report from Lorne, Islay, Tiree and Skye suggests that private stills had, at least for the moment, been effectively suppressed (20.756; 21.135; 21.155; 21.170).[9] The other extreme was comprised of a set of largely industrial districts in central Scotland running from Renfrew to Fife, where there were outlets for every 150 people or fewer: the miners and the weavers here had about six times as many opportunities to go drinking (in a legal way) as the crofters and fishermen of the north. The breakdown by type of community (Table 6.F) shows the same phenomenon: towns and industrial parishes were far better provided with pubs and licensed shops than rural and agricultural parishes. Very broadly, there were most pubs and drink shops where there were most friendly societies and savings banks.

Contemporaries were unclear in their own minds as to whom, among the working classes, were the heaviest drinkers, and why. Some believed that intemperance was found mainly among the poorest (20.245); others, probably better informed, thought that heavy drinking was largely confined to workers with high wages. The statistician Alexander Watt, for instance, poured scorn on the claim (originating with Sheriff Alison) that 30,000 were drunk every weekend in Glasgow: 'This is quite absurd. If it were the case . . . we should have one [adult] in every four or every five drunk every Saturday night. This estimate is quite exaggerated.' He said 'what they pay for their food, and what they receive in wages, are so nearly balanced that they have little in their power to spend in intemperance' (20.364). (See also 22.50; 22.202; 22.243.) Others recognised drinking habits peculiar to certain trades. Nailers were 'proverbial for having a spark in their throats not easily quenched' (20.488). Edinburgh carters were debauched by drinking at toll bars and by selling pilfered coal for whisky at the houses of shady dealers round the city: 'if they begin with one gill they end with a score in a day' (20.166; 22.752). At Tarbat in Easter Ross the herring fishers were allowed 11 gallons of whisky to each boat-crew of four, as well as bounty money from the curers that was spent mainly on whisky: 'there may be a temptation . . . to dram-drinking, on account of their frequent exposure to wet and rain, but they drink during the day when they are at home' (21.55).

Over all, however, it seems clear that there was a positive correlation between the state of wages and the amount consumed in drink. The quantity of spirits distilled and charged for consumption annually in Scotland roughly followed the trade cycle, though the reduction was not dramatic: it fell from 2·36 gallons per head of population in 1840 to 2·14 gallons in 1842, recovering to 2·36 by 1850 (equivalent to about 0·75 pints of whisky per adult per week).[10] Similarly the areas with most drinking places were the areas with most disposable working-class income – the mining areas, the factory areas and the cities – and least was drunk in the rural north and west because the population was very poor there (20.756; 20.758; 21.186; 21.436). Since alcohol was the main non-subsistence consumption good of the workers, and spending money on it was the main alternative to saving, a map of the density of drink outlets is an excellent general guide to the distribution of working-class prosperity.

Nevertheless, within a given district the details of the distribution of pubs and drinking shops were often determined by the degree of social control exercised by the church or the local landowners. Licensed premises – other than respectable inns – were regarded as disorderly, encouragers of profligate waste, solvents of social respect: a man would not wish many on his estate, and rural parishes were often thinly provided. Conversely, where there were independent towns or villages even in the midst of deeply rural areas public houses were often extremely numerous. Such places were generally ancient, self-governing burghs relatively immune from external controls. Thus Dunbar in East Lothian had 53 outlets (one to 83 inhabitants) (23.43), Dunkeld in Perthshire 12 (one to 92) (23.205), Inverury in Aberdeen had 28 (one to 72) (23.335), and Kintore in the same county 12 (one to 108) (23.336). Such little towns were nests of country craftsmen with a surplus to spend, but plainly they also served the dry parishes around as drinking fountains to which farm servants and others would come when they had money to burn. The same could be said of Tranent, with about 52 outlets (one to 76 inhabitants), but this also had a population of rich and thirsty miners (23.41b).

It would, of course, be quite misleading to suggest that, on an individual basis, only those who could afford to drink did so. The whole point of the contemporary anxiety about intemperance was that it could trap otherwise prosperous families into poverty. A surgeon in Girvan told the commissioners, 'those who live soberly are cleanly, and live pretty comfortably; but, when they drink, as many of them do, they are in misery. The wages they receive on Saturday night are gone before Monday morning' (22.442). At Wilton outside Hawick the witness said that in two families of stocking weavers 'he finds in one all that is neat and clean and comfortable, the heads of the family well dressed, the children well dressed and at school; and the other . . . nothing but the most squalid misery – scarcely a bed to sleep on, and very little furniture of any sort . . . the man in the one case is sober and provident, and the other is a drunkard and improvident' (22.661). The minister of Inveresk admitted that 'people in desperation take to drinking' but 'generally . . . intemperance is a very evident and striking cause of pauperism' (22.768).

If the upper classes saw the nature of the problem they were, however, unwilling to impose a solution – restrictions on drinking hours were rudimentary, magistrates were liberal in allowing applications of licences, and the duty on whisky was low. The only determined anti-drink crusade in the early 1840s was a self-help one among the workers themselves. The total abstinence movement was spreading rapidly, and though avowedly non-political in fact it counted many prominent Scottish Chartists among its leaders. It had a great (though perhaps short-lived) impact on Irish immigrants as well as on native Scots due to the preaching tours of the redoubtable Father Matthew. There were varying estimates of the numbers who had signed the pledge – but it amounted to several thousands in both Glasgow and Edinburgh, and many outside the main cities (20.248; 20.322; 20.386). One individual had been forced to take the pledge under pain of eviction by a Glasgow house factor because he 'went around intoxicated with a razor in his pocket . . . he met me sometime ago on the street, and said God would bless me for having compelled him to join the teetotal' (20.395).

It was generally, though not universally, admitted that the temperance movement had helped to reduce the amount of intemperance, evidence to this effect coming from places as widely separated as Glasgow, Fort William and Fraserburgh, though it was always difficult to separate the impact of the anti-drink crusade from that of falling income in the depression (20.289; 20.470; 21.404; 21.708; 21.620; 22.202). Others regarded it as just another movement among the well-paid skilled workers that missed out the destitute and desperate who most needed it and who 'come not within the influence of the blaze of their lights, the harmony of their concerts or the charms of their oratory' (20.482). The Roman Catholic bishop of Edinburgh was bitterly critical (20.113):

> Under the general name of the temperance societies, they are, or may be, spouting and debating societies, political societies, speculating societies, tea and coffee-drinking and dancing societies; in short, anything and everything but what their appellation exclusively implies, viz. *sober* societies . . . They seem to me . . . exceedingly dangerous in principle . . . I myself have been told within my own residence, and by one of a deputation of Catholic teetotallers of my own congregation, that he looked upon me as 'an encourager of drunkenness in Edinburgh'.

Evidently self-help, at least as much as drunkenness, could lead to the dissolution of the traditional respect for authority due from a Catholic to his bishop.

One of the most interesting comments on intemperance in the Poor Law Report came from Sheriff Alison of Glasgow, who related the recent and (as it turned out) temporary decline in alcohol consumption not only to falling wages and the influence of teetotallers but also to the new popularity of music entertainments 'sometimes attracting 2000 people to the city hall two or three times a month' (20.470). It was, ultimately, the rise of other types of recreation than going to the pub and of other forms of consumer good than drink that would first stabilise and then reduce the average consumption of drink in Scotland: but that development was not important until another generation after the 1840s.

4. *Pawnbrokers*

The question on pawnbroking ran as follows:

> Q. 25. Are there any pawnbrokers' shops in your parish? If
>   so, how many? Has the number increased or decreased
>   during the last five years?

824 parishes replied (a 91 per cent. response rate) of which only 42 (5 per cent. of the responding parishes) actually contained pawns. As Map 6.5 shows, almost all of them were either large towns or other urban-industrial parishes: much more than pubs, friendly societies or savings banks they were an urban phenomenon. The answers were, however, totally unreliable as to the number of pawns or whether they had increased or decreased, because the law exercised very imperfect control over them. Commentators divided pawn-shops into those licensed by the magistrates, which were not allowed to exceed 15 per cent. interest on sums over two guineas, or 20 per cent. on sums under two guineas (20.324), and the illegal 'wee pawns' which under cover of a false sale would charge 300 per cent. or more – 'they profess not to take on pledge but to purchase the goods offered to them. They give a very small sum for them and when the party comes to redeem them they charge perhaps 2d. upon each shilling advanced, as interest, before they will give them up.'

It was generally agreed that the wee pawns were much more numerous, though no one knew how many there really were. At Paisley and at Dundee there were said to be about 100 (20.634; 22.166); in Edinburgh, Bailie W. Johnston had counted 46 open in the city on the Sabbath, compared to 193 premises selling spirits (20.207); in Inverness there was one licensed pawn but numerous 'flying pawns' that came in from the countryside, operated for a week or two, and vanished (21.481); in Greenock the wee pawns were said to deal in stolen goods (20.557). In Glasgow, Captain Miller, superintendent of the police, explained the complexities of the trade in more detail:

> There are thirty licensed pawnbrokers, and upwards of 200 small
> unlicensed brokers within the royalty, besides about 300 dealers in old
> clothes etc., who have no shops and reside in various places, both within
> and without the parliamentary district.

There was a regular market for forfeited pledges (mainly old clothes) in Ireland, and some were even shipped to America, possibly for slaves on the cotton plantations. Loans from the licensed brokers alone in Glasgow amounted to about £11,000 a month, or not far off £1 a year per adult inhabitant (20.323).

A licensed pawnbroker in Greenock, Alexander Cairns, appeared in person before the Royal Commission, giving the details of the number of pledges he had taken, month by month, between January 1840 and March 1843. The results appear in Diagram 6.I. He assured the commissioners that the variations were not due to substantial changes in his own share of the market; they expected to find that the number of pledges would increase at the onset of the depression, but he claimed the reverse had occurred (20.557). Others dated the onset of the depression in the town from the early months of

1842 before the relief fund for the able-bodied unemployed came into operation in April and said that 'many families, in fact, pawned or sold all they
could dispose of before coming on the fund for relief' (20.520). That the distress in the county generally grew worse between January and April 1842 is
confirmed by the strain on the relief funds of the Paisley authorities (see below
pp. 156–9). The pawnbroker did take more pledges in the first half of 1842
than in 1841, but less than in the first half of 1840. It is possible that the end of
the pronounced boom in 1840 meant that fewer came to him to pledge articles
for drink that they expected to redeem quickly when they received their next
wage packets, but the onset of deep depression in the early months of 1842
called forth the furniture and clothing of the destitute unemployed who were
pledging articles for food and for their survival. The only variation in the type
of customer Mr. Cairns would admit to was that 'there are a few respectable
persons coming to us that did not come a few years ago' – perhaps they were
labour aristocrats or small tradesmen in distress.

Evidence from Paisley in the same depression suggested that the down-
turn of a trade cycle altered the pattern of the pawnbrokers' trade in a funda-
mental way: in good times only about 4 per cent. of pledges were forfeited,
but in bad times almost all were lost. The pawnbroker was not a gainer in the

6. I MONTHLY NUMBER OF PLEDGES TAKEN BY GREENOCK PAWNBROKER, January 1840 – March 1843

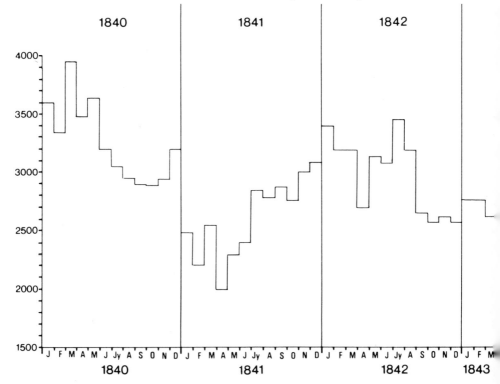

latter situation because he lost interest payments and found it hard to sell the pledges except as trash.[11]

The role of pawnbrokers was a double one. Perhaps Bailie W. Johnston was correct when he said that the main function of the Edinburgh pawn-brokers who opened on Sundays was to receive pledges from people who wished either to prolong their Saturday-night dissipation or to obtain some money to live on for the rest of the week (20.207). But there were as many stories of workmen who pledged their entire household goods to keep them-selves alive when their savings ran out, or who were even driven to theft, like a watchmaker in Fife imprisoned for pledging a watch he was supposed to repair in order to save his wife from starvation (22.286). If the keepers of the licensed pawns and the wee pawns battened on their need it was because the Scottish poor law itself was too mean to keep the unemployed in any other way.

REFERENCES

1. Daniel C. Paton, 'Drink and the Temperance Movement in Nineteenth-Century Scotland', unpublished Ph.D. thesis, University of Edinburgh, 1977.
2. *Report from the Select Committee of the House of Lords on the Provident Associations Fraud Prevention Bill*, P.P. 1847–8, vol. 26, p. 4, quoted in P. H. J. H. Gosden, *Self-Help* (London, 1973), p. 39.
3. For Manchester, see Albert Fishlow, 'The Trustee Savings Banks, 1817–1861', in *Journal of Economic History*, vol. XXI (1961), p. 35. There is also a good discussion in P. L. Payne, 'The Savings Bank of Glasgow, 1836–1914', *Studies in Scottish Business History* (ed. P. L. Payne, London, 1967), pp. 152–86.
4. Henry Duncan, *An Essay on the Nature and Advantage of Parish Banks* (Edinburgh, 1815).
5. S. G. Checkland, *Scottish Banking, a History, 1695–1973* (Glasgow and London, 1975), p. 318.
6. *Ibid.*, p. 367; Professor Checkland discusses rivalry between the savings banks and the joint-stock banks in a post-1870 context – *ibid.*, pp. 487, 531, 633, 646.
7. Paton, *loc. cit.*, p. 135.
8. G. B. Wilson, *Alcohol and the Nation* (London, 1940), Table 25, p. 400. The return is the number of retail excise liquor licences in Scotland, presumably taken from customs and excise data.
9. For this see also T. M. Devine, 'The Rise and Fall of Illicit Whisky-making in Northern Scotland, c. 1780–1840', *Scottish Historical Review*, vol. 54 (1975), pp. 155–77.
10. Calculated from Wilson, *op. cit.*, Table 3, p. 337.
11. *Report of the Select Committee on the Distress in Paisley*, P.P. 1843, vol. 7, p. 119.

TABLE 6.A

*Percentages of Parishes Reporting Friendly Societies and Savings Banks
by District*

	Friendly societies	N	Savings banks (or depositors)	N
1. Shetland	0	12	0	12
2. Orkney	6	18	0	18
3. Caithness	67	12	17	12
4. East Sutherland	36	11	81	11
5. East Ross	7	13	36	14
6. N.-E. Inverness	27	15	29	14
7. North-west coast	0	11	9	11
8. Skye and Outer Hebrides	7	14	0	14
9. West Argyll	6	16	0	15
10. North Argyll	9	11	22	9
11. South Argyll	15	20	18	17
12. Highland Inverness, Banff, Moray	0	11	0	11
13. Highland Perth, Aberdeenshire	20	10	33	9
14. N.-W. Perth	30	13	36	14
15. Nairn, Lowland Moray	25	20	53	19
16. Lowland Banff	27	26	56	27
17. Buchan	42	24	80	25
18. S.-E. Aberdeenshire	35	26	56	27
19. Inner Aberdeenshire	30	20	37	19
20. Kincardine	44	18	61	18
21. Inner Angus	24	34	23	35
22. Coastal Angus	27	26	63	27
23. East Perthshire	5	20	40	20
24. South Perthshire	23	22	41	22
25. East Fife	30	33	27	33
26. West Fife	56	25	62	26
27. North Stirling-Clackmannan	53	17	33	18
28. West Lothian, East Stirling	74	19	23	22
29. Edinburgh area	77	22	20	20
30. Dunbarton, Renfrewshire	75	20	67	21
31. North Ayrshire	83	24	56	25
32. South Ayrshire	71	14	60	15
33. North Lanarks.	95	20	45	20
34. South Lanarks.	42	19	50	20
35. Peeblesshire	50	16	35	17
36. Dunbar area	67	18	11	19
37. South Berwick	43	30	17	30
38. Kelso area	9	22	18	22
39. Hawick area	40	10	56	9
40. Inner Dumfries, Kirkcudbright	14	21	19	21
41. South Dumfries	25	24	29	24
42. South Kirkcudbright	9	21	33	21
43. Wigtown and south tip of Ayr	16	19	7	18
SCOTLAND	35	817	35	821

TABLE 6.B
Numbers and Membership of Different Types of Friendly Societies

	Number (N = 344)	Average membership	Total membership
Burial societies	32	331	10,592
Dividing or yearly societies	57	128	7,296
Occupational:			
Merchants	5	32	160
Trades (not masons)	25	89	2,225
Weavers	8	103	824
Spinners	2	501	1,002
Colliers, quarriers	7	49	343
Sailors, fishermen	6	87	522
Carters	5	82	410
Farmers	3	179	537
Ploughmen	8	168	1,344
Masons or freemasons	39	116	4,524
Affiliated orders:			
Rechabites	13	65	845
Oddfellows	26	98	2,548
Foresters	4	84	336
Gardeners	31	103	3,193
Others:			
Boys, youths	6	220	1,320
Male, unspecified	13	158	2,054
Female	16	205	3,280
Miscellaneous	42	119	4,998

TABLE 6.C
Occupations of Savings Bank Depositors in Four Large Towns

Occupation	% distributions			
	Edinburgh	Glasgow	Paisley	Montrose
Domestic servants	32	17	11	16
Factory workers	1	5	3	4
Other artizans and mechanics	18	25	15	17
Labourers, carters, etc.	4	9	6	6
Clerks, etc.	4	8	} 17	4
Shopkeepers	3	7		
Minors	6	11	14	} 53
Housewives, etc.	24	14	34	
Miscellaneous	8	4	0	
Total	14,503	13,239	1692	753

TABLE 6.D
Mean Savings-Bank Deposits of Working-class Savers in Large Towns (£)

Occupation	Edinburgh	Glasgow	Paisley	Manchester
Domestic servants (female)	12·3	10·6	12·2	26·0[1]
Factory operatives	12·5	10·7	3·9	28·0
Mechanics and artizans	14·5	11·4	13·1	29·0
Labourers	16·3	10·8	14·0	n.a.
Mean of all depositors	14·4	12·0	13·1	27·0

[1] Includes males (about one servant in eight), who generally had larger deposits than women.

TABLE 6.E

Ratio of Public Houses and Other Licensed Outlets to Population, by District

	A Number of people for every pub	B Number of people for every licensed outlet	Column B as % of Scottish mean
1. Shetland	3195	983	512
2. Orkney	367	266	139
3. Caithness	288	286	150
4. East Sutherland	333	309	161
5. East Ross	315	275	143
6. N.-E. Inverness	236	224	117
7. North-west coast	656	543	282
8. Skye and Outer Hebrides	1656	1078	561
9. West Argyll	961	912	475
10. North Argyll	522	296	154
11. South Argyll	204	198	103
12. Highland Inverness, Banff, Moray	345	306	159
13. Highland Perth, Aberdeenshire	252	248	129
14. N.-W. Perth	201	191	99
15. Nairn, Lowland Moray	276	229	119
16. Lowland Banff	291	220	115
17. Buchan	382	238	124
18. S.-E. Aberdeenshire	460	273	142
19. Inner Aberdeenshire	408	287	149
20. Kincardine	264	242	126
21. Inner Angus	207	177	92
22. Coastal Angus	160	146	76
23. East Perthshire	297	242	126
24. South Perthshire	186	173	90
25. East Fife	181	144	75
26. West Fife	150	132	69
27. North Stirling-Clackmannan	164	140	73
28. West Lothian, East Stirling	201	170	89
29. Edinburgh area	151	130	68
30. Dunbarton, Renfrewshire	149	145	75
31. North Ayrshire	174	165	86
32. South Ayrshire	237	225	117
33. North Lanarks.	183	173	90
34. South Lanarks.	269	248	129
35. Peeblesshire	252	179	93
36. Dunbar area	200	153	80
37. South Berwick	240	175	91
38. Kelso area	294	254	132
39. Hawick area	293	235	122
40. Inner Dumfries, Kirkcudbright	403	296	154
41. South Dumfries	251	150	78
42. South Kirkcudbright	253	218	114
43. Wigtown and south tip of Ayr	204	192	100
SCOTLAND	222	192	

TABLE 6.F
Ratio of Public Houses and Other Licensed Outlets to Population,
by Economic Type of Community

	Number of people for every pub	Number of people for every licensed outlet
1.1 Urban-industrial: large towns	146	131
1.2 Urban-industrial: smaller towns, etc.	181	158
2.1 Mixed economy: rural parishes	252	222
2.2 Mixed economy: country towns	157	125
3.1 Agricultural: farming parishes	319	272
3.2 Agricultural: crofting parishes	639	526
SCOTLAND	222	192

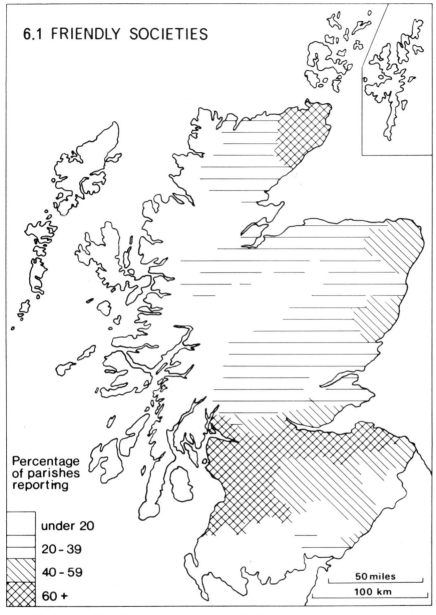

6.1 FRIENDLY SOCIETIES

Percentage
of parishes
reporting

under 20

20 - 39

40 - 59

60 +

50 miles

100 km

See Table 6.A (p. 142) and discussion on pp. 129–32.

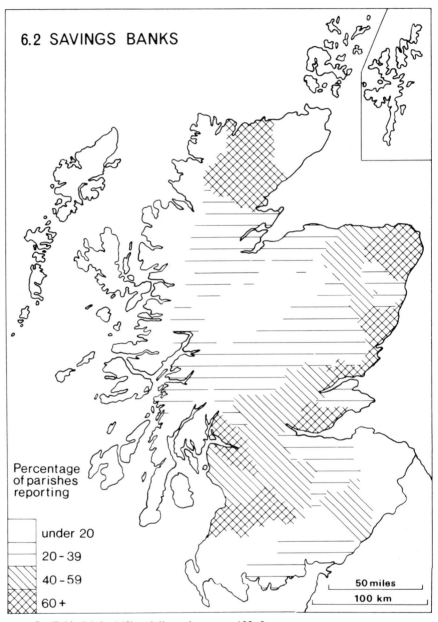

6.2 SAVINGS BANKS

Percentage
of parishes
reporting

under 20

20 - 39

40 - 59

60 +

50 miles

100 km

See Table 6.A (p. 142) and discussion on pp. 132–5.

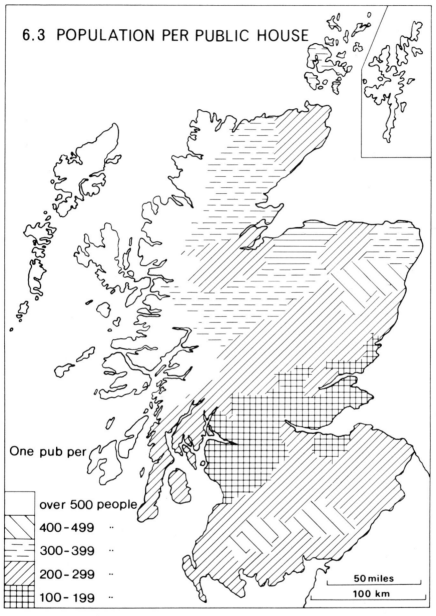

6.3 POPULATION PER PUBLIC HOUSE

One pub per

	over 500 people
	400 – 499 ··
	300 – 399 ··
	200 – 299 ··
	100 – 199 ··

50 miles
100 km

See Table 6.E (p. 145) and discussion on pp. 135–8.

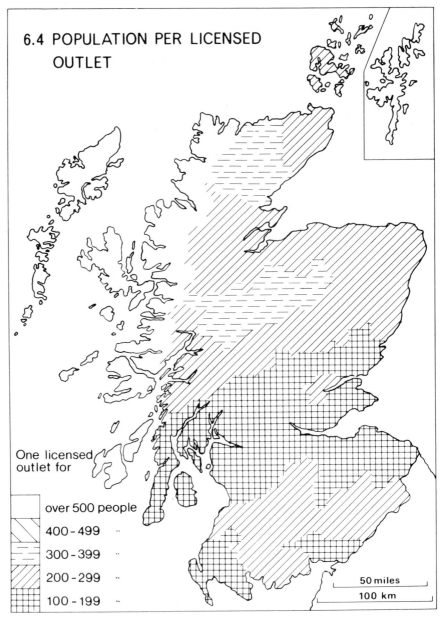

6.4 POPULATION PER LICENSED
OUTLET

One licensed
outlet for

over 500 people
400 - 499   ,,
300 - 399   ,,
200 - 299   ,,
100 - 199   ,,

50 miles
100 km

See Table 6.E (p. 145) and discussion on pp. 135–8.

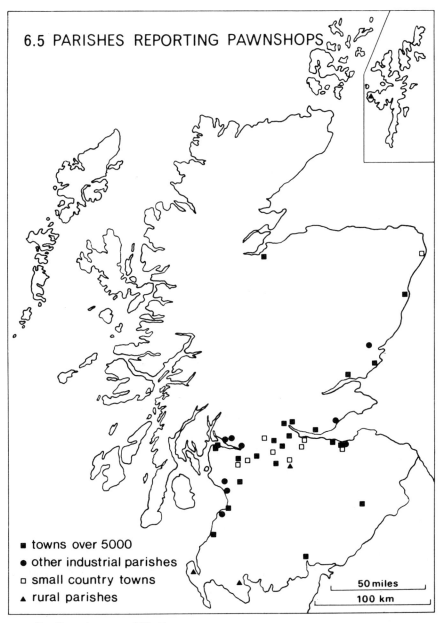

6.5 PARISHES REPORTING PAWNSHOPS

■ towns over 5000
● other industrial parishes
□ small country towns
▲ rural parishes

50 miles
100 km

See discussion on pp. 139–41.

Chapter 7

THE UNEMPLOYED

Of all the distinctions between the poor laws of England and Scotland, none by the mid-nineteenth century appeared so firmly established or so striking as in the treatment of the able-bodied unable to obtain work. In England the unemployed had an entitlement to relief that ran back to the Elizabethan statutes of 1574 and 1601, and which had been confirmed, albeit reluctantly, in the reform of 1834. Sometimes this had meant an extensive dole system, as in the so-called Speenhamland system in the south of England around 1800. Sometimes it meant relief inside a punitive workhouse, as in rural England after 1834. Sometimes it meant outdoor relief on the poor rates after a labour test, as in most English cities in the 1840s.[1] In Scotland, however, after 1800 it was becoming a gradually established point of principle that the unemployed able-bodied man had no entitlement to relief of any sort from the poor fund. Eighteenth-century practice in rural communities had been ambiguous, and law-suits were fought over the problem as unemployment became more of a burden on the parishes. That of *Pollock* v. *Darling* in 1804 raised the question whether a local authority was entitled to impose an assessment to help the 'industrious poor' whose wages were too low in time of harvest failure for them to feed themselves: the Court of Session had decided by one vote and on a technicality that the local authority was justified in this case, but the decision 'was generally interpreted as giving little support to any subsequent appeal by the industrious poor against a local authority which refused to help them'.[2] In 1819, 800 able-bodied unemployed had claimed the right of relief from Abbey Parish, Paisley, and been refused on the grounds that as they were not 'impotent' poor they were not entitled to relief: they had then appealed to the Sheriff, but in 1821 in the case of *Abbey Parish* v. *Richmond* the Court of Session declared such an appeal (i.e., to a Sheriff rather than to themselves) incompetent. In effect this appeared to confirm the exclusion of the unemployed from the poor law, though it could be argued that the point was never finally decided before the emergency died down. Perhaps, indeed, the principle was not so firmly established by statute and law as most commentators made out, and certainly local practice in the parishes was more variable than the authorities cared to admit.

In any case the official line was that, if the harvest failed or if the trade cycle caused thousands of redundancies, the true and proper remedy was (in the words of Lord President Campbell) 'the benevolent attention of their friends and fellow-citizens'.[3] In practice, this might mean the heritors levying a so-called 'voluntary assessment' on themselves outside the strict letter of the poor law, or it might mean the organisation of a charitable fund in a town to relieve the starving, or it might even mean an *ex gratia* payment by the town council or the kirk session to the needy: but it never meant the unemployed had a legal right to a penny.

This feature was indeed regarded as a peculiar glory of the Scottish poor law by all those on the Poor Law Inquiry except Edward Twistleton, the English assistant poor-law commissioner who had been put on the Scottish Royal Commission following his experience in charge of emergency relief at Paisley in 1842.[4] The other commissioners defended it in their report by sanctimonious texts – 'if a man will not work, neither should he eat' (20.xlv) and 'as a man sows he must expect to reap' (20.liv). They regarded many of the able-bodied as work-shy and saw an assessment for their benefit as 'a premium to indolence'. Twistleton alone perceived that this was so much cant in the face of the evidence of hardship they had heard, and wished to allow local authorities the discretionary power to assess the inhabitants for the relief of the unemployed in periods of depression of trade (20.xvii).

The commissioners included one query as to unemployment in their questionnaire. It was a complex one:

Q. 22. Are there, or have there been, within the last ten years, any able-bodied persons, in your parish, willing to work, but unable to procure work? And has there been any general subscription or other provision for their relief, and if so, how often and to what amount?

To the first part of the question they had 827 replies (a 91 per cent. response rate). Of responding parishes, 499 (60 per cent.) reported that they had, indeed, suffered unemployment. Of those that commented upon its seriousness (468 in all), 57 per cent. stated it to have been unusual, rare or not serious as a social problem, 30 per cent. said it was serious in some years and 14 per cent. that it was serious every year. 104 parishes said they suffered from short-term or seasonal unemployment and in 84 per cent. of cases this was associated with the winter. Although they were not asked the causes, 20 parishes volunteered the information that it was associated with failure of trade, 41 with the problems of the handloom weavers and 8 with the coal industry – usually with women becoming unemployed after the passage of Lord Ashley's Act prohibiting female labour below ground. To this can be added another 22 parishes which, from information given in the body of the evidence to the commissioners, plainly also suffered from the downturn of industrial activity during 1841–3.

Table 7.A and Maps 7.1–7.4 summarise this information. Most districts had some unemployment, though there was little of any kind in a few favoured parts of the north-east and the Borders. Short-term unemployment, on the other hand, was commonest in these two areas (and in some parts of the Highlands): no doubt winter unemployment among farm labour caused most distress where there was least access to supplementary industrial earnings.

Serious unemployment (i.e., that described as being serious in some years, or in every year) appears from Map 7.3 to be confined to the western Highlands and Islands and parts of the industrial west central belt. That, in fact, understates the situation in the towns and cities and in certain industrial villages: it should be studied in conjunction with Map 7.4 which shows the location of the parishes affected by 'failure of trade' and by troubles in weaving and mining, and Table 7.B, which shows the incidence of unemployment by type of parish. These show the degree to which serious unemployment was, on the one hand, a critical urban-industrial problem created by the fluctuations of the trade cycle and, on the other, a crofter's problem associated with crop failure and over-population. However pathetic the second, the first was the more important in terms of the numbers of population involved.

The other part of Question 22 referred to the measures taken to relieve the unemployed by charity. It was framed in too complicated a manner for a satisfactory response in terms of how often subscriptions had been raised or how much money had been donated, but 820 parishes reported whether or not any relief had been given. Table 7.C and Map 7.5 show the results. A third of parishes supplied charitable relief of some sort, but although these were broadly in the areas that needed it relief was raised more generally in the central belt and in the south than in the poor Highland fringe. Map 7.6 highlights this very clearly by showing the distribution of parishes that admitted having able-bodied unemployment but which provided no relief for it — they are heavily concentrated in the north and west Highlands.

Despite the findings in *Abbey Parish* v. *Richmond*, and the general assumptions of the time, kirk sessions did fairly often provide for the unemployed by giving a little relief, particularly if it was in a rural area and to meet a small number of cases. Generally, but not invariably, they described (or disguised) this as assistance to what was termed the 'occasional poor', those who had become unemployed solely because of sickness or accident but who were likely to return to the labour market as soon as they had recovered their health. This was a class that had 'seemingly no legal claim' on session poor funds but which was by convention nevertheless allowed relief from one half of the church collection which might be reserved for their benefit.[5] In practice, one may strongly suspect that many such 'occasional poor' were in as good health (or as bad health) as anyone was likely to be after a prolonged spell of unemployment without welfare, and did not differ from thousands of others who were refused relief by the session in other parishes. Some were, according to verbal evidence before the Inquiry, given help because their family was ill, or because it was feared they themselves would become ill. Clearly many parishes hardly troubled even with the subterfuge that the recipients were ill — 29 parishes replied to Question 22 that the kirk session had provided funds for 'able-bodied persons, in your parish, willing to work but unable to procure work' without saying a word about temporary sickness; that was 8 per cent. of the parishes giving relief. Far more than that admitted in their replies to a later question, Question 49, that they gave aid 'on account of want of employment, or of temporary sickness' (see below, Chapter 8, pp. 177–8). Sometimes help is on such a scale as to raise doubts as to whether it could possibly be financed from half the kirk collections. Nevertheless, it is clear that, despite all subterfuges and ambiguities, kirk session help in any form was only marginal to relief of unemployment.

The main channels of unemployment relief, then, were by raising a local subscription among the heritors (or among the middle-class community more widely defined) or by accepting external charity generally from funds based on Edinburgh, Glasgow or London. Map 7.7 shows the distribution of parishes relieved by local subscription – they are virtually all in manufacturing districts, and more densely concentrated in the west than in the east. Map 7.8 shows the distribution of parishes relieved by external subscription: they, too, include the main weaving areas of central Scotland, though with little in the borders or north of the Tay on the east coast. The striking difference, however, is the inclusion of the western Highlands and Islands. If this area was to obtain any relief at all it had to be from external sources: there were so few resident middle-class or even resident heritors (in 1838 it was estimated that three out of four Highland landowners were absentees)[6] that local communities were unable to raise anything extra to combat their own destitution.

The evidence before the Poor Law Commission is not very full or satisfactory in relation to the relief of Highland unemployment, perhaps because the last date when it had been necessary on a large scale was in 1836 and 1837, 'within the last ten years' of Question 22 but not so recent as to be prominent in witnesses' minds. In those years, following partial failure of both the oat and potato harvests combined with a bad season for the fisheries, an appeal has been made, first to the Lowland Scottish public and then to the United Kingdom at large, to rescue 'the inhabitants of the Highlands and Islands . . . from the fell grasp of famine, with all its direful consequences'.[7] £50,000 was raised and distributed among 52 parishes by the Glasgow organising committee, whose chairman and secretary later published an account of the Highland problem.[8] They attributed unemployment basically to over-population, to the continued attachment of Highlanders to subdivided plots of land on which they stayed doing very little even in good seasons and which left them helplessly unprovided for if the crops failed. They added, however, the interesting observation that Irishmen had largely driven the Highlander out of the migrant labour market in the Lowlands, and explained that job opportunities in the Highlands themselves had fallen off with the completion of transport improvements (the Crinan and Caledonian canals, and Telford's Parliamentary roads and bridges), the collapse of the kelp industry and the end of recruiting drives for military service.[9] They did not refer (though they might have done) to the effect on unemployment of the growth of large sheep farms and subsequent clearances: it was felt not only in crofting communities but also in towns on the southern Highland edge, like Crieff, where the local doctor told the commissioners of the extreme poverty of those evicted from the Breadalbane estates (22.193).

There was a sense of hopelessness about the Highlands at this period: one crisis had been averted; there was an expectation that another would follow with the next bad season. When it did, in 1846, it exceeded even the most gloomy forecasts through the total destruction of the potato crop by blight. That great famine wrecked the crofting economy and led to a rapid and immediate decline of population: it did not, however, lead to mass death on an Irish scale largely because the external relief funds once again (and under a much greater test) proved sufficient. In 1846 and the years immediately following £300,000 was raised and spent on the able-bodied Highland unemployed: it was distributed cautiously, even meanly, and after exacting labour on road-building as a test of destitution from men sometimes scarcely fit to lift a spade – but it sustained life.[10]

In 1843, however, all this lay in the future. The commissioners were more interested in the impact of the industrial depression that had commenced in 1841 and was still working its course out in the towns and weaving villages of Scotland when they commenced their hearings in March 1843. Nowhere had the effects of depression been deeper than in Paisley, where the relief of the unemployed became the subject of separate investigations, in this case by a select committee of the House of Commons which reported just as the Royal Commission began its own work.[11]

The story related by the select committee was so extraordinary that it is worth pausing to consider.[12] The staple trade of Paisley was the manufacture of fine hand-woven textiles, especially fancy shawls, though they also took a certain amount of plain work. It was a trade carried on partly by large numbers of small capitalists who survived on credit, and partly by large manufacturers who lived elsewhere but used Paisley as a reserve of skilled labour they could lay on or lay off at will. The onset of depression in 1841 coincided with a change in fashion which made the Paisley shawl less acceptable. Already by May there was a rush of bankruptcies and an alarming increase in the number of destitute weavers: within six weeks an appeal was made by the magistrates to the inhabitants of Paisley to raise money for their relief, and by July 7th there were over 2000 dependent on the funds of the relief committee. The scale of relief at this stage was 2s. a week for a single man and 5s. for a married couple with four children. The numbers on relief had doubled by mid-October and doubled again by mid-November. Little labour was demanded in this first phase in exchange for relief, which was provided in the form of tickets that the weavers could take to a provision shop of their choice and cash for what food they fancied.

By November the fund was in trouble, with 8000 dependent upon it and the numbers rising daily. The appeal was widened to take in first the county of Renfrew and then the country at large, a limited amount of public work was introduced and the scale of allowances slightly improved. Nevertheless the numbers continued to grow: they reached 11,000 by Christmas and almost 15,000 by mid-February 1843 – about a quarter of the entire population of the town were then living on charity. The corporation had gone bankrupt late in 1842 for the sum of £60,000, losing in the process about £20,000 of savings bank money which had been entrusted to its care: and about half the manufacturers in the town also went bankrupt. 'I do not believe', said the Sheriff-substitute of Renfrewshire, 'that there ever happened in the British Empire such a complete prostration of a town.'

It was at this point that, in March 1842, Edward Twistleton, a civil servant and one of the assistant poor law commissioners in England, appeared in the town on a highly peculiar mission, sent, he said, 'on behalf of certain individual members of Her Majesty's Government, to suggest to the relief committee of Paisley the adoption of certain regulations for relief as a condition of the subscriptions of those individual members of the Government'. The individuals (all acting in a private capacity) were Sir Robert Peel, Lord Stanley, Sir James Graham the Home Secretary, along with two outside the government – Lord Abercorn and Queen Victoria herself. The regulations proposed were, firstly the imposition of a strict work test for all able-bodied men – relief only after 10 or 12 hours supervised labour – and, secondly, the replacement of the ticket system by stores run by the relief authorities and giving out only potatoes, oatmeal and bread.

Twistleton's intervention was a clear sign (if a wholly unofficial one), that the government, firstly did not approve of the slapdash way relief had been given hitherto, suspecting with good reason that some of the meal tickets had been exchanged for whisky rather than food, and, secondly, that more money would be forthcoming if the administration was changed. The ace up the sleeve of Westminster was not the government ministers' own private subscriptions but their influence with the Manufacturers' Relief Committee in London: this was a body founded by Sir Robert Peel and the Archbishops of Canterbury and York in 1826 to transmit charitable donations and church collections made after royal appeals, to areas where there was industrial distress. It had been moribund for 15 years, but was revived by Peel in May, 1842.

The initial reaction to Twistleton's intervention was unfriendly: there were working-class demonstrations and agitation in favour of continuing the ticket system and evading the labour test. By May, however, the unreformed relief administration was in a state of collapse, £500 in debt with 10,000 people dependent upon it. On May 9th the Government intervened officially, undertook to supply the unemployed with food on the conditions previously announced, and appointed Twistleton as sole superintendent of the whole of the Paisley Relief Fund. For six weeks he ran it with the assistance of another official, and then handed over to an *ad hoc* committee of twenty nominated, in effect, by himself: for the new committee he chose only those sympathetic to continuing his conditions, and specifically excluded the local clergy on the grounds that they favoured tickets instead of stores.

By May 25th, money began to arrive from the Manufacturers' Relief Committee, and the value of relief was improved to 4s. a week for a single man and 7s. 6d. a week for a man with a wife and four children, after he had laboured at stone-breaking or similar work for 10 hours. The numbers dependent on relief did not materially drop below 10,000 during the period Twistleton was in charge.

After mid-June, when he handed over to the new committee, there was a slow deterioration in relations between the administration at Paisley and the Manufacturers' Relief Committee in London. The latter were unable to understand why they had to pay so much and Paisley raised so little itself: by July they had provided more for this one Scottish town than for all the districts of England put together. They also asked why they were expected to find funds for dependent women and people unable to work who in England would have been supported locally by the poor law. The Paisley committee explained their poverty by the collapse of both manufacturers and of shopkeepers in the town (the government's insistence on a store system must have been a fatal blow to many of them), and they tried hard to raise funds elsewhere in Scotland.

Numbers on relief after June 1842 at first dropped, due to a revival of trade partly associated with a demand for tartan shawls following Queen Victoria's visit to Scotland in the summer: Paisley had made little tartan before, but set to it with a will. There were only 6000 on relief by early October. Then, however, there was a set-back. The revival proved temporary: 10,000 were dependent again by December; scales were again cut to 2s. for men and to 4s. 5d. for a couple with four children. To cap it all, the Manufacturers' Relief Committee, itself running low in funds, progressively cut its weekly drafts to Paisley from £450 in August to £200 in November and threatened to reduce it still further unless the town raised more itself.

The magistrates by the end of 1842 were therefore not far off panic. As they explained in a memorial dated December 5th to Sir James Graham as Home Secretary, the relief money was likely to give out within a week, 'nearly 10,000 persons will have no alternative but either to commence begging *en masse* – to take food where they can find it – or to die quietly of starvation in their houses': at the moment the destitute were receiving only $1\frac{1}{2}$d. a day – 'the cost of the breakfast of a felon in prison' and to give less 'would only mock the people's misery without keeping them in life': there was a threat to public order and of 'the most calamitous consequences'. The Home Secretary replied merely that the government had no money to give Paisley and that 'it will be the duty of the magistrates and of the local authorities to repress *all* attempts to violate the law, either by intimidation or outrage'.

In the event the Manufacturers' Relief Committee continued to send £200 a week and the local relief committee cut costs a little in January 1843 by refusing relief to all Irishmen and their dependants who had not been resident for 10 years. It caused resentment, but there was no civil explosion. In the early months of 1843 before the improvement in trade finally mopped up the residue of the unemployed the allowance was down to 1s. 6d. a week for a single man and 3s. 11d. for a couple with four children. At the end of the day £45,525 had been spent, of which one third had been provided by the Manufacturers' Relief Committee who had, however, given 84 per cent. of the money spent after Twistleton took over in May 1842. Paisley itself contributed less than £3000. The remainder came from voluntary subscriptions in Scotland and England, and from overseas. It seems that relief under Twistleton's rules was rather more economical than previously – therefore the money had supported more people over a longer period: there is no evidence that it was less effective, and as long as he was personally in charge the allowances were more generous than before or afterwards.

Of all the furore in Paisley the Royal Commission on the Poor Law said little: perhaps it regarded the published evidence of the select committee as sufficient, perhaps it found it embarrassing to dwell upon events in which one of its own members had played so conspicuous a part. The body of the evidence did give, however, many details of how the same depression had been met in other Scottish towns. Most only started relief in the spring of 1842 – at Edinburgh in April after a demonstration of large bodies of the unemployed on the Calton Hill (20.200), at Glasgow in May, though there had been some relief given in the spring of 1841 as well (20.389), at Greenock in April (20.515), at Kilmarnock in April, though there had also been some relief from the previous September (20.718), at Aberdeen it had begun in the winter of 1841–2 and continued until May 1843 (21.605–6), at Dundee it lasted from January for the whole of 1842 (22.135), at Dunfermline it did not begin until June 1842 and lasted rather over a year (22.355).

Most large burghs did not begin to organise relief until the distress had been evident for at least six months, and this, as critics of the Scottish poor law said, led to terrible demoralisation among respectable workers who pawned or sold their entire possessions. A witness in Aberdeen described exactly what it meant in one case (21.615):

> I met a poor man, the beginning of this summer, going along the water-side crying – he had been evidently taking some drink. I asked what was the matter with him? He said he had been a workman at one of the factories. He had been out of work for eight or nine months. He had been obliged to sell some articles of furniture: and, last of all, a good room's furniture had been poinded for rent. I went with him to see that his statement was correct, and I found that he had had at one time a room furnished at what would have cost £30. All was packed up to be taken away. He was hopeless of getting anything to relieve himself. He appeared to be a decent man; and if he had had anything like constant employment, even though at reduced wages, he would have been prevented from falling, as he will fall, into the lowest class of destitute characters.

This testimony was echoed elsewhere many times. A minister of Paisley (20.687) said he had known working-class houses of the utmost respectability where 'any person in the higher circles might have taken a meal. There were mirrors, there were window sashes and there was a library well stocked', but on his return after a protracted depression the inhabitants 'had parted with everything, and were lying in the depth of winter, without a blanket'. The commissioners themselves visited such homes in Greenock (22.485) and met, for example, a mason who had been out of work 13 months with a wife and three children dependent on him: he had formerly earned 12–14s. a week. Now 'the bedroom was stripped of every article of furniture, but the house was clean. The amount received by this man from the soup-kitchen was two chopins of soup, and three scones per day.' When asked how he got on, the mason replied, stoically enough, 'while fasting, and whiles getting meat'.

Several towns provided a breakdown of the different occupations who had applied to their relief funds. In Greenock (never a textile town) 44 per cent. of a total of 1482 had been labourers, 24 per cent. woodworkers and 13 per cent. iron workers of various kinds: almost all the remainder were handicraft workers in the building trades, such as masons, painters and slaters, or other artizans like bakers, tailors and ship's riggers (20.518). At Aberdeen, of 502 males, 40 per cent. were labourers, 10 per cent. factory workers, 8 per cent. weavers and all the rest handicraft workers (21.610). In Auchtermuchty almost all the 300 applicants were weavers (22.263). In Dundee almost all the 486 females relieved were mill workers; of 571 males 19 per cent. were labourers, 17 per cent. mill workers, 20 per cent. weavers, 11 per cent. flax dressers and the remaining third other artizans (22.136).

These figures clearly demonstrate how it was, in fact, not only the least well paid or the least prestigious workers who were forced to apply for charitable relief during depression – the most vulnerable after the handloom weavers were often the other handicraft workers or artizans, the backbone of Victorian working-class respectability. As an observer in Paisley put it, 'the first class which suffers is the improvident, but it goes on till it reaches the provident' (20.612). Nor, contrary to popular belief, was it the Irish immigrant who swallowed up most of the funds: in Edinburgh out of 919 applicants asked for their place of birth only a third were Irish; in Glasgow out of 1043 it was 39 per cent. (20.65; 20.374).

Most localities compelled the applicants to labour before they obtained relief: in Edinburgh they worked breaking stones and laying out paths and roads on the Meadows and in Queen's Park, Holyrood; in Dundee they similarly constructed walks; in Dunfermline they broke stones; in Hamilton and Irvine they dug trenches; in Dumfries they made roads; at Dumbarton they deepened the Leven river. In some places (e.g., Kilmarnock and Paisley) webs were given out to unemployed weavers, but this was open to the objection that the relief authorities were undercutting established manufacturers by obtaining work at starvation wages (20.718; 20.618). Nevertheless, the rough physical labour on public works that was the main alternative was often extremely hard on craftsmen unaccustomed to it and already weakened by deprivation: 'it is heart-rending to see such able-bodied and excellent workmen labouring for such small gains', said the treasurer of the Edinburgh relief fund (20.155). In the countryside handloom weavers were often employed by local landowners, sometimes on furrow draining, as at Dunning in Perthshire (22.227), or in general tasks of estate improvement, as at Kettle in Fife (22.284). At Sanquhar in Dumfriesshire the Duke of Buccleuch employed 120 weavers in the winter 1841–2 in making roads and draining around Penpont, and also laid out £800 to keep the remainder at their looms at three-quarters wages until trade improved (22.606).

Another acceptable way of relieving destitution, especially for women, children and the elderly who could not labour at stone-breaking or trenching, was by the soup kitchen. All the main cities and some smaller places like

Largo in Fife, ran them: that in Edinburgh relieved 12,000 to 15,000 people daily in the winter of 1838 and 1839 (20.231), and made a major contribution to the task of keeping the poor alive. One of the few mercies about the crisis of 1842 was that food remained cheap, which greatly helped the managers of the soup kitchens to spin out their money to help as many people as possible.

It is impossible to read the evidence of the destitution among the unemployed in the crisis of 1842 and to retain afterwards much sympathy for the majority report of the Royal Commission, which recommended leaving things as they were, and which was accepted in the subsequent legislation in 1845. A radical motion, in the debate before the Act, to allow assistance to the able-bodied unemployed as a legal right was defeated 2 to 1 in the House of Commons. It was simply untrue to say, as the majority report did, that the relief provided by charity in periods of severe depression was 'not inadequate' (20.lxi): it was grotesquely so, and to allow the law to continue unchanged (as they recommended) was to perpetuate crass social injustice. Even to leave it ambiguous with a general assumption that it disbarred the unemployed was to solve nothing.

The belief at the root of conventional Victorian ideology was that any man who was thrifty and hard-working did have and should have the opportunity to better his lot by upwards social mobility. It was not an ignoble ideal. It was made a lie, however, by a law which allowed six months' accidental unemployment to wipe out at a stroke the thrift of years from one who had perhaps been a model member of a friendly society and a regular contributor to a savings bank. What availed respectability if you ended up sleeping on a pile of straw and queuing for a chopin of soup like your most drunken neighbours?

REFERENCES

1. David Asford, 'The Urban Poor Law' in *The New Poor Law in the Nineteenth Century* (ed. Derek Fraser, London, 1976). pp. 128–48.
2. L. J. Saunders, *Scottish Democracy 1815–40* (Edinburgh, 1950), p. 204.
3. Quoted *ibid.*
4. T. C. Smout, 'The Strange Intervention of Edward Twistleton' in *The Search for Wealth and Stability: Essays in Economic and Social History presented to M. W. Flinn* (ed. T. C. Smout, London, 1979).
5. Saunders, *op. cit.*, pp. 195.
6. A. Fullarton and C. H. Baird, *Remarks on the Evils at Present Affecting the Highlands and Islands of Scotland* (Glasgow, 1838), p. 52.
7. *Ibid.*, p. 5.
8. *Ibidem.*
9. *Ibid.*, pp. 68–9.
10. See *Comparative Aspects of Scottish and Irish Economic and Social History* (eds. L. M. Cullen and T. C. Smout, Edinburgh, 1977), chapters 2 and 4; James Hunter, *The Making of the Crofting Community* (Edinburgh, 1976), Chapter 4.
11. *Report of the Select Committee on the Distress in Paisley*, P.P. 1843, vol. 7.
12. For a fuller account see Smout, *loc. cit.*

TABLE 7.A

Percentages of Parishes reporting Unemployment, by District

	Serious	Not serious	None	N
1. Shetland	36	19	45	11
2. Orkney	47	0	53	19
3. Caithness	25	62	33	12
4. East Sutherland	73	0	28	11
5. East Ross	7	29	64	14
6. N.-E. Inverness	19	31	50	16
7. North-west coast	91	0	10	11
8. Skye and Outer Hebrides	92	0	8	13
9. West Argyll	60	27	13	15
10. North Argyll	9	64	27	11
11. South Argyll	24	35	41	17
12. Highland Inverness, Banff, Moray	33	33	33	12
13. Highland Perth, Aberdeenshire	20	0	80	10
14. N.-W. Perth	21	15	64	14
15. Nairn, Lowland Moray	14	29	57	21
16. Lowland Banff	0	31	69	26
17. Buchan	4	40	56	25
18. S.-E. Aberdeenshire	4	37	59	27
19. Inner Aberdeenshire	0	20	80	20
20. Kincardine	0	50	50	18
21. Inner Angus	3	50	47	34
22. Coastal Angus	11	63	26	27
23. East Perthshire	15	50	35	20
24. South Perthshire	14	48	48	21
25. East Fife	18	53	29	34
26. West Fife	22	63	15	27
27. North Stirling-Clackmannan	44	23	33	18
28. West Lothian, East Stirling	19	52	29	21
29. Edinburgh area	30	61	19	21
30. Dunbarton, Renfrewshire	60	20	20	20
31. North Ayrshire	58	27	15	26
32. South Ayrshire	38	50	12	16
33. North Lanarks.	30	60	10	20
34. South Lanarks.	15	40	45	20
35. Peeblesshire	13	31	56	16
36. Dunbar area	32	21	47	19
37. South Berwick	23	14	53	30
38. Kelso area	5	31	64	22
39. Hawick area	20	40	40	10
40. Inner Dumfries, Kirkcudbright	38	33	29	21
41. South Dumfries	32	36	32	22
42. South Kirkcudbright	33	43	24	21
43. Wigtown and south tip of Ayr	11	27	64	18
SCOTLAND	25	35	40	827

TABLE 7.B

Percentages of Parishes reporting Unemployment,
by Economic Type of Community

	Serious	Not serious	None	N
1.1 Urban-industrial: large towns	64	32	4	28
1.2 Urban-industrial: smaller towns, etc.	40	43	17	114
2.1 Mixed economy: rural parishes	16	51	33	188
2.2 Mixed economy: country towns	29	47	24	42
3.1 Agricultural: farming parishes	12	28	60	360
3.2 Agricultural: crofting parishes	57	17	26	95
SCOTLAND	25	35	40	827

TABLE 7.C
Percentages of Parishes that provided or failed to provide
(Charitable) Unemployment Relief, by District

	Relief needed and given	Relief needed and not given	No relief needed	N
1. Shetland	9	46	45	11
2. Orkney	16	31	53	19
3. Caithness	25	42	33	12
4. East Sutherland	9	63	28	11
5. East Ross	7	29	64	14
6. N.-E. Inverness	13	37	50	16
7. North-west coast	36	54	10	11
8. Skye and Outer Hebrides	54	38	8	13
9. West Argyll	40	47	13	15
10. North Argyll	33	40	27	9
11. South Argyll	24	35	41	17
12. Highland Inverness, Banff, Moray	58	9	33	12
13. Highland Perth, Aberdeenshire	0	20	80	10
14. N.-W. Perth	14	22	64	14
15. Nairn, Lowland Moray	14	30	57	21
16. Lowland Banff	19	12	69	26
17. Buchan	36	8	56	25
18. S.-E. Aberdeenshire	19	22	59	26
19. Inner Aberdeenshire	10	10	80	20
20. Kincardine	39	11	50	18
21. Inner Angus	18	35	47	34
22. Coastal Angus	26	48	26	27
23. East Perthshire	30	35	35	20
24. South Perthshire	24	28	48	21
25. East Fife	38	33	29	34
26. West Fife	63	22	15	27
27. North Stirling-Clackmannan	53	14	33	17
28. West Lothian, East Stirling	50	21	29	20
29. Edinburgh area	45	36	19	20
30. Dunbarton, Renfrewshire	65	15	20	20
31. North Ayrshire	68	17	15	25
32. South Ayrshire	56	36	8	16
33. North Lanarks.	65	25	10	20
34. South Lanarks.	35	20	45	20
35. Peeblesshire	31	13	56	16
36. Dunbar area	5	48	47	19
37. South Berwick	30	17	53	30
38. Kelso area	14	22	64	22
39. Hawick area	40	20	40	10
40. Inner Dumfries, Kirkcudbright	48	33	19	21
41. South Dumfries	55	13	32	22
42. South Kirkcudbright	71	5	24	21
43. Wigtown and south tip of Ayr	11	27	62	18
SCOTLAND	34	28	38	820

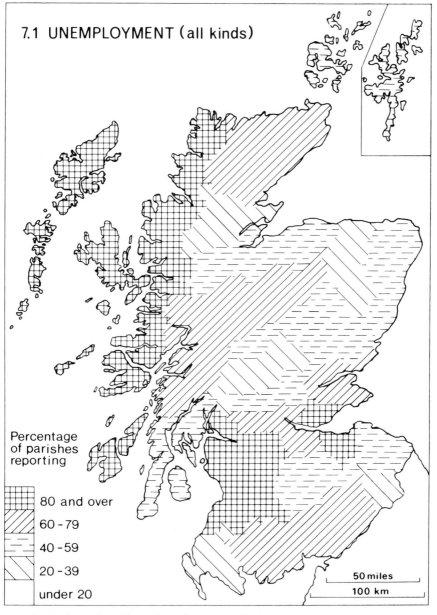

7.1 UNEMPLOYMENT (all kinds)

Percentage
of parishes
reporting

80 and over

60 - 79

40 - 59

20 - 39

under 20

50 miles
100 km

See Table 7.A (p. 162) and discussion on pp. 153–4.

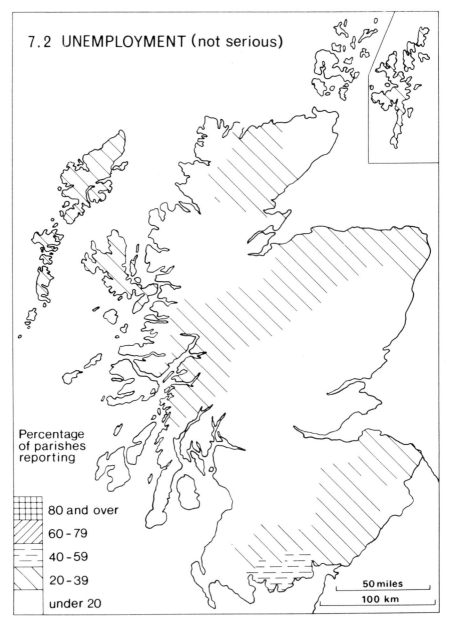

7.2 UNEMPLOYMENT (not serious)

Percentage
of parishes
reporting

80 and over

60 - 79

40 - 59

20 - 39

under 20

50 miles

100 km

See Table 7.A (p. 162) and discussion on pp. 153–4.

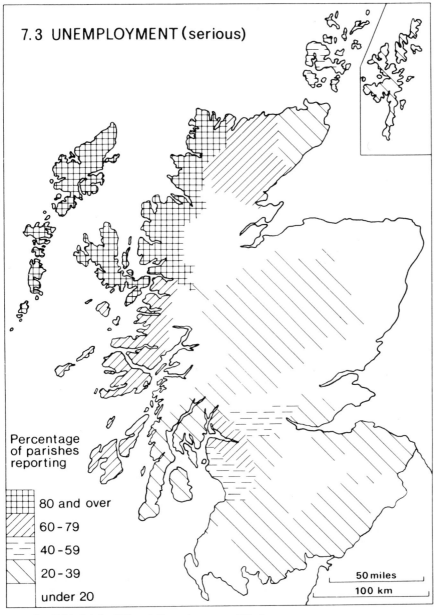

7.3 UNEMPLOYMENT (serious)

Percentage
of parishes
reporting

80 and over
60 - 79
40 - 59
20 - 39
under 20

50 miles
100 km

See Table 7.A (p. 162) and discussion on pp. 153–4.

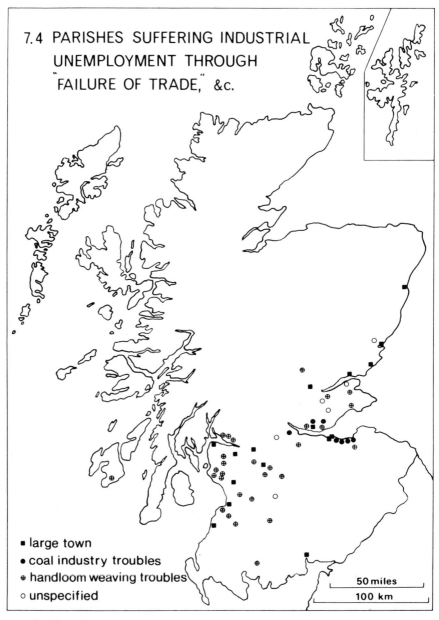

7.4 PARISHES SUFFERING INDUSTRIAL
UNEMPLOYMENT THROUGH
"FAILURE OF TRADE," &c.

■ large town
● coal industry troubles
⊕ handloom weaving troubles
○ unspecified

50 miles
100 km

See discussion on pp. 153–4.

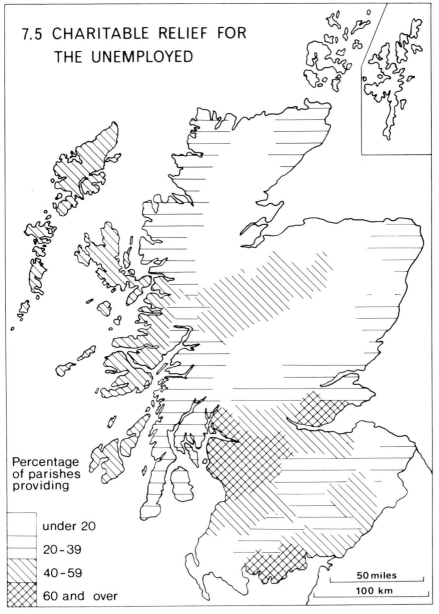

7.5 CHARITABLE RELIEF FOR THE UNEMPLOYED

Percentage
of parishes
providing

under 20

20 - 39

40 - 59

60 and over

50 miles

100 km

See Table 7.C (p. 164) and discussion on pp. 153–4.

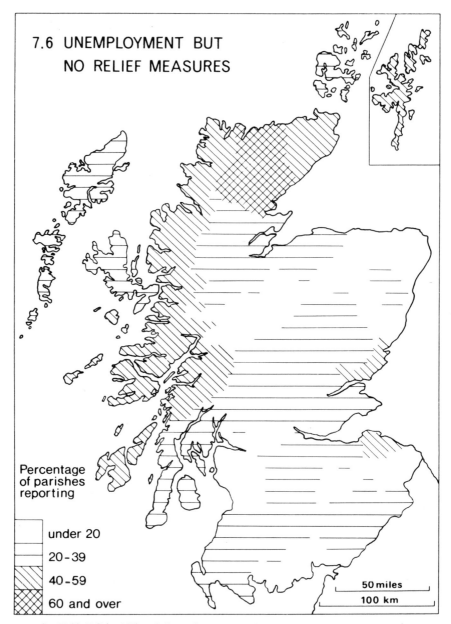

7.6 UNEMPLOYMENT BUT
NO RELIEF MEASURES

Percentage
of parishes
reporting

under 20

20-39

40-59

60 and over

50 miles
100 km

See Table 7.C (p. 164) and discussion on pp. 153–4.

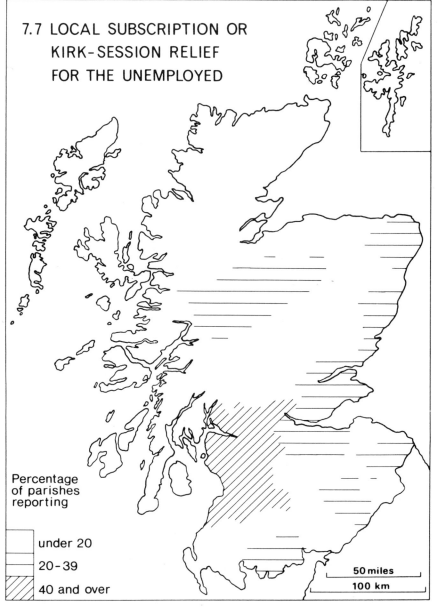

7.7 LOCAL SUBSCRIPTION OR
KIRK-SESSION RELIEF
FOR THE UNEMPLOYED

Percentage
of parishes
reporting

under 20

20-39

40 and over

50 miles

100 km

See discussion on p. 155.

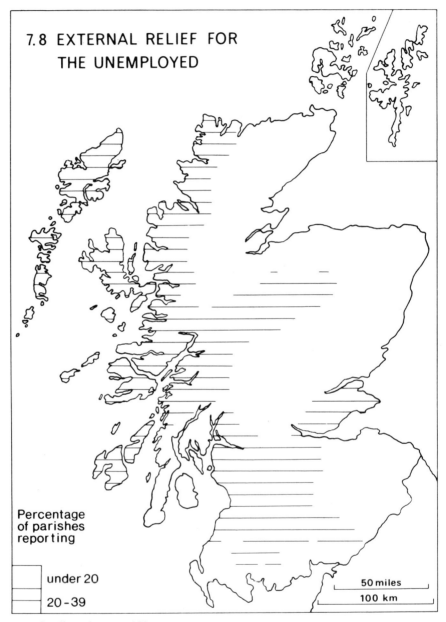

7.8 EXTERNAL RELIEF FOR
THE UNEMPLOYED

Percentage
of parishes
reporting

under 20

20-39

50 miles

100 km

See discussion on p. 155.

Chapter 8

THE OPERATION OF THE POOR LAW ON THE EVE OF REFORM

The primary consideration of the Royal Commission was, as the members said themselves, to make an inquiry into the 'practical operation' of the Scottish poor law and to recommend any necessary alterations in the law and its administration (20.i). What, in 1844, were the law's essential features? Although much of it was ultimately derived from Scottish imitations of sixteenth-century English statutes, it had evolved a distinct ethos and administration; less reliance was placed than in England on a legally imposed assessment, more on voluntary contributions; assistance was normally given to supplement other sources of income, from friends, relations, work and begging; the kirk was still looked on in many places as the main mode of administration; the able-bodied out of work had a very dubious claim to relief; and above all, there were distinct geographical variations, ranging from a non-existent or rudimentary poor law in the north-west to a highly organised, almost English poor law in the south-east.[1] Yet despite this diversity, or perhaps because of it, disputes over its operation and future did not develop until after 1800.[2] Then the acrimony between would-be reformers and their opponents became so intense that its influence on the course of the inquiry has to be grasped, or it will be impossible to comprehend the concern about the salient features of the poor law's operation.

There is no denying that, as a body, the commissioners' philosophical outlook leaned towards the school of thought which was associated with Thomas Chalmers. Thus they could state that

> ... small sums bestowed privately by the minister or elders, whether by way of charity or of loan, will often help to rouse the dormant energies and sustain the drooping spirit; and, by such well-timed assistance, a man may be enabled to get over his difficulties after a season, and resume his station in life, without the consciousness of having been degraded to the state of a pauper (20.xxxvii).

This would seem to follow naturally from Chalmers' own evidence in the Report, where he considered that there was a:

> ... great evil of confounding justice with humanity, in the matter of general indigence [and that the Poor Law] gives to the people the imagination of a right, and so converts that into the subject of an angry

173

and litigious challenge, which should be a pure interchange of goodwill on the one side and gratitude on the other (20.274).

This was, of course, a highly individualistic ethic, which stressed the value of moral self-improvement mediated through the kirk by the discrimimating hand of charity.

It did not go unchallenged. The activities and reputation of Dr. Alison are indicated elsewhere (see pp. 2, 216–7) but, to understand the depth of his attack on the existing orthodoxy, it is necessary to appreciate how far he and his followers had a fundamentally different view of the basis of social welfare:

> I conceive that the poor would be on a more independent footing and would not be so much debased, if it were declared that they had a right to relief which they got, instead of going to ask it as a charity (20.393) ... but when the wants of nature are insufficiently supplied for any length of time, the offer of moral and intellectual enjoyment is looked upon a sheer mockery and will be rejected with contempt, if not with loathing (20.482).

To them, progress, civilisation and a contented society were unobtainable without the recognition that social justice depended on the claims of the poor becoming a legal right. Pauperism, to one witness, grew out of the very conditions of wage labour itself (20.211; 20.98). Even the commissioners were forced to acknowledge that in many areas, the predominance of coalmining and manufacturing had created 'a new order of things' (20.xvi). This altered social and economic relationship had resulted in an atomised and pecuniary society, rather than a paternal one. It was only natural that the structure of social welfare should come to reflect the altered balance of needs and wants.

It was this analysis of the changes that were occurring in Scottish society that led the Alisonians to the opposite pole to the Chalmerians, and which the commissioners, despite their leanings, were forced to admit had to be recognised. The new order was destroying the intimate relationship that the kirk and its ministers had had with the people; within it, it was vital that the church should not take sides between capital and labour, for as one minister put it:

> The cause of the church is independent of anything that could possibly assume the aspect of a bribe: and the spiritual official should not seem to assume that character: for in many cases he might be tempted to make use of it: to the hindrance, also, of his ecclesiastical duties (20.381).

So this was the basis of the acrimony – at one pole there was the belief that the new society could only redeem itself by transplanting the oft-felt traditional values and forms – at the other, the belief that such was impossible because the new environment called for the provision of a legally claimable social minimum. As Chalmers realised, the choice was between a system based on an older consideration of humanity or one based on a new conception of justice.

Given this, how far were the commissioners (and others) able to comprehend the existing poor law? Certainly they went to considerable trouble to ascertain facts and gather opinions. Besides their circulated questionnaire to each parish, they devised a fairly standard form of question for the verbal examinations. One set was used to lead the discussion of rural witnesses, and the other, more flexible, for those from the urban areas. It is interesting to note that urban witnesses were more readily called on to consider poor law matters philosophically, whilst the rural witnesses were kept to more factual topics. Both sets are reproduced in Appendixes III and IV.

Our major concern, however, is with the circulated questionnaire. Three particular areas were considered for analysis: the numbers of people on the poor law and who they were; the policy of giving relief to marginal groups in need; the poor law's sources of income and how it was spent. The commisioners went to great lengths to be clearly understood, issuing, in their supplementary return on an 'analysis of poor', carefully worded instructions, and even an example of how to fill in a particular return. The poor quality of some of the answers dismayed the commissioners, who felt that the lack of uniformity in classifying the poor militated against a complete enumeration of all they had asked for. But the nomenclature they adopted themselves was the one most other contemporary writers used, for all its shortcomings. Thus in Question 53 the commissioners felt it desirable to ask for a return of those on the 'permanent' poor list and those on the 'occasional' poor list. The former, in many eyes, had a clearly established legal right to relief, whilst the latter, which included the able-bodied, had no such right but had to rely on parochial discretion. A similar division was asked for in the 'analysis of the poor'. Even cursory inspection indicates that parishes differed in their use of these categories. Some went as far as to put the able-bodied in their permanent group, others listed widows and the insane as occasional, whilst others had no occasional list at all. St. Quivox, the suburb of Ayr, replied that they had 128 on their roll, but added as a rider, 'to make the distinction betwixt permanent and occasional, we would require to be informed what time constitutes "permanency"' (22.137). Although a majority of parishes did distinguish between occasional and permanent poor, nearly half could not specify this list in terms of the categories the commissioners wanted – the able-bodied, the insane, orphans, deserted families, the elderly, widows, mother with illegitimate children and so on. Many parishes used other criteria .o make that distinction, like moral character, degree of alternative support or length of residence in the parish (22.746).

Despite this, some of the information returned is reasonably satisfactory for analysis. Tables 8.A, 8.B and 8.H and Maps 8.1, 8.2 and 8.3 illustrate some aspects of the commissioners 'analysis of the poor'. The highest number of poor relief recipients as a percentage of the population could be found in the south-west, the eastern Borders, the lower Clyde and the north-east stretching as far up as Sutherland.[3] The areas with the smallest number of poor include Shetland, the western Highlands, Tayside and the upper Forth Valley. The analysis by economic type of community indicates that the geographic spread was underpinned by above-average rates in urban areas. Indeed these areas had nearly half of all the poor (46 per cent.). The agitation by many urban witnesses for more stringent measures to prevent the rural poor, who were allegedly forced to migrate because of housing and job shortages, from congregating in the towns, was no doubt a reflection of this figure (20.xxxix). Virtually every urban witness pressed for an extension of the settlement laws from 3 to at least 7 years and the formal institution of a law of removal, which would enable the authorities to return migrants with less than 7 years residence in a parish to their place of birth.

One of the largest groups on poor relief was the elderly. The returns indicate that they comprised about half of the poor in the Highlands, dropping steadily to around 30 per cent. in the north-east and Tayside and increasing to 40 per cent. in the south-east and in parts of the south-west. But it was in the urban-industrial areas that they formed the smallest proportion (about 25 per cent.) of the total poor. Chapter 10 shows that the Highlands and the south-west had above-average emigration rates, whilst the east coast had below-average rates. An unsupported and ageing population were left to the mercies of parochial relief as younger members of the family with higher earning power left for the towns or overseas (20.646). At the same time the magnetism of the towns, with their greater opportunities for work, begging and general anonymity, enabled the needy to multiply.

The Irish were one new group among the needy. Their poor were heavily concentrated in the south-west, that part nearest to Ireland and the ferry boats, but even in the large towns they were 4·94 per cent. of the total poor. There can be little doubt that the Irish poor law recipients would have been more numerous had the poor law authorities been more willing to assist them. Both Edinburgh and Dundee were notorious in this respect, refusing relief wherever possible, and, when absolutely essential, giving sums far below that afforded to the native population (20.111; 22). The prejudice was exemplified by the Lord Provost of Edinburgh, who in objecting to the introduction of Roman Catholic priests into the local charity workhouse, considered that Catholicism 'had been declared to be not according to the word of God, founded on error, and maintained by delusion' (20.115).

Of all the groups receiving poor relief, the most controversial and the one the commissioners dwelt on at greatest length was certainly the able-bodied. They sought to distinguish between two types of assistance; that given in times of temporary sickness and that given on account of casual failure of trade: unhappily, this distinction was not carried through explicitly enough when they asked about the general policy of giving such relief in Question 49. A sizeable number of parishes were certainly assisting the able-bodied in one form or another. In some districts, like Nairn, South Ayrshire and in the south-west, the numbers assisted formed a sizeable proportion of all those on poor relief: taking dependants into account, one in five of those on poor relief in South Ayrshire was 'able-bodied'. Such high numbers must have constituted a problem where parishes had a small population, and it is doubtful whether there were sufficient voluntary or statutory funds in any size of parish to alleviate large-scale distress, given the prevailing views about taxing property. It is little wonder that witnesses like Sheriff Alison of Glasgow, suggested that 'there should be some gradation of assessment, according to the benefits which the different classes of society have derived from the labour, which produces that pauperism' (20.471).[4]

As we have already explained in Chapter 7, the exact 'rights' of the able-bodied unemployed to claim poor relief from the parish, and the legality of paying such relief, were very uncertain. But parishes often supposed that they were allowed to pay such relief so long as the monies paid out did not come from a legal assessment of ratepayers, although most believed that the poor could not claim it as of legal right. Thus outside the towns and the south-east (where there was most reliance on legal assessment) parishes behaved as though they had a certain amount of discretion to relieve the able-bodied.

Some parishes also conducted what they termed a 'voluntary assessment' exactly as if it was a legal assessment, and assisted the able-bodied occasionally with some proceeds (22.491) – perhaps they were using this terminology to get round what they saw as an inhumane law. There is, however, also evidence that even legally-assessed parishes did sometimes assist the able-bodied out of the assessment, though in a devious way. Take the case of Hamilton – there the returns show a very sizeable number of able-bodied assisted on poor relief, but the verbal evidence indicates that they were assisted only by subscriptions and relief work, at least after 1820. At that time an assessment had been levied to pay the interest on a loan taken out to cover the cost of relief work. The parish was still paying that interest in 1843 (22.376).

One other interesting fact emerges; large towns assisted relatively few able-bodied persons from the poor law, but other industrial areas assisted the greatest number. Perhaps it was easier in the large towns to raise extra-parochial funds for relief, or more speculatively, perhaps the other industrial areas did not feel inclined to be too harsh with the law.

What is certain, however, is that in 1843, fewer than 4000 able-bodied persons were receiving poor relief, under one half per cent. of the population if dependants are included. Many people, including the commissioners, greeted this finding with satisfaction. They also knew, however, that numbers were one thing and that policy in giving relief was another. After all, for the able-bodied, 1843 was a year of reviving prosperity, so that any demand that had existed to assist this group was declining.

The commissioners were always keenly aware that critics of the poor law complained that the administration of it was often arbitrary and discriminatory, so that many who were in need were refused. Question 49 sought to probe this aspect in depth. It asked:

Q. 49. Is relief given in your parish to able-bodied men on
account of want of employment, or of temporary
sickness?

To this, 820 parishes replied (a response rate of 91 per cent.). Tables 8.C, 8.E and Map 8.4 illustrate the replies. Of those which responded, 15 per cent. stated that they definitely did give assistance (but note that there is no specification here as to whether temporay sick or just unemployed). 23 per cent. stated the direct opposite – no assistance given. But between these two poles it was possible to categorise more conditional responses. 59 per cent. replied in a more-or-less positive manner, that is, indicated that at least relief was given occasionally, or sometimes, or in temporary sickness; 41 per cent. replied in a negative manner, that is, if relief was given it was rarely, or seldom, or the parish was never asked. Thus, overall there was a higher 'no' response than 'yes' — but this was offset by a higher conditional 'yes' reply.

Most parishes in Scotland, then, would assist the able-bodied exceptionally and as a matter of discretion but were not too keen on unconditional assistance. The only areas that showed any real inclination to have the latter were spread down the east coast from Banff to Fife, and the only economic type of community, small country towns. But this figure shot up, often dramatically, in many areas, not only from Banff to Fife, but also in the southwest and in parts of central Scotland, when consideration is given to 'positive' replies. The figure for central Scotland is underlined by the replies from industrial areas and large towns. In contrast, the most antagonistic areas to assisting the able-bodied were located in the Highlands, a fact that had been well established before the commission sat. Only a few areas further south approached that antagonism, notably West Lothian and South Lanark. Another question (Q.50) asked about relief to widows with one child and to single able-bodied women. The results closely followed those of Question 49.

Another group which evidently interested the commissioners and many witnesses were mothers with illegitimate children. The returns show a very marked district pattern. A disproportionate number of the mothers who were relieved were located down the east coast. The Highlands and central Scotland had relatively few cases, but small country towns show an above average proportion of cases. This pattern can in part be illuminated by reference to Question 56, which asked:

> Q. 56. Is bastardy on the increase, or on the decrease, amongst
>   the labouring classes or in your parish?

Although the ministers could not possibly have had accurate statistical knowledge of any trend, the pattern of replies was so pronounced, 80 per cent. of parishes in the Highlands reporting a decrease in bastardy, compared with 46 per cent. in Scotland as a whole, that it is worth mentioning. Moreover, it underpins to some degree the trends of assistance and numbers of this group in the poor law.

On actual relief to mothers with illegitimate children they asked in Question 51:

> Q. 51. Is relief given in your parish to single women, mothers
>   of illegitimate children?

817 parishes replied (a response rate of 90 per cent.). Tables 8.D, 8.F and Map 8.5 illustrate the replies. To this question a higher number replied than to the question on the able-bodied that they definitely gave assistance — 31 per cent. But a greater number replied that they definitely did not — 29 per cent. Moreover, fewer replied in a more-or-less positive manner, a mere 45 per cent. (with 55 per cent. negatively). It would seem that poor law relief to this group was more morally repugnant, even if conditions were attached to it, than

to the able-bodied. A broadly similar distribution of replies occurred, with the most generous areas for giving relief (if there was a demand) from Banff to Fife, in parts of the central Lowlands, in large towns and in other industrial areas. The worst was again the Highlands, the area that had the fewest cases on the poor roll and had stated declining bastardy. But it is interesting to note that the extreme south-west, an area well known for its high rate of bastardy, was also less willing to give relief. It would seem to be not just a question of how many cases there were likely to be in the parish, but also of the appropriateness of giving relief to this type of case. Many said assistance would place a premium on sin, and that was not to be countenanced. A further question (52) discussed the relief of deserted women, and the pattern closely followed the answers on illegitimacy.

In many respects, Question 49 and Question 51 strike at the heart of the poor law debate in the 1840s. To the Chalmerians, assistance would undermine the moral fibre of the nation. To the Alisonians, meeting need was the first call. To most parish officers and ministers, however, there was no fine line to distinguish the two concepts; they had to work on the practicalities. Not giving assistance to the occasional able-bodied case may have resulted in greater numbers at a later stage, if the labourer was unable to 'restore himself' because he could not support his relations. Not assisting the wanton mother may have led to her death, and the parish supporting orphans. Many, like the minister at Dolphinton, gave help 'grudgingly' (22.804). Some, however, were often more anxious to keep costs low rather than to relieve even the most deserving. When the commissionsers were in the Inverness area, Edward Twistleton asked one of the witnesses: 'Have not the impotent poor of Scotland a right to relief, irrespective of the fact whether there is an assessment or not?' He received the reply: 'Yes, under the statute; but we have tried to conceal that from them as much as possible . . .' (21.501). The respondent was franker than most poor law administrators would have been, but many would have agreed fully with his approach. What these responses seem to indicate, is that some areas, and in particular, those along parts of the east coast, had a wider sense of the 'practicalities' of relief than others.

It is possible to carry the analysis a little further. Table 8.G breaks down the relief to various types of poor by poor law income, that is it shows where parishes relied primarily on legal assessment, or voluntary assessment, or in fact were non-assessed and just used church-door collections or mortifications. In general, those parishes which had legal assessment had the most poor and the most lenient policy, while those relying on unassessed sources of income had the least poor and the harshest policy. Those legally assessed had slightly fewer able-bodied and mothers with illegitimate children, but hardly significant in relation to the low proportions assisted in an unassessed group. It is interesting to note that the legally assessed had proportionately fewer elderly, whilst the unassessed group had the greatest. This was no doubt a reflection of the greater amount of cash available to the first group (see below), which enabled it to broaden the categories it could assist, like the insane, the widows and orphans, in contrast to the small amounts available to the unassessed group, which could only assist (if that is the right word) the most 'needy' and those unable through age to fend for themselves. There is, however, one other interesting point. Those legally assessed, while having the most positive replies to the giving of relief, had, nevertheless, an equal 'yes' score with those voluntarily assessed. It would seem that, while relief was more plentiful than elsewhere, it was tied to conditions – an indication that legal assessment was not a panacea for indiscriminate relief.

Whatever the polemics of giving relief, policy without money was merely talk. It had long been realised that the regular imposition of legal assessment implied a secure and high source of income with which to pay what was called 'needful sustentation'. But legal assessment in the years preceding 1840 had been disparaged by many, including Chalmers, as a morally incorrect system of welfare. A parish was not obliged to impose a legal assessment, as the law left the method of raising poor relief funds to local discretion. Theoretically, all that was required was enough to meet 'needful sustentation'. But for the poor person by 1843 the ability to enforce any rights that the sixteenth-century legislature had envisaged was practically non-existent.[5] The parish was the final arbiter. Thus how much you got, if anything, was dependent on a number of factors; the wealth of the local community; custom; attitude towards the poor by heritors and common-folk alike; regional notions of what constituted a minimum standard of subsistence; the availability of work, such as winding pirns, which would enable the parish to avoid giving a full allowance; appropriateness of begging.

A parish like Greenlaw in Berwickshire was well organised (22.737) with heritors and kirk session meeting twice a year, conjointly, to impose a legal assessment and fix the allowances:

> Application for relief is usually made first to the minister, and he always makes inquiry into the circumstances of the applicant, and makes a report to the heritors previous to their final decision. The heritors' clerk is likewise always required, for the behoof of the heritors to become acquainted with the circumstances of each applicant. If a person requires relief between the half-yearly meetings, such relief is afforded, either from the sessional funds, which are left entirely at the disposal of the kirk session, or from the assessment, by the heritors' clerk.

The allowances given to an elderly person would normally exceed 2s. per week, well in excess of the usual amount.

Greenlaw was in the rich south-east; the poor in many other areas were less fortunate. At Stranraer, for example, they were simply given a badge which would license them to beg (22.522). Rosskeen (Ross-shire) is representative of the Moray Firth parishes: there the poor were 'supported by their neighbours. They go about begging, and to those that do not, their neighbours contribute' (21.45). Further north, in Orkney and Shetland, the poor were frequently deposited in rotation on neighbouring farmsteads, with each farmstead providing food and shelter. It was called 'quartering' (21.195). Further west, on Barra, Harris and South Uist, the community was so poor and the heritors so concerned about encouraging emigration, that they did not bother about having a poor roll at all (21.362).

In short, the heritors or the kirk session could either impose a legal assessment with all the problems of assessing and collecting from property holders and others, or the heritors could agree to collect from themselves through a voluntary collection without legal sanctions against any who declined to pay (often referred to as a 'voluntary assessment'); but failing that, the kirk session (or magistrates in burghs) would have to fall back on church-door collections, contributed by all, 'mortified' income (legacies or 'mortifications') left by the wealthier parish residents, mortcloth dues (for the hire of a black cloth to go over the coffin) and fines. Beyond that, irregular voluntary contributions from heritors were often given. An example of mortification can be seen at Lonmay (Aberdeenshire) which received in 1842, '£50, being a periodical payment, once in eight or nine years, from Burnett's mortification ... also £26 19s., interest of funds lent out; also 17s. 10d. mortcloth' (24.347c). Another at Brechin, which received, 'Mortcloth dues £5 13s.; sale of deceased pauper's effects, £10 4s. 5d.; proceeds of money mortified in the session, £7 1s. 8d.; garden rents, £8 18s.; rents of seats in the church, £17 5s. 11d.' Examples of voluntary contributions can be seen at Kilfinan (Argyll) which received '10s. and a fat cow, by Mr Oldham, one of the heritors', and at Lauder where, 'a donation of £10 given by Lady Lauderdale, for purchasing coals for the poor; and clothes given by the clothing society, to the amount of £14 11s. 8½d.' was made (24.71c, 185c). With a wide range of possible sources of income, any one parish could select those sources which it thought most suitable to its particular circumstances. Theoretically, there was no need to remain year after year adhering to any particular source or sources; indeed the legislature seemed to imply the likelihood of changing them, or of supplementing them, to meet any emergencies like a famine. But despite the intention of the legislature, the pattern of Scottish history had, by 1840, led to widespread differences in the method of raising income and in its expenditure.

The answers to five other questions on the questionnaire illustrate how deep these divisions were. Question 33 asked, 'Was there a legal assessment for the relief of the poor in your parish during the year 1842? If yes, what was its amount?' Question 34 asked, 'Was there a Voluntary Contribution by the heritors for the relief of the poor in your parish during the year 1842? If yes, what was its amount?' Question 35 asked, 'What was the amount of the collection made at the church doors during that year?' Question 36 asked, 'What was the amount of other voluntary contributions for the relief of the poor in your parish during that year?' Question 37 asked, 'What was the amount of mortifications, mortcloth dues, and other sessional funds in your parish during that year?' Overall some 840 parishes replied to these questions, 93 per cent. of total parishes.

Tables 8.I, 8.J and Maps 8.6, 8.7, 8.8 and 8.9 refer to those parishes replying that they had certain types of income (irrespective of amount). Church-door collections (Question 35) were left out of our tables and maps as almost every parish that replied had them. Only the south-east, Lanarkshire, South Dumfries and the large towns imposed a legal assessment to any significant degree, though outcrops were reported north of the Tay and into the south-west. Voluntary assessment (Question 34) was rare in the large towns and in crofting communities, but geographically was spread in a crescent shape beyond the core areas reporting legal assessment. Voluntary contributions (Question 36), apart from the crofting communities, were spread fairly evenly between different economic types with the smaller urban-industrial communities the highest. But, this time, it was geographically concentrated (over 50 per cent.) in the north-east, the Forth valley and on Clydeside. It would seem from this table that assessment did not preclude further charity from the better-off. Mortified and other sessional funds, although scoring high at 84 per cent., were low in the large towns, in crofting communities, but touched 100 per cent. in the north-east. Reports of this type of income remained consistently high all down the east coast, dipping only significantly in the far south. In aggregate, whilst virtually every parish had some sort of church-door income and most had mortifications, less than half could rely on any other form of voluntary contribution. Moreover, only 67 per cent. had an assessment, either voluntary or legal.

How important was each source of income? Tables 8.K and 8.L refer to the distribution of certain types of income as a percentage ot total income. For the 840 parishes, what looms largest is the proportion of legally-assessed income, accounting for nearly 49 per cent. of the total. Voluntary assessment vies with church-door collections at about 18 per cent. of the total. Mortifications and voluntary contributions follow with 10 per cent. and 5 per cent. respectively. The large towns can be seen as relying almost totally on assessment, but crofting areas at the other end of the spectrum rely for over half of their income on church-door collections. Other communities depended on more of a mixture, though assessments never fall below 54 per cent. of total income.

Large towns were excluded from the district table (8.K) because they would bias certain districts with high legal assessment incomes; nevertheless, it can be seen that some southern areas had an overwhelming dependence on legal assessment, reaching 91 per cent. in the Kelso district. The same cannot be said for voluntary assessment. For instance, 68 per cent. of East Fife parishes used it, but it formed only 32 per cent. of that district's income. Voluntary assessment, despite raising quite considerable sums (generally more than could be raised by any non-assessed means), was decidedly inferior to legal assessment. The areas in which church-door collections were dominant lay in the north and west and in the extreme south-west, with areas like Nairn relying for more than 60 per cent. of their income from this source. It seems that it is in these areas heritors did least to support the poor law. Mortications fluctuated between 10 per cent. and 20 per cent. of total income, except where there was legal assessment and in the north-east, where in one district, Buchan, it almost equalled that raised through the church. Voluntary contributions seemed to have flowed remarkably well in the industrial areas of central Scotland, despite assessment. Overall, a marked regional pattern emerges from this table and certainly underpins contemporary comments that legal assessment, where it predominated, dwarfted other forms of income.

Did legal assessment lead to a real reduction in the amounts given by other sources of income, as was often claimed by its opponents? Tables 8.M and 8.N refer to funds per head, broken down by type. Total poor law income per head of population averaged £0·08, but varied dramatically from £0·10 in the towns to just over £0·01 in crofting areas – a phenomenal factor of 10. But this becomes a factor of 40 at the extreme, South Berwick and Skye, when the district table is considered. This table, because it considers poor law income per head of population, is a particularly apt method of considering church collections – they came from the community at large. This source of income was particularly strong in agricultural areas, reaching twice the Scottish average in the north-east, Tayside and the south-west. But reasonable amounts were still forthcoming from all other areas except the Highlands.

Another way of considering income is in relation to valuation (see above, Chapter 1, pp. 8–9). Tables 8.O and 8.P refer to imcome per £1 of gross valuation, broken down by type of income. This gives an indication of what each area was willing to, or had to, 'contribute' in terms of its property valuation, and while perhaps being less apt for church collections, is more so for assessments and mortifications. The same wide variations by community and area, from less than £0·01 in the north and west, to over £0·04 in large urban areas, is noticeable again. But here the magnitude is far less, a factor of 7 at its greatest (contrast Dunbarton and Renfrew with Skye). It would seem that amounts given were far more constrained by valuation than by population. Particularly high were large towns, most of central and southern Scotland and the extreme north-east. Indeed Banff, an area where assessment was not particularly predominant, had a higher figure than many of those areas which did. This is in stark contrast with the previous table on population, where if anything the reverse was true.

To the commissioners, income represented only one side of the monetary equation. The other was expenditure. Question 38 asked, 'What was the amount of money distributed by your parish amongst paupers on the Permanent Roll during the year 1842?' Question 39 asked, 'What was the amount of money distributed by your parish amongst paupers on the Occasional Roll during the year 1842?'

827 parishes (91 per cent.) replied sufficiently well for the data to be used in the computer. Tables 8.Q and 8.R, Maps 10, 11 and 12, refer to expenditure per recipient (in pounds per annum), per head of population (in new pence) and per £1 of gross valuation (in new pence).[6] Apart from crofting areas, where expenditure averaged a miserly £0·34 per recipient, there was very little difference between economic type of community. But by district, a much greater difference can be seen. In the Hawick area, nearly £4·00 per recipient was spent, compared with £0·19 in Skye and £1·81 for Scotland as a whole. Because the poor law roll was made up of different types of applicant, it is difficult to generalise accurately on expenditure per recipient.

The Alisonians thought that £3 to £4 per year was needed to sustain a person properly, but even after allowing for differences in income needs between adults, children and the elderly, only the south-east approached the Alisonian minimum.[7] For the poor in other areas south of the Highlands, poor law income was clearly supplementary to other sources. For instance, at Kirkcudbright, only a quarter of total income per recipient came from poor law funds, with a further 41 per cent. from the recipient's own work and the rest, 34 per cent., from friends and begging (22.540). It cannot therefore be argued that poor law income was the mainstay of the poor in most areas: rather it was their own labours and the kindliness of their friends that saw them through their misfortune. In the Highlands, the amount given was so derisory that it would have needed massive supplementation from other sources to support life decently; this was certainly not forthcoming.

The figures relating to expenditure per head of population and expenditure per £1 of gross valuation complement what has already been said on poor law income per head of population and valuation. Again greater differences can be seen with population than with valuation.

These maps and tables represent some of the statistical material on the poor law with which the commissioners had to work. There can be little doubt that they were shaken by much of what they read, saw and heard, despite the gloss of their report. It was appalling to them that the poor law varied so much in the numbers assisted, the policies pursued and the amounts raised and given. All the moralising in the world could not justify these wide disparities in a society that was responding ever more quickly to the pace of industrial growth. Greater wealth meant that greater disparities had to be justified to those less fortunate, and the break-up of the traditional agrarian communities meant that justifications could not be localised but had to be national. The commissioners understood this, and in the long run the Alisonians won. The Lord Advocate, when introducing the subsequent Bill in 1845, almost reiterated their clarion call, by stating that his aim was:

> ... To facilitate to the party entitled to relief the means of admission to the receipt of relief ... [and] ... to secure due attention to his condition after his right was admitted.[8]

Thus legal assessments and a bureaucratic approach to the Poor Law were to become the norm. The kirk was out. But the victory was not total. The Alisonians could not break down the growing concern of capital for a free and unfettered labour force. The question of relief to the able-bodied out of work was held in abeyance, with one side claiming it could be given under certain circumstances and the other that it could not. Neither was absolutely sure, and the resolution of that question, through the courts, belongs to another and later chapter of Poor Law history.

REFERENCES

1. There are many references to the law and practice of the old Scottish poor law. The following are illustrative: *Royal Commission on the Poor Laws: Report on Scotland, part*

III – Historical Development [by William Smart], P.P. 1909, vol. XXXVIII; J. E. Graham, 'The History of the Poor Law of Scotland previous to 1845', *Poor Law Magazine*, vols. XVII–III (1917–18); R. Mitchison, 'The Making of the Old Scots Poor Law', *Past and Present*, no. 163 (1974).

2. The positions can be best summarised by the following: *Report by a Committee of the General Assembly on the Management of the Poor in Scotland*, P.P. 1839, vol. XX; W. P. Alison, *Illustrations of the Practical Operation of the Scottish System of the Management of the Poor* (London 1840), and *Observations on the Management of the Poor in Scotland* (Edinburgh 1840).

3. 'Poor relief recipient' has been used here in preference to the more value-laden 'pauper', a word many witnesses to the commission did not use. Throughout the text, 'poor' is taken to be poor relief recipient.

4. It was the small-scale parish that led to the poor law's ultimate demise, when mass unemployment in the 1920s left a trail of bankrupt parishes. See I. Levitt, 'The Scottish Poor Law and Unemployment 1890–1929' in *The Search for Wealth and Stability: Essays in Economic and Social History presented to M. W. Flinn* (ed. T. C. Smout, London, 1979).

5. *Duncan* v. *Heritors of Ceres*, February 14th, 1843 (20.xvi). The Court of Session indicated they would support claims by the poor for higher allowances.

6. The income and expenditure figures in the tables are not identical because, firstly, some of the church-door income was not spent on the poor but on other ecclesiastical expenses; secondly the expenditure figures are net of administration costs (in the south of Scotland about 5 per cent. of income); and thirdly not all that was income in one year was necessarily spent in the same year – lump sums in the shape of mortifications, etc., were still often invested in loans to landowners and others to ensure a steady flow of interest.

7. The commissioners attempted to show that there was no commonly held social minimum (20.xvii). The verbal evidence indicates, however, that the majority of witnesses held views on the minimum amount of income similar to the Alisonians.

8. *Hansard*, vol. 73, p. 1409.

TABLE 8.A
Breakdown of Certain Numbers on Poor Relief, by District

	1. % of population on poor relief	2. Mothers with illegitimate children as % of poor relief recipients	3. 'Able-bodied' (unemployed plus temporary sick) as % of poor relief recipients
1. Shetland	2·58	0·25	2·03
2. Orkney	3·20	1·55	2·55
3. Caithness	3·42	0·31	0
4. East Sutherland	5·24	0·11	2·81
5. East Ross	4·53	0·82	1·56
6. N.-E. Inverness	3·76	0·16	0·22
7. North-west coast	2·99	0	0
8. Skye and Outer Hebrides	1·97	0·10	0·55
9. West Argyll	1·52	0·92	1·67
10. North Argyll	2·62	1·00	0·84
11. South Argyll	3·16	0·46	3·94
12. Highland Inverness, Banff, Moray	4·84	2·42	3·05
13. Highland Perth, Aberdeenshire	2·63	0·78	3·58
14. N.-W. Perth	3·75	1·56	1·41
15. Nairn, Lowland Moray	4·23	1·22	8·38
16. Lowland Banff	3·72	2·38	5·75
17. Buchan	3·48	2·59	4·31
18. S.-E. Aberdeenshire	4·23	0·79	1·33
19. Inner Aberdeenshire	3·13	1·99	4·82
20. Kincardine	4·38	1·87	2·23
21. Inner Angus	3·53	2·86	8·48
22. Coastal Angus	2·92	2·62	2·76
23. East Perthshire	3·44	1·61	3·21
24. South Perthshire	2·63	2·86	6·75
25. East Fife	2·54	1·86	6·85
26. West Fife	3·44	1·81	9·01
27. North Stirling-Clackmannan	2·57	1·59	5·48
28. West Lothian, East Stirling	2·94	1·62	4·25
29. Edinburgh area	4·05	0·83	1·06
30. Dunbarton, Renfrewshire	4·35	0·46	4·46
31. North Ayrshire	4·25	0·78	5·56
32. South Ayrshire	3·42	0·86	12·48
33. North Lanarks.	3·62	0·29	5·86
34. South Lanarks.	3·01	1·98	4·23
35. Peeblesshire	3·99	3·70	5·25
36. Dunbar area	3·70	1·14	4·02
37. South Berwick	4·57	1·67	3·13
38. Kelso area	4·24	1·89	4·30
39. Hawick area	3·72	4·09	2·73
40. Inner Dumfries, Kirkcudbright	3·57	1·80	4·67
41. South Dumfries	5·77	1·69	8·32
42. South Kirkcudbright	6·14	2·19	8·91
43. Wigtown and south tip of Ayr	3·20	2·20	2·56
SCOTLAND	3·64	1·22	4·43

TABLE 8.A *continued*

4. 'Able-bodied' (unemployed only) as % of poor relief recipients	N for columns 1–4	5. Irish as % of poor relief recipients	N for column 5	6. Those aged over 60 as % of poor relief recipients	N ·for column 6
0	14	0	14	63	6
0·78	19	0	19	37	13
0	12	0	12	58	9
2·70	11	0	11	44	5
1·39	14	0·08	14	49	8
0·05	15	0·11	15	52	9
0	11	0	11	56	8
0·21	14	0	14	58	10
0·58	14	0·56	14	47	12
0·33	12	0·16	12	69	6
2·08	20	1·08	20	47	15
1·78	12	0	12	55	10
0	10	0	10	65	9
0·14	14	0	13	51	10
4·89	21	0	21	50	11
2·59	24	0·16	27	47	21
1·34	25	0·14	25	47	22
0·37	27	0	27	32	25
1·50	20	0·07	20	47	19
0·58	18	0	18	38	14
5·21	35	0·27	35	28	31
0·77	27	3·09	27	41	20
1·32	19	1·17	19	24	13
3·78	21	0	21	31	15
3·01	35	0·19	35	36	32
6·43	27	0·60	27	16	22
2·30	18	5·33	17	28	14
2·15	22	5·42	21	38	14
0·54	22	0·33	20	31	16
1·60	21	7·71	20	26	20
1·62	25	16·07	21	27	17
4·94	17	26·16	12	36	11
4·40	21	6·45	16	14	12
2·43	20	4·13	20	30	17
2·53	17	1·14	17	28	16
1·86	19	0·31	19	39	16
1·40	30	0·67	30	40	29
0·53	23	0·15	23	41	17
0·24	11	0	11	28	9
2·28	21	6·12	19	38	17
3·37	24	3·30	24	33	20
4·19	21	7·96	20	30	18
0·66	19	24·90	9	42	13
2·27	845	3·23	812	35	651

TABLE 8.B

Breakdown of Certain Numbers on Poor Relief, by Economic Type of Community

	1	2	3	4		5	
	% of population on poor relief	Mothers with illegitimate children as % of poor relief recipients	'Able-bodied' (unemployed plus temporary sick) as % of poor relief recipients	'Able-bodied' (unemployed only) as % of poor relief recipients	N for columns 1–4	Those aged over 60 as % of poor relief recipients	N for column 5
1.1. Urban-industrial: large towns	4·04	0·70	3·67	2·18	32	26	19
1.2. Urban-industrial: smaller towns, etc.	4·14	2·06	5·57	2·45	44	40	32
2.1. Mixed economy: rural parishes	3·30	1·75	4·43	1·70	192	38	158
2.2. Mixed economy: country towns	3·20	1·70	8·56	4·48	114	27	88
3.1. Agricultural: farming parishes	3·72	1·51	3·53	1·68	364	44	294
3.2. Agricultural: crofting parishes	2·72	0·51	1·34	0·60	99	49	66
SCOTLAND	3·64	1·22	4·43	2·27	845	35	651

TABLE 8.C

Answers to the Question, 'Is Poor-law Relief given to Able-bodied Men, either Unemployed or Temporarily Sick?': Percentage of Parishes making Different Responses, by District.

	Positive ('yes', 'occasional', 'sometimes' or 'in temporary sickness only')	Only unqualified 'yes'	Negative ('no', 'rarely', 'never asked', 'seldom')	Only unqualified 'no'	N
1. Shetland	20	0	80	60	10
2. Orkney	28	6	72	28	18
3. Caithness	17	0	83	58	12
4. East Sutherland	27	0	73	55	11
5. East Ross	33	0	67	50	12
6. N.-E. Inverness	33	7	67	53	15
7. North-west coast	0	0	100	60	10
8. Skye and Outer Hebrides	7	0	93	64	14
9. West Argyll	40	27	60	47	15
10. North Argyll	27	0	73	55	11
11. South Argyll	39	11	61	39	18
12. Highland Inverness, Banff, Moray	33	17	67	33	12
13. Highland Perth, Aberdeenshire	40	20	60	50	10
14. N.-W. Perth	39	8	61	54	13
15. Nairn, Lowland Moray	60	0	40	20	20
16. Lowland Banff	77	23	23	8	26
17. Buchan	72	16	28	16	25
18. S.-E. Aberdeenshire	82	26	18	11	27
19. Inner Aberdeenshire	65	25	35	10	20
20. Kincardine	63	19	37	6	16
21. Inner Angus	70	21	30	18	33
22. Coastal Angus	82	26	18	7	27
23. East Perthshire	70	20	30	5	20
24. South Perthshire	59	23	41	23	22
25. East Fife	68	32	32	12	34
26. West Fife	78	26	28	22	27
27. North Stirling-Clackmannan	67	11	33	28	18
28. West Lothian, East Stirling	36	14	64	41	22
29. Edinburgh area	78	21	22	11	19
30. Dunbarton, Renfrewshire	76	19	24	14	21
31. North Ayrshire	60	8	40	20	25
32. South Ayrshire	63	6	37	25	16
33. North Lanarks.	84	16	16	11	19
34. South Lanarks.	40	10	60	20	20
35. Peeblesshire	65	35	35	18	17
36. Dunbar area	56	17	44	28	18
37. South Berwick	72	17	28	10	29
38. Kelso area	57	9	43	13	23
39. Hawick area	70	10	30	10	10
40. Inner Dumfries, Kirkcudbright	71	10	29	14	21
41. South Dumfries	75	17	25	8	24
42. South Kirkcudbright	71	10	29	5	21
43. Wigtown and south tip of Ayr	63	8	27	11	19
SCOTLAND	59	15	41	23	820

TABLE 8.D
Answers to the Question, 'Is Poor-law Relief given to Mothers with Illegitimate Children?': Percentage of Parishes making Different Responses, by District.

	Positive ('yes', 'occasional', 'sometimes')	Only unqualified 'yes'	Negative ('no', 'rarely', 'never asked', 'seldom')	Only unqualified 'no'	N
1. Shetland	33	33	67	67	12
2. Orkney	18	18	82	47	17
3. Caithness	18	18	82	73	11
4. East Sutherland	9	9	91	46	11
5. East Ross	23	8	77	77	13
6. N.-E. Inverness	27	13	73	60	15
7. North-west coast	10	10	90	50	10
8. Skye and Outer Hebrides	0	0	100	64	14
9. West Argyll	20	7	80	53	15
10. North Argyll	27	27	73	36	11
11. South Argyll	0	0	100	56	16
12. Highland Inverness, Banff, Moray	50	50	50	33	12
13. Highland Perth, Aberdeenshire	40	20	60	30	10
14. N.-W. Perth	36	29	64	36	14
15. Nairn, Lowland Moray	32	21	68	47	19
16. Lowland Banff	59	48	41	11	27
17. Buchan	56	20	44	20	25
18. S.-E. Aberdeenshire	62	50	38	8	26
19. Inner Aberdeenshire	60	45	40	10	20
20. Kincardine	61	56	39	17	18
21. Inner Angus	56	47	44	19	32
22. Coastal Angus	63	59	37	22	27
23. East Perthshire	40	35	60	50	20
24. South Perthshire	67	48	33	19	21
25. East Fife	59	44	41	24	34
26. West Fife	77	58	23	12	26
27. North Stirling-Clackmannan	50	28	50	22	18
28. West Lothian, East Stirling	50	32	50	41	22
29. Edinburgh area	45	30	55	20	20
30. Dunbarton, Renfrewshire	48	29	52	33	21
31. North Ayrshire	52	24	48	20	25
32. South Ayrshire	33	13	67	33	15
33. North Lanarks.	68	32	32	6	19
34. South Lanarks.	60	35	40	20	20
35. Peeblesshire	35	35	65	35	17
36. Dunbar area	29	24	71	41	17
37. South Berwick	31	24	69	28	29
38. Kelso area	44	35	56	22	23
39. Hawick area	60	30	40	20	10
40. Inner Dumfries, Kirkcudbright	48	24	52	14	21
41. South Dumfries	58	33	42	25	24
42. South Kirkcudbright	33	24	67	14	21
43. Wigtown and south tip of Ayr	21	11	79	16	19
SCOTLAND	45	31	55	29	817

TABLE 8.E

Answers to the question, 'Is Poor-law Relief given to Able-bodied Men, either Unemployed or Temporarily Sick?': Percentage of Parishes making Different Responses, by Economic Type of Community

	Positive ('yes', 'occasional', 'sometimes', or 'in temporary sickness only')	Only unqualified 'yes'	Negative ('no', 'rarely', 'never asked', 'seldom')	Only unqualified 'no'	N
1.1. Urban-industrial: large towns	90	17	10	3	29
1.2. Urban-industrial: smaller towns, etc.	75	25	25	11	44
2.1. Mixed economy: rural parishes	65	19	35	19	189
2.2. Mixed economy: country towns	77	16	23	14	114
3.1. Agricultural: farming parishes	56	15	44	23	350
3.2. Agricultural: crofting parishes	20	5	80	52	94
SCOTLAND	59	15	41	23	820

TABLE 8.F

Answers to the Question, 'Is Poor-relief given to Mothers with Illegitimate Children?': Percentage of Parishes making Different Responses, by Economic Type of Community

	Positive ('yes', 'occasional', 'sometimes')	Only unqualified 'yes'	Negative ('no', 'rarely', 'never asked', 'seldom')	Only unqualified 'no'	N
1.1. Urban-industrial: large towns	72	48	32	3	29
1.2. Urban-industrial: smaller towns, etc.	59	43	41	16	44
2.1. Mixed economy: rural parishes	50	33	50	32	188
2.2. Mixed economy: country towns	65	45	35	12	113
3.1. Agricultural: farming parishes	39	28	61	29	350
3.2. Agricultural: crofting parishes	15	13	85	58	93
SCOTLAND	45	31	55	29	817

TABLE 8.G

How Aspects of Poor-relief varied according to the Type of Poor-law Income in the Parishes, all Scotland

Type of poor law income	% of parishes replying with an unqualified 'yes' to the question on relief of able-bodied poor or temporary sick	N	% of parishes replying with an unqualified 'yes' to the question on relief for mothers with illegitimate children	N	Total poor in such parishes as % of population	N	'Able-bodied' poor as % of total poor	N	Poor-law recipients aged over 60 as % of total poor	N
Legal assessment	15	198	34	198	4·2	198	5·4	199	30	158
Voluntary assessment	18	355	34	352	3·4	352	6·0	359	37	276
No assessment	13	262	26	263	3·1	263	2·7	273	46	211
All	15	815	31	813	3·6	813	4·4	831	35	645

TABLE 8.H

*What Percentage of Scottish Poor-law Recipients of Various Types
occurred in Selected Districts*

	Total recipients	Recipients aged over 60	Mothers with illegitimate children	'Able-bodied'
2. Orkney	1·02	1·30	1·30	0·58
5. East Ross	1·37	1·95	0·93	0·48
8. Skye and Outer Hebrides	1·03	2·08	0·09	0·13
17. Buchan	2·43	4·84	5·19	2·36
21. Inner Angus	2·49	3·11	5·84	4·75
29. Edinburgh area	5·69	2·31	6·58	2·31
34. South Lanarks.	16·35	6·58	3·89	21·61
37. South Berwicks.	1·69	3·22	2·32	6·36
42. South Kirkcudbright	2·31	2·99	4·17	1·20
Total for Scotland	88,692 (100%)	18,559 (100%)	1078 (100%)	3933 (100%)
N	845	651	845	845

TABLE 8.I

Percentages of Parishes receiving Certain Categories of
Poor-law Income, by District

	Legal assessment	Voluntary assessment	Voluntary contributions	Mortifications	N
1. Shetland	0	0	21	79	14
2. Orkney	0	11	26	79	19
3. Caithness	0	25	75	100	12
4. East Sutherland	0	64	55	46	11
5. East Ross	0	36	36	79	14
6. N.-E. Inverness	0	31	56	81	16
7. North-west coast	0	20	30	50	10
8. Skye and Outer Hebrides	0	7	21	21	14
9. West Argyll	0	47	13	60	15
10. North Argyll	18	23	18	91	11
11. South Argyll	5	53	37	63	19
12. Highland Inverness, Banff, Moray	0	58	75	58	12
13. Highland Perth, Aberdeenshire	0	50	40	90	10
14. N.-W. Perth	0	64	43	86	14
15. Nairn, Lowland Moray	0	43	52	81	21
16. Lowland Banff	4	52	59	96	27
17. Buchan	4	48	56	100	25
18. S.-E. Aberdeenshire	7	33	63	100	27
19. Inner Aberdeenshire	0	50	45	95	20
20. Kincardine	6	39	72	100	18
21. Inner Angus	20	43	31	97	35
22. Coastal Angus	22	56	44	89	27
23. East Perthshire	20	40	15	90	20
24. South Perthshire	10	81	29	95	21
25. East Fife	6	68	44	91	34,
26. West Fife	7	74	59	89	27
27. North Stirling-Clackmannan	11	56	50	89	18
28. West Lothian, East Stirling	23	59	59	86	22
29. Edinburgh area	82	18	55	96	22
30. Dunbarton, Renfrewshire	33	62	81	91	21
31. North Ayrshire	36	52	56	80	25
32. South Ayrshire	6	94	59	100	17
33. North Lanarks.	72	17	61	72	18
34. South Lanarks.	45	40	55	85	20
35. Peeblesshire	41	47	41	94	17
36. Dunbar area	79	0	42	90	19
37. South Berwick	97	3	33	90	30
38. Kelso area	100	0	13	61	23
39. Hawick area	100	0	20	60	10
40. Inner Dumfries, Kirkcudbright	24	62	43	76	21
41. South Dumfries	63	25	33	75	24
42. South Kirkcudbright	14	62	62	67	21
43. Wigtown and south tip of Ayr	0	84	42	100	19
SCOTLAND	24	43	45	84	840

TABLE 8.J

What Percentage of Parishes received Certain Categories of Poor Law Income,
by Economic Type of Community

	Legal assessment	Voluntary assessment	Voluntary contribution	Mortifications etc.	N
1.1. Urban-industrial, large towns	79	14	41	76	29
1.2. Urban-industrial, smaller towns, etc.	30	50	43	84	44
2.1. Mixed economy, rural parishes	22	53	51	91	192
2.2. Mixed economy: country towns	35	53	57	89	113
3.1. Agricultural: farming parishes	23	42	43	86	363
3.2. Agricultural: crofting parishes	1	23	32	62	99
SCOTLAND	24	36	45	84	840

TABLE 8.K

How Total Parish Poor Law Income was Divided between Different Categories of Income, Percentages by District
(excluding Large Towns)

	Legal assessment	Voluntary assessment	Voluntary contributions	Church-door collections	Mortifications etc.	Total district income (£ p.a.)	N
1. Shetland	0	0	9	69	22	244	14
2. Orkney	0	2	3	76	18	327	19
3. Caithness	0	17	8	52	23	739	12
4. East Sutherland	0	27	12	45	16	439	11
5. East Ross	0	19	12	52	17	681	14
6. N.-E. Inverness	0	22	9	48	20	687	15
7. North-west coast	0	7	20	59	14	148	10
8. Skye and Outer Hebrides	0	22	10	65	3	175	14
9. West Argyll	0	21	2	61	16	306	15
10. North Argyll	12	16	4	31	14	563	11
11. South Argyll	0	52	6	35	7	1630	17
12. Highland Inverness, Banff, Moray	0	22	11	46	20	499	12
13. Highland Perth, Aberdeenshire	0	29	5	45	21	734	10
14. N.-W. Perth	0	43	8	35	14	1375	14
15. Nairn, Lowland Moray	0	20	6	61	13	1499	21
16. Lowland Banff	8	26	12	34	20	3543	27
17. Buchan	17	6	18	37	32	4152	25
18. S.-E. Aberdeenshire	0	10	9	45	36	2039	25
19. Inner Aberdeenshire	0	10	10	46	33	1121	20
20. Kincardine	16	17	6	40	21	2835	18
21. Inner Angus	49	20	1	22	8	4895	34
22. Coastal Angus	10	28	7	29	14	2631	22
23. East Perthshire	22	23	4	31	20	2031	20
24. South Perthshire	10	49	4	26	11	2805	21
25. East Fife	10	32	7	30	21	4530	34
26. West Fife	0	56	8	23	12	4156	26
27. North Stirling-Clackmannan	22	34	6	26	11	2809	16
28. West Lothian, East Stirling	12	37	9	20	22	3024	21
	70	0			7	6304	21

	% provided by legal assessment	% provided by voluntary assessment	% provided by voluntary contribution	% provided by church door collections	% provided by mortifications etc.	Total	N
31. North Ayrshire	35	35	6	13	11	7620	22
32. South Ayrshire	12	49	5	27	7	2332	16
33. North Lanarks.	76	3	6	9	6	4196	14
34. South Lanarks.	50	18	12	11	10	3634	20
35. Peeblesshire	34	35	3	14	14	2067	17
36. Dunbar area	76	0	3	10	11	3747	19
37. South Berwick	87	0	2	7	3	6632	30
38. Kelso area	91	0	0	6	2	5079	23
39. Hawick area	88	0	2	6	4	2354	9
40. Inner Dumfries, Kirkcudbright	25	26	4	31	15	2187	21
41. South Dumfries	72	9	3	11	5	4956	23
42. South Kirkcudbright	37	25	7	22	8	3854	21
43. Wigtown and south tip of Ayr	0	42	5	39	14	2599	19
SCOTLAND	37	23	6	22	12	115,063	811

TABLE 8.L

How Total Parish Poor Law Income was Divided between Different Categories of Income, by Economic Type of Community

	% provided by legal assessment	% provided by voluntary assessment	% provided by voluntary contribution	% provided by church door collections	% provided by mortifications etc.	N
1.1. Urban-industrial: large towns	82	4	2	7	4	29
1.2. Urban-industrial: smaller towns, etc.	48	12	5	21	15	44
2.1. Mixed economy: rural parishes	33	26	5	24	12	192
2.2. Mixed economy: country towns	42	30	8	14	8	113
3.1. Agricultural: farming parishes	34	20	5	27	15	363
3.2. Agricultural: crofting parishes	7	17	7	51	17	99
SCOTLAND	49	18	5	18	10	840

TABLE 8.M

Parish Poor Law Income per Head of Population, in Pence (p.), by Categories of Income and by District (excluding Large Towns) (N as Table 8.K)

	Total income	Legal assessment	Voluntary assessment	Voluntary contributions	Church-door collections	Mortifications etc.
1. Shetland	0·79	0	0	0·07	0·55	0·17
2. Orkney	1·16	0	0·03	0·04	0·88	0·21
3. Caithness	1·96	0	0·34	0·15	1·02	0·45
4. East Sutherland	2·59	0	0·69	0·31	1·17	0·42
5. East Ross	2·54	0	0·48	0·31	1·32	0·43
6. N.-E. Inverness	1·98	0	0·44	0·19	0·95	0·40
7. North-west coast	0·87	0	0·06	0·17	0·52	0·12
8. Skye and Outer Hebrides	0·42	0	0·08	0·04	0·29	0·01
9. West Argyll	0·84	0	0·17	0·02	0·51	0·14
10. North Argyll	2·33	0·67	0·41	0·10	0·80	0·35
11. South Argyll	5·47	0	2·84	0·32	1·92	0·39
12. Highland Inverness, Banff, Moray	3·08	0	0·69	0·35	1·42	0·62
13. Highland Perth, Aberdeenshire	4·94	0	1·43	0·23	2·26	1·02
14. N.-W. Perth	7·27	0	3·12	0·59	2·57	0·99
15. Nairn, Lowland Moray	3·69	0	0·75	0·23	2·25	0·46
16. Lowland Banff	6·84	0·58	1·77	0·83	2·31	1·35
17. Buchan	6·94	1·17	0·42	0·58	2·58	2·24
18. S.-E. Aberdeenshire	6·89	0	0·72	0·62	3·08	2·47
19. Inner Aberdeenshire	5·84	0	0·60	0·60	2·71	1·93
20. Kincardine	8·95	1·64	1·48	0·53	3·62	1·88
21. Inner Angus	9·31	4·53	1·88	0·13	2·06	0·71
22. Coastal Angus	8·74	0·88	2·42	0·61	2·52	2·31
23. East Perthshire	9·13	2·05	2·09	0·32	2·86	1·81
24. South Perthshire	7·53	0·74	3·69	0·32	1·98	0·80
25. East Fife	8·44	0·84	2·74	0·60	2·52	1·74

	Total	Legal assessment	Voluntary assessment	Voluntary contribution	Church-door collections	Mortifications etc.
(…)			0·42		1·72	0·78
28. West Lothian, East Stirling	7·34	0·90	2·72	0·65	1·47	1·60
29. Edinburgh area	12·94	9·11	1·21	0·47	1·21	0·97
30. Dunbarton, Renfrewshire	10·71	3·41	4·71	0·94	1·25	0·40
31. North Ayrshire	8·73	3·05	3·06	0·53	1·17	0·92
32. South Ayrshire	6·28	0·73	3·10	0·31	1·69	0·45
33. North Lanarks.	6·41	4·88	0·20	0·39	0·55	0·39
34. South Lanarks.	9·85	4·88	1·78	1·18	1·04	0·97
35. Peeblesshire	16·05	5·39	5·57	0·51	2·26	2·32
36. Dunbar area	14·29	10·86	0	0·45	1·40	1·58
37. South Berwick	20·17	17·62	0	0·46	1·49	0·60
38. Kelso area	16·21	14·75	0	0·17	0·91	0·38
39. Hawick area	16·19	14·23	0	0·36	1·02	0·58
40. Inner Dumfries, Kirkcudbright	9·24	2·32	2·42	0·34	2·88	1·38
41. South Dumfries	13·42	9·66	1·25	0·37	1·50	0·64
42. South Kirkcudbright	11·55	4·31	2·88	0·84	2·56	0·96
43. Wigtown and south tip of Ayr	6·11	0	2·57	0·30	2·37	0·87
SCOTLAND	7·42	2·74	1·70	0·43	1·64	0·91

TABLE 8.N

Parish Poor Law Income per Head of Population, in Pence, by Categories of Income and Economic Type of Community

	Total	Legal assessment	Voluntary assessment	Voluntary contribution	Church-door collections	Mortifications etc.	N
1.1. Urban-industrial: large towns	10·01	8·23	0·40	0·19	0·75	0·44	29
1.2. Urban-industrial: smaller towns, etc.	10·03	4·82	1·20	0·47	2·06	1·48	44
2.1. Mixed economy: rural parishes	8·70	2·89	2·26	0·43	2·04	1·08	192
2.2. Mixed economy: country towns	8·64	3·61	2·42	0·66	1·24	0·71	133
3.1. Agricultural: farming parishes	7·54	2·58	1·45	0·39	2·01	1·11	363
3.2. Agricultural: crofting parishes	1·29	0·09	0·22	0·10	0·66	0·22	99
SCOTLAND	8·05	3·96	1·42	0·39	1·46	0·82	840

TABLE 8.O

Parish Poor Law Income per £1 of Gross Valuation, in Pence, by Categories of Income and by District
(excluding Large Towns)

	Total	Legal assessment	Voluntary assessment	Voluntary contributions	Church-door collections	Mortifications
1. Shetland	1·07	0	0	0·10	0·74	0·23
2. Orkney	1·51	0	0·04	0·05	1·15	0·27
3. Caithness	1·09	0	0·19	0·08	0·57	0·25
4. East Sutherland	1·66	0	0·44	0·20	0·75	0·27
5. East Ross	1·43	0	0·48	0·14	0·61	0·20
6. N.-E. Inverness	2·10	0	0·26	0·10	1·53	0·21
7. North-west coast	0·69	0	0·05	0·13	0·41	0·10
8. Skye and Outer Hebrides	0·46	0	0·10	0·05	0·29	0·02
9. West Argyll	0·54	0	0·10	0·01	0·29	0·14
10. North Argyll	0·74	0·26	0·12	0·03	0·23	0·10
11. South Argyll	1·87	0	0·97	0·11	0·66	0·13
12. Highland Inverness, Banff, Moray	0·95	0	0·21	0·11	0·44	0·19
13. Highland Perth, Aberdeenshire	1·21	0	0·35	0·06	0·55	0·25
14. N.-W. Perth	1·49	0	0·64	0·12	0·53	0·20
15. Nairn, Lowland Moray	1·43	0	0·29	0·09	0·87	0·18
16. Lowland Banff	2·69	0·23	0·69	0·33	0·91	0·53
17. Buchan	2·27	0·38	0·14	0·19	0·83	0·73
18. S.-E. Aberdeenshire	1·68	0	0·18	0·15	0·75	0·60
19. Inner Aberdeenshire	1·60	0	0·17	0·16	0·74	0·53
20. Kincardine	2·18	0·35	0·36	0·13	0·88	0·46
21. Inner Angus	2·31	1·14	0·46	0·03	0·50	0·18
22. Coastal Angus	1·76	0·18	0·49	0·12	0·51	0·46
23. East Perthshire	1·43	0·32	0·33	0·05	0·45	0·28
24. South Perthshire	1·63	0·16	0·80	0·07	0·43	0·17

	Total	Legal assessment	Voluntary assessment	Church-door contributions	Church-door collections	Mortifications
27. North Stirling, Clackmannan	1·61	0·56	0·55	0·10	0·41	0·19
28. West Lothian, East Stirling	1·69	0·21	0·62	0·15	0·34	0·37
29. Edinburgh area	2·46	1·85	0·25	0·09	0·25	0·20
30. Dunbarton, Renfrewshire	2·89	0·92	1·27	0·25	0·34	0·11
31. North Ayrshire	2·71	0·95	0·95	0·16	0·36	0·29
32. South Ayrshire	1·20	0·18	0·41	0·08	0·42	0·11
33. North Lanarks.	1·25	0·94	0·04	0·08	0·11	0·08
34. South Lanarks.	2·35	1·17	0·42	0·28	0·25	0·23
35. Peeblesshire	2·06	0·69	0·71	0·07	0·29	0·30
36. Dunbar area	1·82	1·38	0	0·06	0·18	0·20
37. South Berwick	2·81	2·46	0	0·06	0·21	0·08
38. Kelso area	2·48	2·25	0	0·03	0·14	0·06
39. Hawick area	2·70	2·37	0	0·06	0·17	0·10
40. Inner Dumfries, Kirkcudbright	1·63	0·41	0·42	0·06	0·50	0·24
41. South Dumfries	3·14	2·26	0·29	0·09	0·35	0·15
42. South Kirkcudbright	2·58	0·97	0·64	0·19	0·57	0·21
43. Wigtown and south tip of Ayr	1·62	0	0·68	0·08	0·63	0·23
SCOTLAND	1·98	0·73	0·45	0·12	0·44	0·24

TABLE 8.P

Parish Poor Law Income per £1 of Gross Valuation, in Pence, by Categories of Income and by Economic Type of Community

	Total	Legal assessment	Voluntary assessment	Church-door contributions	Church-door collections	Mortifications
1.1. Urban-industrial: large towns	4·34	3·57	0·17	0·08	0·32	0·19
1.2. Urban-industrial: smaller towns, etc.	3·02	1·45	0·36	0·14	0·62	0·45
2.1. Mixed economy: rural parishes	1·82	0·60	0·47	0·09	0·43	0·23
2.2. Mixed economy: country towns	2·28	0·88	0·67	0·18	0·35	0·20
3.1. Agricultural: farming parishes	2·14	1·00	0·34	0·09	0·46	0·25
3.2. Agricultural: crofting parishes	0·93	0·06	0·16	0·07	0·48	0·16
SCOTLAND	2·32	1·14	0·41	0·11	0·42	0·23

TABLE 8.Q
Parish Poor Law Expenditure, by District (excluding Large Towns)

	Per recipient		Per head of population		Per £1 gross valuation		N
	£ per annum	% of Scottish mean	Pence per annum	% of Scottish mean	Pence per annum	% of Scottish mean	
1. Shetland	0·21	12	0·59	10	0·76	44	13
2. Orkney	0·24	13	0·76	12	0·99	60	19
3. Caithness	0·44	24	1·49	24	0·83	50	12
4. East Sutherland	0·37	21	1·92	31	1·24	75	11
5. East Ross	0·52	29	2·35	38	1·08	65	14
6. N.-E. Inverness	0·33	18	1·32	21	0·71·	43	13
7. North-west coast	0·25	14	0·72	12	0·57	35	10
8. Skye and Outer Hebrides	0·19	11	0·38	6	0·46	28	14
9. West Argyll	0·35	19	0·56	9	0·31	19	14
10. North Argyll	0·81	45	2·07	33	0·60	36	11
11. South Argyll	0·92	51	2·71	44	0·92	56	18
12. Highland Inverness, Banff, Moray	0·54	30	2·55	41	0·83	50	11
13. Highland Perth, Aberdeenshire	1·66	92	4·36	70	1·06	64	10
14. N.-W. Perth	1·84	102	6·90	111	1·42	86	14
15. Nairn, Lowland Moray	0·66	37	2·80	45	1·07	65	20
16. Lowland Banff	1·37	76	5·09	82	2·00	121	27
17. Buchan	1·59	88	5·74	93	1·88	114	25
18. S.-E. Aberdeenshire	1·61	89	6·36	103	1·55	94	25
19. Inner Aberdeenshire	1·59	88	5·00	81	1·37	84	20
20. Kincardine	1·91	106	8·38	135	2·05	124	18
21. Inner Angus	2·27	126	8·30	134	2·09	127	34
22. Coastal Angus	2·32	129	8·27	133	1·66	101	22
23. East Perthshire	2·47	137	7·74	125	1·23	75	19
24. South Perthshire	2·18	121	5·74	93	1·24	75	21
25. East Fife	2·44	136	6·97	112	1·51	92	34
26. West Fife	1·93	107	5·59	90	1·83	111	25
27. North Stirling-Clackmannan	2·01	112	5·42	87	1·31	79	16
28. West Lothian, East Stirling	2·12	118	6·99	113	1·60	97	19

	£ per annum	% of Scottish mean	pence per annum	% of Scottish mean	pence per annum	% of Scottish mean	N
31. North Ayrshire	1·79	99	6·91	111	2·14	130	22
32. South Ayrshire	1·64	91	5·62	91	1·37	83	16
33. North Lanarks.	2·26	126	5·56	90	1·07	65	14
34. South Lanarks.	2·38	132	7·49	121	1·78	108	20
35. Peeblesshire	2·64	147	10·81	174	1·39	84	17
36. Dunbar area	3·18	175	11·75	190	1·49	90	19
37. South Berwick	3·36	187	15·36	247	2·15	130	30
38. Kelso area	3·39	188	14·36	232	2·19	133	23
39. Hawick area	3·85	214	15·48	250	2·58	156	9
40. Inner Dumfries, Kirkcudbright	2·50	139	8·91	144	1·56	95	21
41. South Dumfries	2·80	156	12·86	207	3·01	182	23
42. South Kirkcudbright	1·53	85	9·42	152	2·11	128	21
43. Wigtown and south tip of Ayr	1·62	90	5·21	84	1·40	85	19
SCOTLAND	1·80	100	6·20	100	1·65	100	800

TABLE 8.R

Parish Poor Law Expenditure, by Economic Type of Community

	Per recipient		Per head of population		Per £1 gross valuation		
	£ per annum	% of Scottish mean	Pence per annum	% of Scottish mean	Pence per annum	% of Scottish mean	N
1.1. Urban-industrial: large towns	1·84	102	8·28	125	3·54	187	27
1.2. Urban-industrial: smaller towns, etc.	1·94	107	8·04	122	2·42	128	44
2.1. Mixed economy: rural	2·22	123	7·48	113	1·57	83	189
2.2. Mixed economy: country towns	2·21	122	7·34	111	2·04	108	113
3.1. Agricultural: farming parishes	1·64	91	6·14	93	1·39	74	357
3.2. Agricultural: crofting parishes	0·34	19	0·94	14	0·68	36	97
SCOTLAND	1·81	100	6·60	100	1·89	100	827

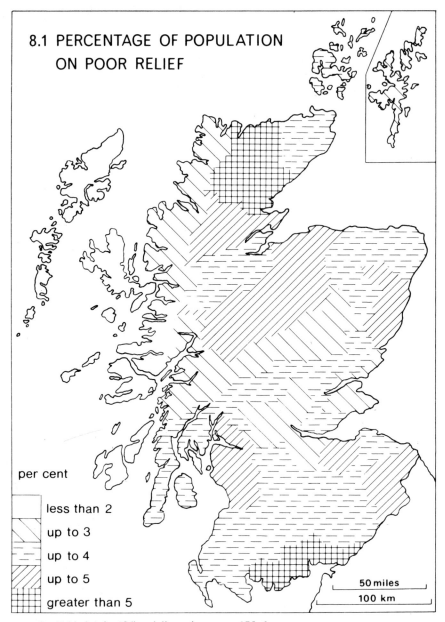

8.1 PERCENTAGE OF POPULATION ON POOR RELIEF

per cent

less than 2
up to 3
up to 4
up to 5
greater than 5

50 miles
100 km

See Table 8.A (p. 186) and discussion on pp. 175–6.

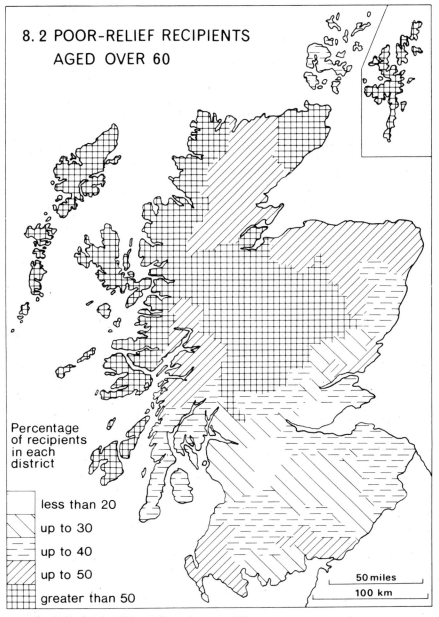

8.2 POOR-RELIEF RECIPIENTS AGED OVER 60

Percentage
of recipients
in each
district

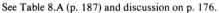

less than 20
up to 30
up to 40
up to 50
greater than 50

50 miles
100 km

See Table 8.A (p. 187) and discussion on p. 176.

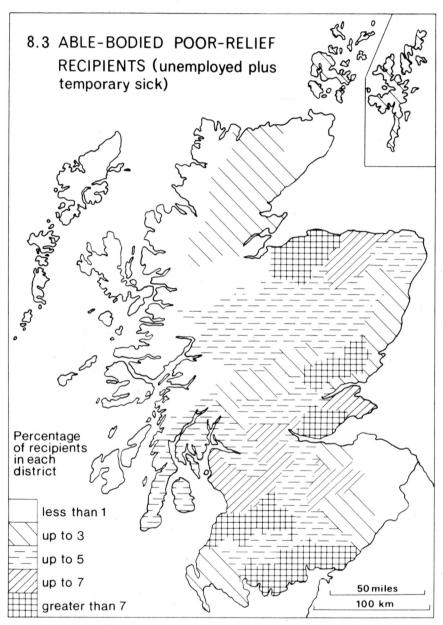

8.3 ABLE-BODIED POOR-RELIEF RECIPIENTS (unemployed plus temporary sick)

Percentage of recipients in each district

less than 1
up to 3
up to 5
up to 7
greater than 7

50 miles
100 km

See Table 8.A (p. 186) and discussion on pp. 176–8.

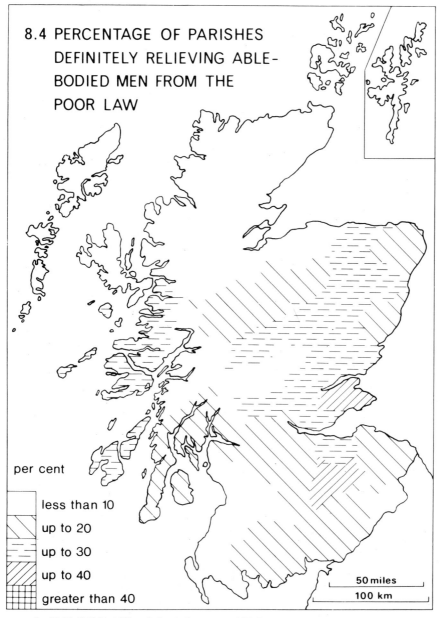

8.4 PERCENTAGE OF PARISHES
DEFINITELY RELIEVING ABLE-
BODIED MEN FROM THE
POOR LAW

per cent

less than 10
up to 20
up to 30
up to 40
greater than 40

50 miles
100 km

See Table 8.C (p. 189) and discussion on pp. 177–8.

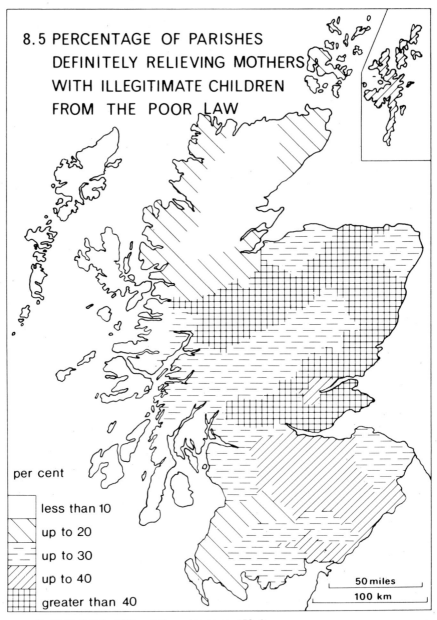

8.5 PERCENTAGE OF PARISHES
     DEFINITELY RELIEVING MOTHERS
     WITH ILLEGITIMATE CHILDREN
     FROM THE POOR LAW

per cent

less than 10
up to 20
up to 30
up to 40
greater than 40

50 miles
100 km

See Table 8.D (p. 190) and discussion on pp. 178–9.

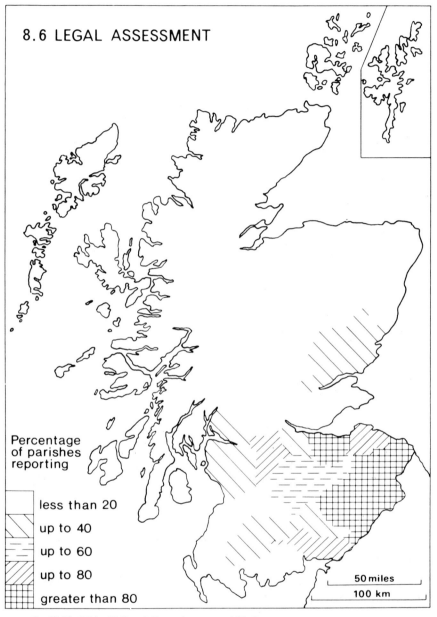

8.6 LEGAL ASSESSMENT

Percentage
of parishes
reporting

less than 20
up to 40
up to 60
up to 80
greater than 80

50 miles
100 km

See Table 8.I (p. 194) and discussion on pp. 181–3.

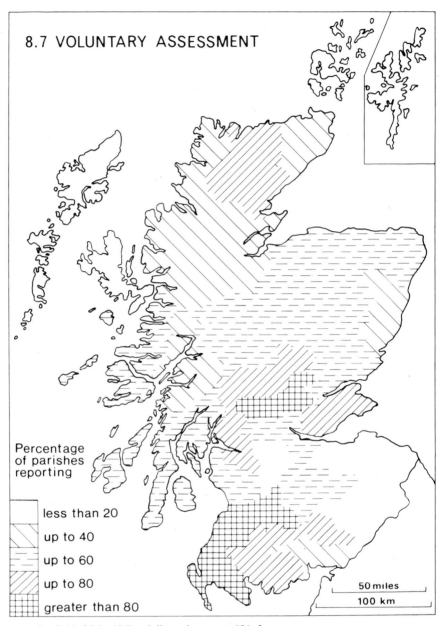

8.7 VOLUNTARY ASSESSMENT

Percentage
of parishes
reporting

less than 20
up to 40
up to 60
up to 80
greater than 80

50 miles
100 km

See Table 8.I (p. 194) and discussion on pp. 181–3.

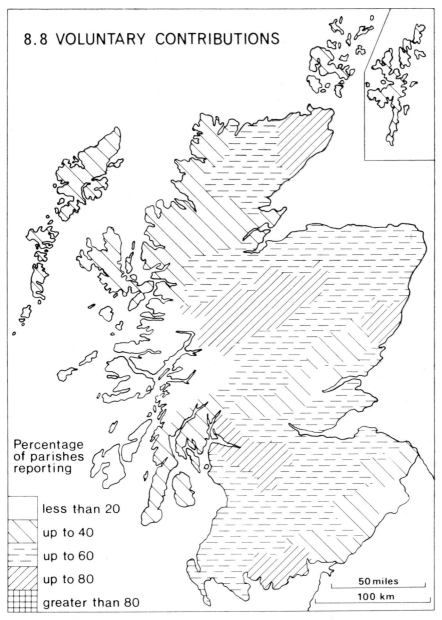

8.8 VOLUNTARY CONTRIBUTIONS

Percentage
of parishes
reporting

less than 20
up to 40
up to 60
up to 80
greater than 80

50 miles
100 km

See Table 8.I (p. 194) and discussion on pp. 181–3.

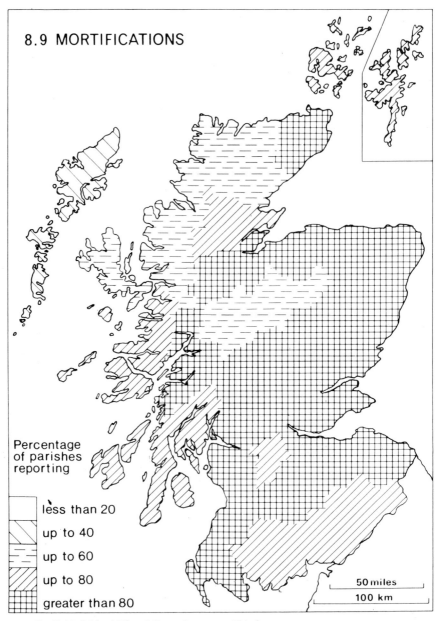

8.9 MORTIFICATIONS

Percentage
of parishes
reporting

less than 20
up to 40
up to 60
up to 80
greater than 80

50 miles
100 km

See Table 8.I (p. 194) and discussion on pp. 181–3.

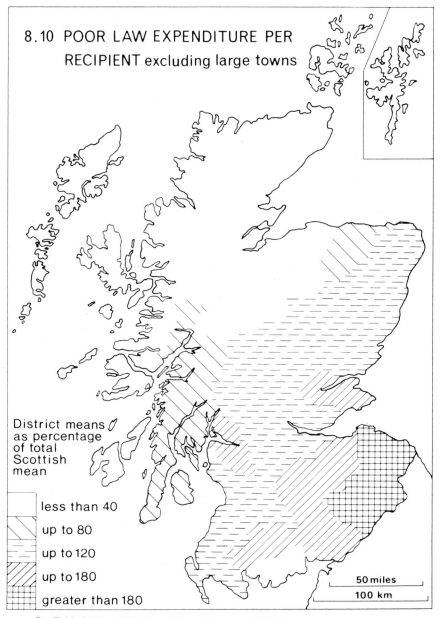

8.10 POOR LAW EXPENDITURE PER
       RECIPIENT excluding large towns

District means
as percentage
of total
Scottish
mean

less than 40
up to 80
up to 120
up to 180
greater than 180

50 miles
100 km

See Table 8.Q (pp. 202–3) and discussion on pp. 183–4.

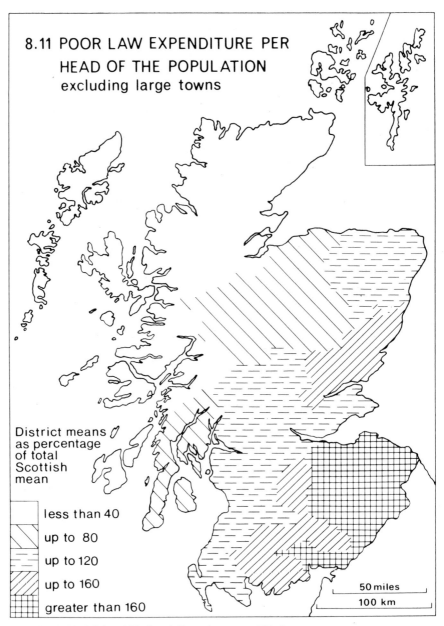

8.11 POOR LAW EXPENDITURE PER HEAD OF THE POPULATION excluding large towns

District means
as percentage
of total
Scottish
mean

less than 40
up to 80
up to 120
up to 160
greater than 160

50 miles
100 km

See Table 8.Q (pp. 202–3) and discussion on pp. 183–4.

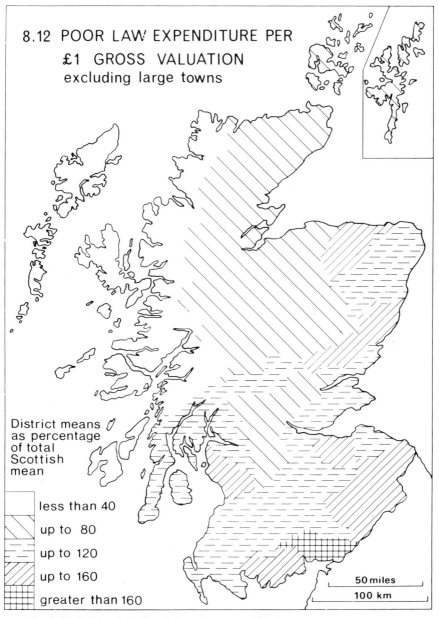

8.12 POOR LAW EXPENDITURE PER
£1 GROSS VALUATION
excluding large towns

District means
as percentage
of total
Scottish
mean

less than 40
up to 80
up to 120
up to 160
greater than 160

50 miles
100 km

See Table 8.Q (pp. 202–3) and discussion on pp. 183–4.

Chapter 9

THE SICK POOR

One of the main roots of the agitation for the reform of the Scottish poor law was the dissatisfaction of the medical profession with the amount and quality of relief provided for the sick poor. The greatest crusader for reform was, of course, W. P. Alison, Professor of Medicine at Edinburgh University, whose *Observations on the Management of the Poor in Scotland* (Edinburgh, 1840) provided the most damning indictment of the voluntary system that had been made hitherto. He did not stand alone. Men like Adam Farrie, treasurer of Greenock Infirmary, and Dr. Handyside, acting surgeon of Edinburgh Royal Infirmary, played an important part in the campaign of the Society for Obtaining an Official Inquiry into Pauperism in Scotland and gave effective evidence before the Commissioners (20.133; 20.550). Indeed, throughout the volumes of evidence of the Report the most trenchant criticism of the existing poor law in town and country alike came from the doctors, scores of whom were called upon to give their views.

Alison's main lines of attack were related to his knowledge of great towns. Firstly, he maintained that poverty unalleviated by adequate allowances was itself a major cause of ill-health and high death rates: in this he differed in emphasis from Edwin Chadwick, whose epoch-making *Report on the Sanitary Condition of the Labouring Population* of 1842 had attributed high urban death rates mainly to the dreadful state of town sanitation.[1] Secondly, and more materially to this chapter, Alison complained of the 'irregularity and frequent inadequacy of gratuitous medical aid to the poor in Scotland'. It was especially bad, he said, in country areas where paupers were treated not in infirmaries or in dispensaries but in their own homes (22.906). Even where it was adequate it was usually at the expense of individual benevolent physicians who worked unpaid rather than of the parish authorities who would not contribute sufficient to pay either for medicine or fees. In the towns the voluntary dispensaries and infirmaries provided care only in a haphazard way, good in some areas but bad in others even within the same community. The remedy, he said, would be to follow the English practice of appointing district medical officers to each poor law authority, charged with the duty of treating the sick poor and supplying them with drugs at public expense. As an Episcopalian, Alison no doubt felt fewer qualms about recommending English practice than most Presbyterians, who perhaps felt that a system associated with their own church had to be kept free of southern influences.

216

It was against this background that the Royal Commission asked two questions of their parish respondents:

    Q. 54. What was the sum of money expended in your parish
           for the medical relief of paupers during the year 1842;
           and what was the precise remuneration from parochial
           funds of the medical practitioners for their attendance
           during that period?

    Q. 55. Is there any dispensary in your parish? or do you sub-
           scribe to any dispensary in your neighbourhood?

To Question 54 there were 813 replies (a 90 per cent. response rate), of which only 230 (28 per cent. of the responding parishes) indicated that their parishes had paid anything at all in medical relief in the form of physicians' fees or cash for medicine. The replies to the second half of the question were too sparse or vague to analyse. To Question 55 there were 792 replies (an 88 per cent. response rate), of which 244 (30 per cent. of the responding parishes) indicated parishes with a dispensary or infirmary, or subscribing to one. Altogether 388 parishes (48 per cent. of those replying to Question 54) indicated that they paid either something towards a doctor or something towards dispensary or infirmary provision: but only 85 (10 per cent.) provided both. Table 9.A and Maps 9.1–9.4 describe the geographical distribution of these parishes.

It can at once be seen that there was seldom anything paid for medical relief from doctors north and west of a line from Dunbarton to Buchan, and that the only district with more than three-quarters of the parishes with such help was round Hawick. The maps of provision for dispensaries and in-infirmaries show a more eccentric pattern; with slightly more generous provision in the north (though not in the remote western areas of the Highlands nor in the northern isles), but less in the central belt outside the main cities themselves. Putting together the previous data, Map 9.4 shows those parishes with paid medical help of any kind. The Borders and some industrial areas appear as the best provided, the rural west and the far north as the worst.

At first glance this might be interpreted, not as good, but as rather more adequate than W. P. Alison and his lobby were suggesting. If almost half the parishes obtained some form of medical help, was the situation critical? Table 9.B shows the breakdown by different types of economic community – most urban and industrial parishes have medical provision in some form though most agricultural ones do not and crofting ones have very little of any kind.

The most revealing table about the inadequacy of medical relief is, however, Table 9.B (and Map 9.5), which shows how much was actually spent on doctors per head of the population on the poor roll. The Scottish average was £0·0154, or no more than $3\frac{3}{4}$d. per pauper per year in the old money. There was, admittedly, some variation from virtually nothing in the Highlands to almost 2s. per pauper (9·45p.) in the Hawick area – but only one other district had an expenditure as much as half the latter sum. Considered by the type of economic community the large towns came out best, but even they provided only 6d. per head of pauper: and ordinary Lowland rural parishes were not paying half that. The bleak statistic that the responding parishes, with a population of 1,865,874 souls, were only paying £1017 in medical relief, about £1 for every 2000 people, does more than anything to justify the vehemence of Alison's criticisms.

What actually happened, then, to the sick poor in the face of so feeble an attempt by the poor law to come to their aid? The worst situation shown in the maps and tables prevailed in the crofting districts of the north and west, as is fully borne out by verbal evidence before the commission.

Here, over very wide areas of the mainland, there were simply no doctors at all, or none of adequate calibre, or none who would stay. The minister of Shieldaig in Wester Ross said that able-bodied men who became sick were left in the hands of providence because there was hardly a doctor within sixty or seventy miles of the coast: 'my brother, who had studied medicine lived with me; but he gave up practising in disgust, and did not remain, because he got nothing from it' (20.726). At Ullapool they had had until recently no doctor nearer than Dingwall, fifty miles away on the opposite coast; now there were 'two young men here who are expectants of a better situation hereafter else-where ... Ullapool is too poor to make it worth their while to remain' (21.423). In Morvern the minister explained that the nearest doctor was at Strontian or Tobermory: 'it would take a man five or six hours, having to cross a ferry besides, to walk from his house to Strontian; and from his house to Tobermory is a distance of seven miles by land, and three of a ferry' (21.181). As he observed, in places like these not only the poor but all classes of the community suffered from the want of qualified medical attention.

The situation was no better on the islands. In Shetland there were few doctors outside Lerwick – 'which is twenty miles from the manse, and there are two arms of the sea intervening', as the minister of Sandsting and Aith-sting pointed out (21.184). At Stromness in Orkney there were four medical men – good provision, but two had only been partially educated (20.744). On Mull there were one or two doctors for a population of 10,000: 'medical men will not set themselves down in such districts' (20.647). Accounts like these make comprehensible Sir Archibald Geikie's story of the man of Canna who smashed his leg building a wall; he was taken to Arisaig, twenty-five miles away over the open sea, only to find the doctor had gone away inland and would not return for two days. As there was no time to lose, the boatmen took the patient round Ardnamurchan point to Tobermory, where the leg was successfully amputated thirty-six hours after the accident. The amputated limb was buried in the churchyard, but when the victim recovered he insisted on having the decomposing remains disinterred and towed back in another boat ten yards behind him home to Canna on the grounds that he would certainly need it again: 'D'ye think I'm to gang tramp-tramping aboot at the Last Day lookin' for my leg'.[2]

The basic problem of the north and west was that most communities were too poor to support any kind of doctor, either for paying patients or for others. Sometimes a solution was found by the generosity of a great landowner, as on the estates of the Duke of Sutherland who paid part of the salary of a doctor in Tongue to enable him to visit the poor in the parishes of Farr and Reay, the remainder of the salary being found by a subscription among the farmers who used him themselves. The Duke also subsidised physicians elsewhere in the county, or paid for medicine for the poor (21.282; 21.287; 21.357). Unfortunately other landowners were forgetful or half-hearted. The Duke of Argyll had told the minister of Inveraray to discontinue collecting a fund for providing the poor with medicines as 'he would desire his own medical man to attend the poor', but 'within this month . . . that arrangement has been discontinued' (21.141). Some medical men in the Highlands spent a good deal of their own money providing free medicine to the poor – at Fort William it could amount to £20 a year (21.401). In other cases the laird kept a medicine chest (20.760).

Left without doctors, others very often tried to take their place. The minister, in particular, was commonly called on for his healing powers, as at Kildonan on Islay where the poor attributed 'certain virtue' to relief from the manse (21.280). Often he or his wife kept a medicine chest for the poor; sometimes the minister had even gone to the trouble of acquiring the rudiments of a medical education, as at Sandwick in Orkney where he had obtained a diploma (21.261) and at Gairloch in Wester Ross where he had 'attended a few lectures in anatomy' (20.735). It must not be imagined, however, that their standard was very high; the minister of Fetlar and North Yell in Shetland prescribed 'in simples, like the honest man in England "laudamy and calamy"' (20.770) and his colleague at Deerness in Orkney also kept 'a little laudanum and some other trifling medicines' (21.244). The surgeon in Tain understandably commented that the clergy were liable to make mistakes (21.50). Other members of the community reckoned wise in these things also gave medical help: at South Knapdale in Argyll the kirk treasurer was a farmer who 'bleeds and prescribes for the people occasionally, he is reckoned skilful, particularly in bone setting' (21.145), and at Sandwick in Shetland there was an old man who although 'not regularly bred to it, understands a good deal about medicine, and the people have a good deal of confidence in him' (21.183).

The Highlands and Islands also had special problems in medical care that were more severe than elsewhere. The institutional care of lunatics was totally lacking. 'They are left as long as they possibly can be', said one medical witness, 'at large, wandering about through the country, and, when they become dangerous, they are tied with ropes, chained, handcuffed, confined in outhouses, or in some house apart from others, and occasionally in some of the cottars' houses' (20.672). On Stronsay, Orkney, for example, there was a girl who had cut off the privy parts of her brother while he was asleep. Nothing was done to her but she became disabled from sleeping in an outhouse and was ultimately taken in to the home of a kindly married couple who were given £2 a year by the session for her maintenance (20.249). Unqualified midwives were another problem: at Glenelg the minister believed that many deaths had been occasioned by their ignorance (20.438). Then there was the difficulty of vaccinating the children against smallpox. Strenuous efforts were made by the ministers and by such medical men as there were, to obtain lymph from Glasgow or London and to attend as many households as possible, but coverage was not good – it was found in one epidemic in Glasgow (where there had been 2196 deaths from smallpox in five years) that in a sample of 95 victims 70 had come from Highland parishes (20.659).

In the Lowlands the problem was not an absolute shortage of doctors but rather a lack of will to provide for the sick poor. It took different form in town and country. In the main towns help for the poor was focused on infirmaries and dispensaries, which were supported by voluntary subscriptions, and on certain other charitable bodies such as Destitute Sick Societies. In Edinburgh, for example, the Royal Infirmary was used almost exclusively by the poor. It was supplemented by two large dispensaries and some lesser ones which both saw the poor as out-patients and visited them in their own homes – the Royal Dispensary (the largest) had 12 medical officers on the permanent staff and a number of students attached to them as deputies. The Destitute Sick Society, for its part, tried to help those temporarily unemployed through sickness by giving them small grants for subsistence – they relieved 3517 cases in the capital in 1842 (20.130–47). In addition there was a Lying-in Hospital which provided care at childbirth for about 200 mothers a year in the building, and for about 500 in their own homes (20.147) and a Lock Hospital with accommodation for 30 to 50 women suffering from venereal diseases (20.170–1). There was also a Fever Hospital, but it was not in 1843 used as such: fever cases (suffering from typhus and typhoid) were treated in the wards of the Royal Infirmary mixed in with other patients (20.131).

The situation in other large burghs did not differ in kind, though it varied in detail. Glasgow had 17 'district surgeons' appointed at a salary of £21 a year from the funds of the Town's Hospital (a poor law institution) – an enlightened though limited measure of public involvement (20.285–9). Similar provision was made in Paisley (20.562) and Kilmarnock (20.714). In Glasgow and Perth fever victims were isolated from the other patients in the wards of the Infirmaries (20.249; 20.429). Dundee and Aberdeen provided the commissioners with tabular statements of the patients admitted to their infirmaries: they were almost all working-class, Dundee admitting within a year 2162 and Aberdeen 1956 (21.619; 22.152).

What was the actual quality of urban medical provision? Almost everyone agreed that it placed a great strain on the charity of the doctors themselves: 'I do not know a class of men that deserve more gratitude from the public than medical men', said a minister in Paisley, 'and I know that the one half of them have been themselves pushed for the means of support. The times have pressed on that class of men very painfully' (20.562). At the same time, astute observers saw that even the most public-spirited doctors could not be equal to their task as long as medical relief rested on a voluntary and charitable basis. The dispensaries were not adequately staffed. 'The amount of disease among the poor', exclaimed Dr. Handyside of Edinburgh, 'is such that all the pupils, with all the medical men of the dispensaries, are insufficient to overtake it'

(20.135). The infirmaries were too small and made no provision for after-care. Both Glasgow and Greenock were said to turn their patients out before they had fully recovered, unable to work and penniless – Glasgow Infirmary shipped her Irishmen and Highlanders down the water on steamboats, and they were often removed from the ships at Greenock as being unable to pay the rest of their passage (20.559). The evidence before the commissioners creates a picture of a middle-class pleased and impressed by its own charitable efforts, which were in reality scarcely touching the surface of the problems they purported to relieve.

Individual cases strengthen this impression. In Paisley the Rev. Brewster had visited a squalid household fatally infected with typhus: he found the children crawling about the floor, the mother lying in her coffin, the father too ill to raise his head, and one or two daughters similarly prostrate on the only bed: 'great neglect had taken place on the part of the parish officers', he said, 'The poor are staved off in every way when they apply' (20.601–2). Another case was related by a surgeon in Port Glasgow who had been called to see a woman from Edinburgh found sitting on a grocer's stair in a state of collapse from fever. He had tried to have her admitted to Greenock Infirmary, but it was full; eventually an Irish labourer and his wife took pity on her, accepting her into their home – all the family subsequently caught fever, the wife and one child dying of it (20.483). The commissioners themselves interviewed an Edinburgh baker, aged 21, who had been ill for four months with an ulcerated leg: 'I have not been in the infirmary. I applied to be admitted, but it was quite full and there was no room for me.' He had received 2s. 6d. a week from the Destitute Sick Society for three weeks, but it was discontinued 'as they said I ought to get into the infirmary'. He had then pawned all his furniture, wearing apparel and blankets apart from a bedstead, three chairs and the clothes on his back in order to buy food for himself and his wife who 'has a young bairn at her breast and cannot work' (22.920). In these three cases there was a hopeless gap between the scale of the individuals' misfortunes and the provision made by society to relieve them.

Was the situation in the Lowlands better away from the fever-ridden slums of the large towns? As the maps suggest, it varied very widely from place to place. Many country parishes paid subscriptions, usually from the poor fund but sometimes through an individual, entitling their paupers to use infirmaries or dispensaries in near-by towns (see Map 9.3). Gray's Hospital in Elgin was open to all the inhabitants of Morayshire whether they subscribed or not (21.513). Sometimes landowners or employers were private subscribers, buying the right of treatment for their own dependants if they were ill. Even quite small towns in rural areas, such as Huntly or Coldstream, might have a dispensary of their own, and where they did not it was common for the local heritors to keep a medicine chest as a charity.

Where there was no attachment to a medical institution the parish might pay something for medicines or medical fees, and this, too, was supplemented by charity of various kinds outside the poor law. In industrial areas, factories occasionally provided their own doctors to attend accidents, as at Rothesay

(21.72) and New Lanark, where care extended to ordinary sickness and the provision of medicines (22.405). Such consideration was, however, rare in the iron and coal works of Lanarkshire (22.372), while the colliers of Gladsmuir in East Lothian paid for their own doctor (by a weekly contribution) to visit them and their families in sickness (22.798).

The main weaknesses in the voluntary system were the same here as elsewhere. The doctor's generosity was presumed upon, sometimes to an extraordinary degree. The surgeon at Kincardine O'Neil in Aberdeenshire, for example, was morally expected to give his medical attention for nothing, often to provide medicines free, and to act as go-between in arranging extra food for the sick poor from heritors or farmers. 'I feel my attendance upon the poor to be a heavy burden', he said. 'It is a serious inroad on my time and I think the amount of charity thus exacted . . . is disproportionate. . . . At the same time I cannot feel at liberty to refuse to give attendance upon paupers' (21.740). It was a situation where even the most benevolent might become exhausted, or give only minimal help. 'Medical men will get tired of it, and I know they are tired of it', said a doctor at Scone in Perthshire, who had had a long tussle with the kirk session over the payment of a £6 bill. 'At present I have nothing to do with the poor, unless when I get a written order' (22.868).

Admittedly it was an open question what medicine could do in cases of serious illness, and in some parishes there were reports of a distrust of the medical profession (21.525; 21.533; 21.736; 21.33). The minister of Kilmaronock in Dunbartonshire reported that his session had provided, on medical advice, ten days' supply of alcohol to a family suffering from fever – four glasses of port wine a day for the man, three glasses for the woman, two glasses for the two eldest children and a glass each for the four younger. It was generous, and a cheerier cure than the laudanum prescribed by the minister in Shetland, but there is no evidence that it was more efficacious (22.454).

One problem that was often acute in small communities and hardly faced up to in the Lowlands more than in the Highlands was the care of lunatics. There were seven asylums, all in large towns – Edinburgh accommodated 250, Glasgow 450, Perth 180, Dumfries about 150, Montrose 100, Aberdeen 200, Dundee 220 (20.674). In Inverness there were eight cells set apart in the Infirmary, which was supposed to minister for all the lunatics in the five northern counties (21.470). These town asylums often drew upon a wide area – the Crichton Institute at Dumfries had 46 poor and pauper patients at the end of 1843, of whom 29 were supported by their parishes – 15 from the county of Dumfries, 7 from Kirkcudbright, 3 from Wigtown, 2 from Ayrshire, 1 from Selkirk and 1 from England (22.603).

The pauper lunatics brought to the Crichton Institute from the country had generally arrived 'bound – galled – in a state of shocking filth; crouching with their limbs contracted, showing that they had been long confined, or that they had been long in bed' (22.604). An Edinburgh gas-fitter drew the attention of the commissioners to the case of a mad woman in parochial care at St. Andrews, who had been similarly chained in brutal conditions to the floor of a garret-room containing an unglazed window and a bed unfit for the use of a human being (22.868). On the Isle of Arran, 123 lunatics were illegally boarded out with crofters and farmers, having been placed there by industrial parishes in the west of Scotland – 'poor half-fed, half-clothed wretches who are sent here to linger out a miserable life without medical or any other attendance', as a correspondent described them, 'they may die like beasts without anyone to look after, or care for them' (20.949–59).

One problem actually exacerbated by the Scottish poor law was that of poor people taken ill far from their original homes, who were liable to be transported by cart back to their parish of legal settlement. This led to pathetic cases of suffering in the parishes along the main roads – the minister of Tranent said up to 50 a year were carted through his parish, many of them Irish reapers, and the minister of East Kilpatrick recalled two instances of women dying in outhouses or deserted buildings in his parish after becoming too ill to be carted further (22.455; 22.802). A desperately sick man sent from Girvan to Glasgow in April 1843 passed on the way through the hands of 15 different parochial authorities in four days, only to be refused admittance to Glasgow Town's Hospital because the official there did not accept his proof of settlement. This was legalised torment of the poor (20.463).

If there was one area of Scotland that won praise from Alison and his friends it was the Borders, where assessment was more general and medical care apparently more widespread and generous (as Maps 9.2 and 9.4 show). It was, however, the opinion of Dr. James Douglas who had practised medicine in Kelso for 39 years, that at least in Roxburghshire the poor were much worse off than over the English side of the Border: in England when a pauper was taken ill he was attended by doctors employed by the parish, but in and around Kelso they had to depend on the local dispensary supported by charity, and even so 'many want medical assistance' (22.690). In the Hawick district, however, there were far more paid doctors but no dispensary. It is as though the parochial authorities even here regarded the existence of an efficient charitable organisation as an excuse for them to provide nothing further for the aid of the poor.

How did the commissioners react to the overwhelming evidence of the sufferings of the sick poor and the inability or unwillingness of parish authorities to relieve them? The majority report recommended that 'medical relief should be supplied more extensively to the poor', that the legal ambiguity that still existed regarding whether it was legal to give medical relief to someone probably only temporarily sick be resolved in favour of giving relief and that dispensaries should be attached to poorhouses where it was found expedient to build them; they further recommended that insane paupers be sent immediately to asylums unless central authority released parochial boards from the duty of doing so (20.xxvi–xxxi). Edward Twistleton in his minority report criticised in a short paragraph the lack of powers actually compelling the managers of the poor to provide medical help, and the absence of any fixed scale for the fees for doctors attending the poor. If these matters were to be left to the local authorities, he observed, they 'may deem that they have a direct pecuniary interest in fixing the scale as low as possible, or in throwing altogether upon medical practitioners, as is very frequently the case at present, the burden of attending the sick poor gratuitously' (20.lxvi). Exhortation, he plainly believed, was humbug when so much needed doing so urgently.

There was one other question asked by the commissioners that had a bearing on the unfit poor, and which was also worth analysis. It ran as follows:

Q. 23.   Have farm servants who have become unfit for hard work any difficulty in obtaining dwellings in your parish? And do you know any instance of such persons, who, on this account, have migrated to country towns or to the large towns?

To this there were 809 replies (an 89 per cent. response rate), of which 237 (29 per cent. of the responding parishes) stated that farm servants had indeed had difficulty in obtaining dwellings. Table 9.C and Map 9.6 show how these parishes were distributed. Almost all the replies associated difficulty in obtaining houses with internal migration: in 220 cases they reported that servants moved to nearby villages or country towns, only in 51 cases did they move to the large towns. Though a problem, it was evidently not thought to be a severe one: 38 per cent. of the positive responses were qualified with the remark that it only happened occasionally.

Map 9.6 shows, indeed, a curious distribution of the positive replies. It is not surprising that there were few from the northern crofting districts, as there were few farm servants there in any case. That there should be few in central Scotland may be explicable in terms of mobility occurring earlier: perhaps farm servants moved into new houses and new jobs while they were still fit and young, because in industrial districts there were simply more and better-paid jobs near at hand. Certainly the problem seemed to be most widespread – or the migration most visible – in deeply rural areas of the Borders, the southern Highlands and the north-east. On the other hand it also seemed to be serious in Angus, where there was still much employment available in the village linen industry.

Evidence heard before the commissioners indicated the nature of the problem. Farm workers became unfit for heavy work in middle age – estimates varied from 45 to 60 (22.656; 22.727). Since rural poor law provision was so inadequate for the sick or the old, they often attempted to get a new job away from their former community. Middle-class observers suspected that they came to the big cities in order to sponge on charity, or to hide away for three years so that they could then claim legal settlement in an assessed urban parish, but it was not so. Rev. Thomas Guthrie who had worked in Angus explained the realities: (20.90)

Take the case of a ploughman. When unable to do his work, he is turned off: his cottage is transferred to another. The next best thing he can do is to turn carter, and for that purpose he comes to town; but such persons do not migrate from the idea that they will be better off on account of the charities, or for any other reason than that they expect to get many small jobs which they could not get in the country.

If he did not become a carter (see also 21.468; 22.12; 22.130) he might seek employment as a weaver, as a pirn-winder, as a gardener, or in some other less strenuous job – 'in all towns there are more light jobs than in the country. Hence towns become centres of attraction to old people' (22.273). Historians have frequently dwelt on the migration of the young: the migration of the old and the ill seeking to survive in a harsh world is less often noticed but might sometimes be even more compelling.

REFERENCES

1. *Report on the Sanitary Condition of the Labouring Population of Great Britain* (M. W. Flinn, ed., Edinburgh, 1965). The introduction contains a useful account of the issues in dispute between the two reformers.
2. Archibald Geikie, *Scottish Reminiscences* (Glasgow, 1904), pp. 162–4.

TABLE 9.A

Percentages of Parishes providing Medical Relief, by District

	Paying a doctor	Subscribing to a hospital dispensary	By doctor or dispensary, etc.	N
1. Shetland	0	0	0	13
2. Orkney	16	0	16	19
3. Caithness	8	0	8	12
4. East Sutherland	0	36	36	11
5. East Ross	14	7	21	14
6. N.-E. Inverness	7	47	53	15
7. North-west coast	0	18	18	11
8. Skye and Outer Hebrides	0	0	0	14
9. West Argyll	7	0	7	14
10. North Argyll	10	0	10	10
11. South Argyll	17	6	19	16
12. Highland Inverness, Banff, Moray	0	17	17	12
13. Highland Perth, Aberdeenshire	10	30	30	10
14. N.-W. Perth	29	7	36	14
15. Nairn, Lowland Moray	0	33	33	21
16. Lowland Banff	15	33	41	27
17. Buchan	32	40	64	25
18. S.-E. Aberdeenshire	4	50	50	26
19. Inner Aberdeenshire	30	60	70	20
20. Kincardine	22	67	72	18
21. Inner Angus	34	40	54	35
22. Coastal Angus	39	65	81	26
23. East Perthshire	35	50	65	20
24. South Perthshire	36	36	59	22
25. East Fife	29	5	35	34
26. West Fife	19	14	30	27
27. North Stirling-Clackmannan	33	33	56	18
28. West Lothian, East Stirling	41	15	59	17
29. Edinburgh area	56	33	67	18
30. Dunbarton, Renfrewshire	57	57	81	21
31. North Ayrshire	36	20	52	25
32. South Ayrshire	40	0	40	15
33. North Lanarks.	37	42	63	19
34. South Lanarks.	35	15	40	20
35. Peeblesshire	31	6	38	16
36. Dunbar area	47	33	53	15
37. South Berwick	43	27	60	30
38. Kelso area	44	78	87	23
39. Hawick area	80	0	80	10
40. Inner Dumfries, Kirkcudbright	52	38	62	21
41. South Dumfries	43	52	70	23
42. South Kirkcudbright	33	33	48	21
43. Wigtown and south tip of Ayr	20	20	20	15
SCOTLAND	28	30	48	813

TABLE 9.B

Percentages of Parishes providing Medical Relief,
by Economic Type of Community

	Percentage of parishes of each type reporting:			
	a Paying a doctor	*b* Subscribing to a hospital or dispensary	*a + b* Subscribing to either a doctor or a hospital or dispensary	N
1.1. Urban-industrial: large towns	61	64	86	28
1.2 Urban-industrial: smaller towns, etc.	42	35	66	113
2.1. Mixed economy: rural parishes	35	33	56	181
2.2 Mixed economy: country towns	28	26	42	43
3.1. Agricultural: farming parishes	24	31	45	353
3.2. Agricultural: crofting parishes	5	6	12	95
SCOTLAND	28	30	48	813

TABLE 9.C

Amount of Medical Relief paid per Pauper, by District

	New pence (p) per pauper	N
1. Shetland	0	13
2. Orkney	0·44	19
3. Caithness	0·23	12
4. East Sutherland	0	11
5. East Ross	0·41	14
6. N.-E. Inverness	0	15
7. North-west coast	0	10
8. Skye and Outer Hebrides	0	14
9. West Argyll	2·00	13
10. North Argyll	0	10
11. South Argyll	0·73	16
12. Highland Inverness, Banff, Moray	0	12
13. Highland Perth, Aberdeenshire	0	10
14. N.-W. Perth	2·68	14
15. Nairn, Lowland Moray	0	21
16. Lowland Banff	0·23	27
17. Buchan	0·69	25
18. S.-E. Aberdeenshire	0·66	26
19. Inner Aberdeenshire	1·16	20
20. Kincardine	0·58	18
21. Inner Angus	1·18	35
22. Coastal Angus	2·98	26
23. East Perthshire	2·75	19
24. South Perthshire	2·15	21
25. East Fife	1·82	34
26. West Fife	1·48	26
27. North Stirling-Clackmannan	3·65	18
28. West Lothian, East Stirling	1·78	17
29. Edinburgh area	2·16	17
30. Dunbarton, Renfrewshire	2·30	21
31. North Ayrshire	0·51	25
32. South Ayrshire	0·84	15
33. North Lanarks.	0·56	19
34. South Lanarks.	1·98	20
35. Peeblesshire	2·98	16
36. Dunbar area	3·70	15
37. South Berwick	3·33	30
38. Kelso area	1·81	23
39. Hawick area	9·45	10
40. Inner Dumfries, Kirkcudbright	4·43	21
41. South Dumfries	1·40	23
42. South Kirkcudbright	2·14	21
43. Wigtown and south tip of Ayr	0·56	15
SCOTLAND	1·54	807

TABLE 9.D
Percentages of Parishes reporting Unfit Farm Workers as Migrants,
by District

	Percentage	N
1. Shetland	0	12
2. Orkney	17	18
3. Caithness	46	11
4. East Sutherland	18	11
5. East Ross	64	11
6. N.-E. Inverness	40	15
7. North-west coast	9	11
8. Skye and Outer Hebrides	8	13
9. West Argyll	47	15
10. North Argyll	44	9
11. South Argyll	24	17
12. Highland Inverness, Banff, Moray	50	12
13. Highland Perth, Aberdeenshire	20	10
14. N.-W. Perth	14	14
15. Nairn, Lowland Moray	14	21
16. Lowland Banff	31	26
17. Buchan	54	24
18. S.-E. Aberdeenshire	50	26
19. Inner Aberdeenshire	60	20
20. Kincardine	56	18
21. Inner Angus	40	35
22. Coastal Angus	44	27
23. East Perthshire	22	18
24. South Perthshire	19	21
25. East Fife	12	33
26. West Fife	7	27
27. North Stirling-Clackmannan	18	17
28. West Lothian, East Stirling	19	21
29. Edinburgh area	25	20
30. Dunbarton, Renfrewshire	24	21
31. North Ayrshire	12	26
32. South Ayrshire	31	16
33. North Lanarks.	11	19
34. South Lanarks.	5	20
35. Peeblesshire	19	16
36. Dunbar area	11	18
37. South Berwick	31	29
38. Kelso area	29	21
39. Hawick area	50	10
40. Inner Dumfries, Kirkcudbright	50	20
41. South Dumfries	32	22
42. South Kirkcudbright	43	21
43. Wigtown and south tip of Ayr	24	17
SCOTLAND	29	809

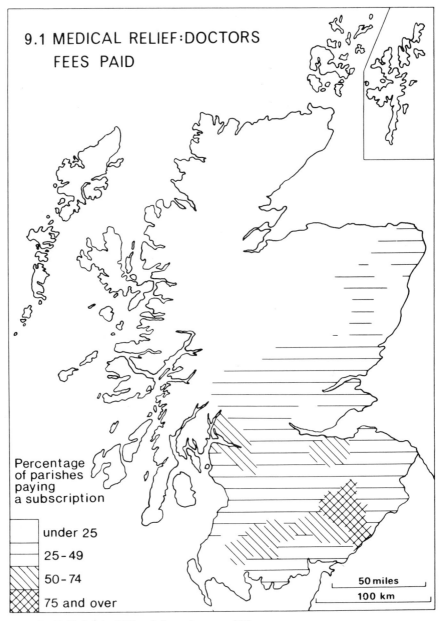

9.1 MEDICAL RELIEF:DOCTORS FEES PAID

Percentage
of parishes
paying
a subscription

under 25

25-49

50-74

75 and over

50 miles

100 km

See Table 9.A (p. 226) and discussion on p. 217.

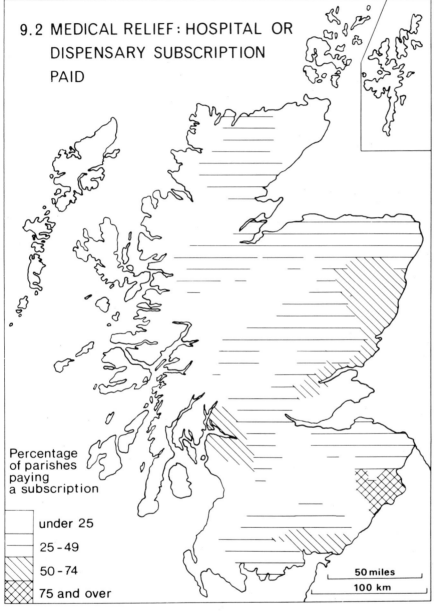

9.2 MEDICAL RELIEF: HOSPITAL OR DISPENSARY SUBSCRIPTION PAID

Percentage of parishes paying a subscription

under 25

25 - 49

50 - 74

75 and over

50 miles

100 km

See Table 9.A (p. 226) and discussion on p. 217.

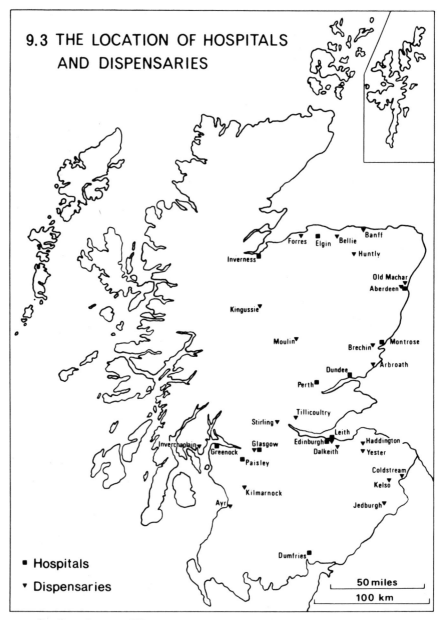

9.3 THE LOCATION OF HOSPITALS AND DISPENSARIES

- Hospitals
▼ Dispensaries

50 miles
100 km

See discussion on p. 217.

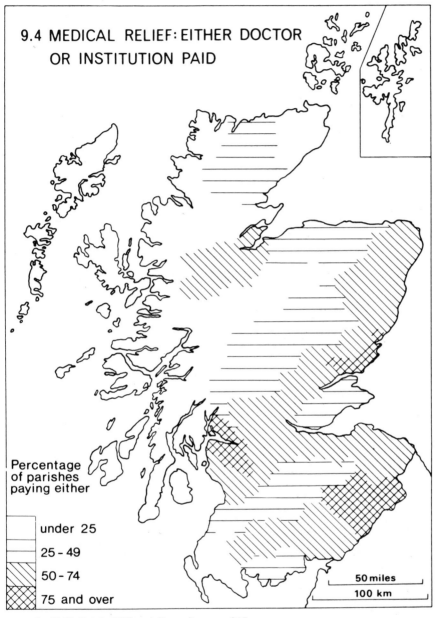

9.4 MEDICAL RELIEF: EITHER DOCTOR
OR INSTITUTION PAID

Percentage
of parishes
paying either

under 25
25 - 49
50 - 74
75 and over

50 miles
100 km

See Table 9.A (p. 226) and discussion on p. 217.

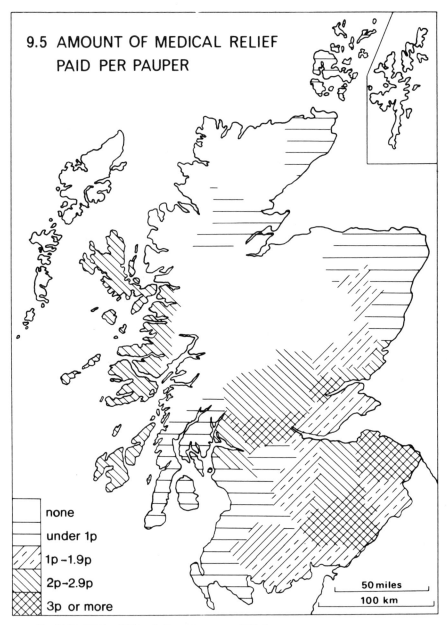

9.5 AMOUNT OF MEDICAL RELIEF
PAID PER PAUPER

under 1p

1p –1.9p

2p–2.9p

3p or more

50 miles

100 km

See Table 9.C (p. 228) and discussion on pp. 217–8.

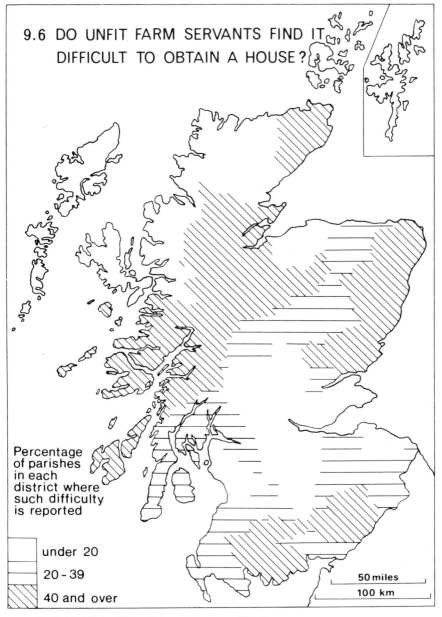

9.6 DO UNFIT FARM SERVANTS FIND IT DIFFICULT TO OBTAIN A HOUSE?

Percentage of parishes in each district where such difficulty is reported

under 20

20 - 39

40 and over

50 miles
100 km

See Table 9.D (p. 229) and discussion on pp. 224–5.

Chapter 10

EMIGRATION

If a working-class person found life hard, how likely was he to leave the country? 'The paucity of good statistical records' has long been recognised as a hindrance to the detailed study of nineteenth-century migration from the British Isles,[1] for Scotland no less than for other constituent parts.[2] The principal sources hitherto used by historians of the early Victorian period are the figures collected by customs officers, inspecting the muster rolls required to be provided by the captain of each vessel carrying emigrants under the Passenger Acts. These record the ports of departure and the destinations of the emigrants, but say nothing of their geographical origins or their occupations. N. H. Carrier and J. R. Jeffery have conveniently tabulated these.[3] Other statistical sources of potential value are U.S. sources recording inward movement of migrants arranged by their country of birth, also tabulated by Carrier and Jeffery[4] although, as we shall see, the U.S. registration of those of Scottish birth appears to be extremely inaccurate. Finally, there are Australian immigration records, particularly detailed between 1837 and 1842 for migrants whose fares were subsidised. D. S. Macmillan has made admirable use of these to delineate the birthplace and occupations of nearly 3000 such passengers from Scotland.[5]

What additional light can the Royal Commission Report throw on this dark corner of population history? Three of the questions dealt with emigration. They ran as follows:

Q. 30. What number of emigrants, and of what description have left your parish during each of the last three years?

Q. 31. To what country have they gone?

Q. 32. Have they received any, and what, assistance for the purpose of emigration?

Question 30 dealt with the overall numbers. It was answered for 793 Scottish parishes (87 per cent. of the whole) but the urban sector was unusually deficient – not only were Edinburgh (with Leith), Glasgow, Paisley and Perth missing as usual, but also in this case Dundee and Aberdeen appear unreliable.[6] This is unfortunate, as we know from the Australian shipping records that there were quite heavy (though not necessarily disproportionate) movements of people born in Edinburgh and Glasgow.[7] The respondents seldom differentiated between migration in each of the three years as they were asked to do, so we have treated the totals as a single sum aggregating emigration over 1840–2. They were also sometimes uncertain themselves as to exact numbers, expecially if they were very high, and tended in those circumstances to state round figures, or to qualify their reply with 'about' or 'approximately'. Sometimes they replied in terms of families rather than individuals: in interpreting these we used a multiplier of 5 to a family after inspection of a variety of cases where the actual members of those in a family emigrating were given. Furthermore, 99 of the responding parishes replied to the first part of the question only in a non-numerical way ('a few', 'many' etc.). We have not tried to put a number to such vague terms.

Despite these shortcomings and imprecisions one has a very strong over-all impression here as elsewhere of the respondents struggling to be accurate, and not normally giving ignorant or slapdash replies. Our analysis therefore concentrated on 693 parishes that responded either to say that there had been no emigration (there were 214 of these, 27 per cent. of the original sample), or with a positive and numerical answer to say how many people had emi-grated (479 parishes, 60 per cent. of the original sample).

How many Scots left, and what proportion of the total population did they represent? In 1841 the population of the 693 parishes was 1,294,000: their replies accounted for the emigration of about 11,700 people, or 0·90 per cent. of that population. On the other hand the official customs returns stated that 32,979 souls left from all Scottish ports 1840–2, or 1·25 per cent. of total population.[8]

This discrepancy between the questionnaire returns and official statistics is susceptible to a variety of explanations. Firstly, the official statistics of those leaving from the Clyde ports of Glasgow and Greenock probably include substantial numbers of Irishmen using these as their final port of departure for a Transatlantic crossing:[9] on the other hand, of course, they make no allowance for potentially large numbers of Scots leaving from English ports.[10] Secondly, the official statistics take no account of re-migration, of those who left for a time and then returned to Scotland; in the early twentieth century when there is first information on re-entrants they amount to between a quarter and a third of the number of migrants.[11] The questionnaire returns in 1843 were perhaps more likely to ignore short-term movement of this kind and to give an estimate for 'net' migration. Thirdly, the ministers might have been unaware of the full extent of migration over-seas, and under-estimated it, especially if their parishes were large or urban. Fourthly, the sample of 693 parishes might be improperly skewed towards those that had few or no emigrants, since it is obviously easier to be precise about small numbers than about large ones. Unfortunately, there seems to be no way of deciding which of these four factors had most weight or which estimate approximates to the true proportion of the population emigrating.

The main value, then, of the answers to Question 30 lies in the details they can provide on over 11,700 emigrants, at least a third of those who left Scotland between 1840 and 1842. In particular, they throw a light on the regional distribution of the migrants that cannot be readily obtained in any other way. Table 10.A and Map 10.1 lay these data out.

The degree to which emigration was a Highland phenomenon is immediately apparent – two-fifths left from the western Highlands and almost half from the Highlands as a whole. It was also, to a striking degree, a west coast phenomenon: 65 per cent. of the emigrants left from districts along the western seaboard. Considered from the alternative perspective of which areas lost the largest percentages of their populations by emigration, the same features re-emerge: the western Highlands easily top the league, losing over 3 per cent. of their 1841 populations within these three years. The absence of satisfactory data from the largest cities makes it hard to judge what they lost, but it is perhaps significant that almost the lowest emigration rates are reported from regions which were nearest to the large cities.

This suggests that the rural surplus in such regions was more likely to be absorbed in the cities, at least in the first instance,[12] than to emigrate overseas, whereas when the remotest areas shed population they were more likely to head straight for the New World. It was explained, for instance, before the Select Committee on Emigration (1841) that the inhabitants of the Outer Hebrides were unwilling to go to Glasgow 'because of the distance: the expense of going is great and they find the work so much taken up by Irish labourers'; but they were happy to go to the wild colony of Cape Breton where so many of their contrymen had already gone.[13]

Looked at in detail, Table 10.A and Map 10.1 show great variation between districts in close propinquity. Shetland, for example, had an extremely low rate, which can be explained in terms of the current mode of production whereby fishermen-crofters were discouraged from any kind of mobility by the lairds who marketed their catch and kept them trapped in a truck relationship; this consideration did not apply to Orkney or to Caithness on the mainland, a Lowland county with a Highland rate of migration at this period. Caithness had been the receptacle for many cleared from the Sutherland estate in the first quarter of the nineteenth century and was now seriously overcrowded itself.

The opposite pole to the Shetland situation was to be found in the western isles, where the landowners of Skye and the Outer Hebrides were trying by force or persuasion to get rid of a crofting tenantry for whom, since the collapse of the kelp industry, they could find no economic function. The Select Committee on Emigration abounded with evidence of the poverty of the area and of the determination of landlords not to allow themselves to be burdened by it. On the estate of Macleod of Macleod on Skye, for instance, there had been disturbances and 'inflammatory proclamations' on church doors when clearance was threatened. In Harris the military had been called in by Lord Dunmore to quell similar resistance to eviction, and assisted emigration had followed with Lord Dunmore paying £1000 towards the expenses of the emigrants.[14] Everyone remembered the famine of 1837 and feared a recurrence: it was to happen in 1846 on an even greater scale than had been anticipated.

The most systematic attempts to encourage Hebridean emigration in these years originated in the co-operation between Lord Macdonald, who owned North Uist and about half of Skye, and the trustees of the fund for the relief of Highland destitution which had been set up to save the population from the effects of famine in 1836–7. After the immediate danger had passed, the surplus funds were partly diverted into subsidising emigration. The inspiration came from Dr. Norman Macleod of St. Columba's, Glasgow, the best-known Highland churchman of his day, who ran a regular column in his newspaper *Gaelic Miscellany* devoted to disseminating reliable information in Gaelic about prospects in Canada and elsewhere overseas. The trustees arranged to pay 10s. a head to every emigrant to whom the landowner would also pay 10s. (or more) and under this scheme 3250 individuals left Lord Macdonald's estates on Skye and North Uist in the four years 1839–42 (20.648 ff.; 20.736). Some had left voluntarily under this scheme, but others were plainly forced out: 'the numbers thus offering to emigrate were increased by Lord Macdonald's giving notice of removal to those crofters who were inhabiting the less fertile parts of the parish', explained a Sheriff-substitute, '(this) had the effect of deciding some to emigrate who were previously doubtful' (21.367). That was one way of putting it.

Even in Skye and the Outer Hebrides, however, where according to our estimates $7\frac{1}{2}$ per cent. of the population emigrated in the years 1840–2, and where the biggest incentive to emigration existed of anywhere in the country, the extent of movement varied enormously from parish to parish. In the Presbytery of Skye, for instance, the 1843 returns speak of 500 emigrating from Portree, about 500 in 1841 from Kilmuir, and a 'considerable number' from Snizort; yet the reply from Duirnish was 'a few, three years ago', from Sleat 'four families', and from the Small Isles, one family. In the Outer Hebrides, North Uist lost 950 (21 per cent. of its 1841 population) – the largest total and the largest percentage of any parish in the country: but several parishes on Lewis lost few or none. Obviously, a great deal depended on the patchy and spasmodic way eviction and assisted emigration were carried out, and in the early 1840s primordially overcrowded parishes with everyone struggling to live off potatoes on bad land by the sea must have co-existed with those from which a substantial proportion had already left to find a new life in British North America. Had it not been so, the famine of 1846 – which was apparently contained without great loss of life, despite the enormous social and economic dislocation it caused – would probably have been as uncontrollable as it was in parts of Ireland.

Skye and the Outer Hebrides had a much larger emigration rate than the rest of the Highland districts, even though these also tended to be considerably above the national mean. Argyll was an interesting case of variation within one county. North Argyll (focused on the Oban area) had a very low rate; the Rev. Norman Macleod in his evidence to the 1841 Committee described this as an area of large farms from which emigration had already drained the surplus population.[15] South Argyll, however, had a high rate, although here again there were large differences in a small compass. Six parishes in the Presbytery of Kintyre reported, for example, as follows – Gigha had had no emigrants, 34 had left Campbeltown, 35 Saddell and Skipness, 'not above a family or two yearly' from Kilbride, 70 from Kilcolmonell and Kilberry, but 'about 400' from Killean and Kilchenzie. The latter figure was equivalent to 17 per cent. of its 1841 population.

The migration from Argyll was not primarily from crofting parishes as the term was understood in the islands or the north-west, but from an area of small farms organised on the old joint-tenant principle of the eighteenth century that was only at this point beginning to undergo reorganisation – and then not so much for sheep as for cattle. The movement also seems to have been connected with the recent failure of the herring fishing in Loch Fyne and the Firth of Lorne.[16]

In the eastern Lowlands, with lower proportions emigrating, there tended to be less variation between districts within the same area. What there was could hardly be related to the push factor of eviction, though the lowest figures might be due to the pull influence of large towns in the neighbourhood. The low figures in the immediate neighbourhood of Edinburgh compared to North Stirlingshire or the eastern Borders, of coastal Angus compared to Perthshire, and of the districts near Aberdeen compared to Banffshire all support this interpretation: instead of going abroad, people were going to the towns if they already lived close to them.[17]

In the west central region of the Lowlands, however, this relationship does not hold. Slightly more people, proportionately, were leaving North Lanarkshire, where Glasgow was situated, than other districts in the region. This has to be seen, however, against the background of depressed handloom weaving in the numerous industrial villages of the west of Scotland – weavers were notoriously difficult to employ in factories or mines, and were said to be only too anxious to leave. Sheriff Alison in Glasgow knew of 'thirty or forty' voluntary emigration societies devoted to getting workers in the city across the

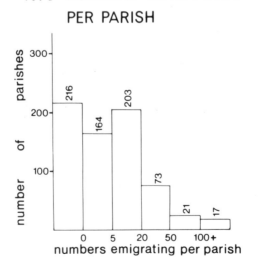

10. I NUMBERS EMIGRATING PER PARISH

Atlantic (20.473). People in the west, too, were generally readier to emigrate than in the east. Presumably this was because the Clyde ports and the other outlets were in almost daily contact with America, and the voyage held fewer terrors than to an easterner living 40 or 50 miles from such a port. It might also be partly due to the fact that there were more people of Irish birth in the west — those who had moved once, might, it is often suggested, be readier to move again.[18]

In the western Borders, South Dumfries and the Hawick district had appreciably higher emigration than elsewhere in the Lowlands. It was a poor area and deeply rural, with a tradition of independence in the ordering of its affairs that can be traced back to the days of the Covenanters: evidently when under pressure now they looked to a new life in America or Australia rather than as part of the industrial proletariat of the central belt. Neither to the west nor to the east of this area was there high migration — in Wigtownshire it was perhaps because this was the one district in which the Irish peasant had settled on Scottish land; they already had what they wanted. In the eastern borders wages were high, there was little distress and poor relief was well organised. Even in the Hawick district half the emigrants came from the single parish of Castleton adjacent to Dumfriesshire and furthest from the incipient industrial centres at Galashiels, Hawick itself, and Selkirk.

· This picture of wide regional variation should be borne in mind in considering the national aggregations illustrated in Diagrams 10.I and 10.II. Both are heavily skewed to the left, showing that the typical experience of a parish was to lose less than 20 of its inhabitants and less than 1 per cent. of its population. Nevertheless, most migrants came from a small number of parishes: 78 per cent. of the people came from 15 per cent. of the parishes (which lost 20 inhabitants or more); 55 per cent. came from 6 per cent. of the parishes (which

10. II PERCENTAGES OF POPULATION EMIGRATING PER PARISH

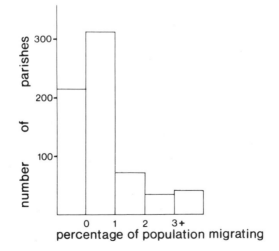

lost 50 inhabitants or more); 44 per cent. came from 3 per cent. of the parishes (which lost 100 inhabitants or more). Put in another way, 43 per cent. of the people came from $5\frac{1}{2}$ per cent. of the parishes losing more than 3 per cent. of their population. The distribution of this critical minority of parishes is shown on Maps 10.2 and 10.3. They both show the importance of the rural west and of the Highlands in contributing disproportionately to the migration. Map 10.2 also shows how several burghs (even some on the east: Brechin, Forfar, Cupar, Arbroath) sent quite high numbers of people even though these did not amount to a large percentage of the towns' populations.

Another way to summarise the date is by considering the economic structure of the parishes providing emigrants in relation to the loss of population they suffered. Such an exercise shows that most economic types of parish sent migrants roughly in the proportions one would expect, but crofting parishes, 12 per cent. of the total, provided a third of those parishes sending over 3 per cent. of their population abroad. This is explicable in terms of the heavy concentration of the crofting parishes in the north and west Highland area from which we have already noted such a high propensity to migrate.

Where did the migrants go to? Question 31 dealt with destinations, as Question 30 dealt with numbers, but it is seldom possible to match the two exactly: it was common to state that, for example, 12 people had left for Canada and Australia, but unusual to explain that 8 had left for Canada and 4 for Australia: enough answers in the second form were made to enable us to use them for illustrative purposes, but not enough to construct a detailed breakdown. All we can do is to state how many parishes reported migrants bound for different destinations, implying that they had at least one individual going to the area in question. 568 parishes reported destinations. Of these, 502 (88 per cent.) reported migrants to North America, 205 (36 per cent.) migrants to Australasia, and only 38 (7 per cent.) migrants elsewhere. Of the parishes reporting migration to North America, 192 did not distinguish between the British possessions and the United States; 266 said British America and 111 said the United States. Of the parishes reporting migration to Australasia, 188 said Australia and 29 New Zealand. Of parishes reporting migration elsewhere, about half named British colonies, mainly in the West Indies. Only about a dozen parishes reported migration to anywhere except an English-speaking (or at least Gaelic-speaking) society: only about a fifth reported migration to anywhere outside the British Empire – and that was almost always to the U.S.A. British North America, or those territories now called Canada, was the most widely popular destination, especially for parishes in the Highlands and those parts of the rural Lowlands without much industry. It looks like the first choice of the poor and land-hungry.

Within the territories of British North America, Ontario was much the most popular destination. One reaches this conclusion slightly obliquely. Two-thirds of the parishes reporting emigration to British North America simply described the destination as 'Canada': in contemporary usage this implied either Lower Canada (Quebec) or Upper Canada (Ontario); it excluded the Maritime provinces. It is extremely unlikely that more than a small proportion of the emigrants were heading for French-speaking Quebec, though some were: six parishes refer to emigration to the 'Canadas', which surely implies both Ontario and Quebec, and occasionally there was an explicit reference to Lower Canada alone – it was, for instance, the destination of 94 people from Barvas in Lewis. On the other hand, a further 42 parishes explicitly refer to Upper Canada alone as the destination of their migrants: the Huron district was being settled in these years and proved a magnet for Highlander and Lowlander alike, Norman Macleod reporting that Paisley weavers as well as Lewismen had done well there – 'there is not one who is not contented' (20.651). There was an interesting discussion in the Select Committee on Emigration on the relative popularity of Upper and Lower Canada.[19] It explained that by far the largest number of Scots went to Upper Canada, and that of those who went to Lower Canada few cared to stay except as labourers in the towns, or as servants to such British residents as there were in that province. It seems reasonable to assume that more than 200 of the parishes reporting emigration to British North America, or about four-fifths of the whole, were sending emigrants to Ontario. This compares with 3 parishes sending emigrants to Prince Edward Island, 11 to Cape Breton, 13 to Nova Scotia, 2 to New Brunswick and 1 to the Hudson Bay Territories.

Migrants to Ontario came from all over Scotland, often in small numbers from Lowland parishes, in larger numbers from parts of the Highlands, especially Argyll. Some localities – the five parishes of Islay for instance – made it their speciality: 'Canada' was the only destination mentioned on the island (except at Kilarrow which had also sent a few to Australia).

Migration to the Maritimes, however, was much more concentrated on certain strongholds and was clearly more important in numerical terms than appears from the above figures of the parishes. Map 10.4 shows how it was only the north and west Highlands, Gaelic-speaking parishes for the most part, who sent migrants there. Of the parishes sending to Prince Edward Island, two were on Skye and one (Shieldaig) was in Wester Ross. Of those sending to Cape Breton, all were in the Outer Hebrides except for one in Skye, Shieldaig again, and Strontian in Argyll. Nova Scotia drew from parishes in Easter Ross, Sutherland and Moray, as well as Argyll and the north-west. The Hebridean parishes in particular had very heavy emigration to the Maritimes: the 950 who left North Uist were heading for Ontario and Cape Breton. 350 who left Harris were destined for Cape Breton and 500 from Kilmuir were divided between Cape Breton and Prince Edward Island.

This kind of concentrated, coagulated emigration was very different from the trickle of families or individuals who often left Lowland parishes to other parts of North America. Hebridean migrants to the Maritimes were transplanting a whole society, and rejecting the other avenue of escape by becoming Lowland workers in Glasgow and the other cities. Many Gaels chose their destination on clannish grounds: 'their principal inducement for preferring to go to Cape Breton is that there are a great many of their own countrymen there.'[20] Similarly, Norman Macleod said many Hebrideans liked to travel to Nova Scotia 'because their friends are there' (20.648). Conditions when they arrived in the Maritimes were often worse than what they would have been in more fertile colonies. On Prince Edward Island destitute immigrants were received by a committee that tried to direct them to where there was employment (20.651), but they were also exposed (uniquely, in the New World) to the very landlordism that they had sought to escape in leaving Skye. If they had pressed on to Ontario (as did many from other parts of the Highlands) they would still have found a Gaelic culture, 'very considerable in Glengarry and in a few other parts: Zora, for instance'.[21] But that had originated in a slightly earlier period, and the Outer Hebrideans of the 1840s seemed to have few lively contacts with it. In choosing the Maritimes they found, at least, better places to survive in than the overcrowded islands they had left.

Emigration to the United States was quite different in origin from emigration to Canada, and relatively few Highland parishes reported it in 1843. This confirms observations to the effect that Gaels firmly believed 'the United States is not a country for Highlanders. In Canada you will be welcomed; here you will be repulsed.'[22] One must also bear in mind, however, that apart from any cultural considerations, the cost of travelling to New York was substantially above the cost of travelling to Canada, because the migrant to Canada had the benefit of travelling as cheap return freights on timber-importing boats that would otherwise have had to sail to British North America empty. It is also possible, however, that many emigrants to Canada ultimately went over the border to the United States when they had saved enough to undertake the next leg of the journey and had discovered that prospects were better in the south.[23]

The typical emigrant from Scotland to the United States, then, was a Lowlander, often from the western districts, and probably better off than the average Highland cottar. There is insufficient information to reveal which states they favoured, although the first U.S. census to give birthplace, taken in 1850, shows that Scots greatly preferred the northern states to the southern, and the older states to the new.[24] Some details in the replies to the questionnaire show how local knowledge could produce a continuing trickle of migrants to a particular destination. Thus, at Tough, Aberdeenshire, there had left 'about nine each year; two carpenters with their families, the rest labourers. All to Ohio, United States.' It was not always like that, however. At Fearn (Angus) 'the blacksmith went to Australia and the tailor to New York'; at Loch Carron (Wester Ross) the weaver (who would be a Gael) took his family to Canada in the established way, but the shepherd and his wife (who would almost certainly have been Borderers in origin) went to Illinois (24.294c; 330c, 417c).

There is a remarkable difference in the picture given of the overall number of Scottish emigrants to the U.S.A. according to whether one uses the British or American sources. The British customs officers' sources report 7518 people leaving Scotland for the U.S.A., 1840–2, the American sources only 105 people of Scottish birth arriving in the U.S.A.[25] In theory, this could be explained entirely by Irish emigration through Scottish ports – i.e., by almost all those leaving Scotland being on transit, or at least of Irish birth moving for a second time, and not true Scottish emigrants at all. But it is really inconceivable that only 105 Scots went in these years, given the fact that the Poor Law Inquiry records emigration from 114 Scottish parishes to the U.S.A., and emigration from another 190 parishes to an unspecified part of 'America'. Admittedly, there is little to suggest the movement of several hundreds of agricultural migrants from an individual parish of the kind one gets for Canadian destinations but certainly, as at Tough, whole families often moved together, and sometimes far more than that; at Dalry, Ayrshire, the report was that 'upwards of 100 labourers and artizans' had moved 'principally [to] the United States' (24.142c). Whatever the real figure (and that is impossible to discover) it must be very well above what the American records suggest. This implies, too, that the decision of Carrier and Jeffery to amend one of their main tables of British emigrants by replacing the British statistics of movement to the U.S.A. by American ones was unwise.[26]

Scottish emigration to Australia in this period has been the subject of D. S. Macmillan's excellent study using Australian data which allow a careful breakdown by geographical origins and occupations of over 2500 bounty immigrants brought into New South Wales by private operators.[27] Our data are much less comprehensive than his, and not strictly comparable, both on account of the parish basis of our returns and because we deal only with the years 1840–2 while he deals with 1838–42. Nevertheless, our findings broadly conform with his.

The geographical distribution of migration to Australia was intermediate in character between migration to Canada and migration to the U.S.A. Like migration to Canada, it had a substantial Highland component, but like emigration to the United States, it was more widespread in parts of the Lowlands. Unlike either, however, it had an eastern bias: there were more parishes around Tayside and east-central Scotland reporting movement to Australia than to either Canada or the United States. This is not, however, so evident in the statistics of actual numbers of emigrants gathered by Macmillan, either because on average more people left from western parishes than eastern or because (as suggested by Balfour) most Highland movement to Australia occurred in the years immediately before 1840.[28] There is, indeed, evidence of suspicion and hostility in the Highlands towards going to Australia at this period. Stories were circulating round Ullapool, for example, of the 'dangers from the natives and bush-rangers' (21.426): at Morvern the population 'heard of the depressed state of matters, and of the scattered state of the population in Australia, and friends separated from each other' (21.180). Clearly, clansmen much preferred the security and closer settlement of Canada (21.519; 21.402; 21.415).

It is difficult to obtain a clear picture of which parts of Australia were favoured by Scottish emigrants, though New South Wales is the most frequently mentioned destination, followed by Tasmania. Most respondents, however, did not specify any other destination than 'Australia'.

It is also hard to be quite sure who was leaving from the 1843 reports:

Macmillan's data on occupation are again more directly useful. Nevertheless, there are some clues: the 400 emigrants from Killearn and Kilchenzie (Argyll) 'mostly cottars, with a few tenants' were divided between Canada and New South Wales — otherwise there is little sign of the mass movement of crofters. Shepherds and agricultural labourers on the other hand, often left in small numbers, like the 25 'single men, chiefly shepherds', who left Glenorchy (Argyll) for Australia. Lowlanders were a mixture, with craftsmen often relatively numerous. Thus Ratho (Midlothian) provided 'three females, one mason, one baker, one smith, married; unmarried, one mason, two labourers and two females', Largo (Fife) sent 'twenty to thirty, principally colliers', and Kilconquhar next door 'about a dozen carpenters and agricultural labourers'.

Of the migration to destinations outside North America and Australia little can be said. New Zealand, which was expensive to reach and demanded some capital, was not at this date at all popular: almost all the parishes sending migrants there were situated in the Lowlands (see Map 10.5). Most sent very few thence — typical were a blacksmith and his family from North Berwick, 2 or 3 ships carpenters from Dumbarton, and a farmer's son from Logie Pert in Angus (24.35c, 170c, 295c). The weavers of Kilbarchan were offered government help towards their passage, but they were frightened 'of the character of the natives there' (22.412).

There was also a small movement to the West Indies from Lowland parishes — for example, two ploughmen from Manor in Peebles, a clergyman from Kirkpatrick-Irongray in Dumfries, and 18 individuals who had their passage paid for them to Jamaica from Keith, Aberdeenshire. The rest were highly miscellaneous — the occasional missionary or gentleman's son to India, a few labourers to the Cape of Good Hope or South America, two or three flaxdressers from Kinghorn in Fife to Boulogne, and so forth (24.25c, 99c, 365c, 251c).

For the three main destinations of Canada, the United States and Australia it is possible to check whether the economic structure of the parish influenced the probability of sending migrants to one of them. Table 10.B shows the results. Of the 793 parishes replying to Question 30, a third reported migration to Canada — but the proportion was over half in the large towns and in the crofting communities: for the U.S.A. disproportionate numbers came from the urban-industrial areas (especially smaller towns and heavily industrialised parishes with textiles and mines), while for Australia the urban-industrial bias was still more marked. From all the evidence we obtain a picture of the three main destinations being attractive to all kinds of Scot, but in differing degrees depending on exactly where they lived and what they did.

It is possible to consider in greater detail the occupations of emigrating Scots, though unfortunately, as was the case with the study of destinations, the data do not relate to the number of *individuals* following each occupation but to the number of *parishes* that reported emigrants of each occupation. There were 344 parishes that provided information of this kind. 24 (7·5 per cent.) reported middle-class migrants; 196 (57 per cent.) reported the emi-

grations of those involved in farming or crofting; 84 (24 per cent.) reported
the emigration of unspecified labourers; 154 (46 per cent.) reported the emigration of artizans and tradesmen. Table 10.C lays this out in greater detail.
As some parishes reported the migration of more than one description of
artizan or agriculturalist, the totals are not identical with those above. Some
things are obvious at a glance. The emigrants were seldom of high social
status. Even adding 'farmers' to the 'middle class' only provides 70 parishes
(20 per cent.) sending propertied emigrants, and they usually left in ones and
twos. The great majority of emigrants were involved in manual work and, if in
industry, often in skilled work. The large number of parishes sending artizans
is interesting. On the other hand, 'labourers' of one sort or another occurred
in 192 parishes (56 per cent.) if one adds the agricultural labourers to the
unspecified labourers: this is more parishes than the artizans, and as there
were probably often many more individuals involved in areas from which
agricultural labourers left than in areas from which artizans left, it is a fair
guess that those of the lowest status far outnumbered artizans and tradesmen.

Among the artizan group the migration of weavers (hard pressed though
they were by the contemporary problems of the handloom-weaving industry
in Scotland) was reported from only about half as many parishes as the migration of construction workers (carpenters, wrights and masons), though this
was an age of the rapid growth of towns and both occupations were very
widespread among Scottish parishes. Similarly, in the agricultural group the
migration of farmers and tenants of at least some substance was reported from
twice as many parishes as the migration of those poorer people described
merely as crofters and small tenants, although the latter were under pressure
from the Highland clearances. This does not mean, of course, that *more*
farmers and building workers left than crofters and weavers, only that the
migration of the former was more widespread in its geographical origins within Scotland. It brings out the importance of a group of migrants often over-
looked in Scottish history, people not necessarily rich or established, but not
destitute or on the edge of desperation either. Farmers and building workers
presumably went in search of larger holdings and improved prospects, ambitious men pulled out by the attractions of the New World rather than driven
out by the horrors of the old.

On the other hand, at least half of the three-year period was taken up by a
slump that produced a great deal of unemployment even among the skilled
workers in Scottish towns. Perhaps this down-turn in the trade cycle, even
though only a short-term phenomenon, proved the last straw to competent
and frustrated men anxious to better themselves. Sheriff Alison was among
those who believed that the onset of a trade depression increased the propensity for respectable working men to migrate, but if it continued so long
that artizans became destitute they lost the will to help themselves (20.473–4).
The United States in particular appeared to offer security in time of slump, as
people believed there would generally be safe jobs there.[29]

The available evidence, then, suggests, that artizan emigration favoured
Canada and the U.S.A., and certainly did not despise Australia, while the

agriculturalists particularly favoured Canada, with Australia as a second choice preferred to the U.S.A.

Finally, there is the problem of how widespread was the practice of assisting the emigrant by paying all, or some, of his passage, which was dealt with in Question 32. In only 91 parishes (16 per cent. of those reporting emigration) did respondents report that the emigrants had received any assistance. Table 10.D shows the various ways in which this was done. The figures are, however, open to some doubt. Firstly, only in about half of the instances did the ministers indicate the actual number helped, but even if one doubles the figure in the right-hand column, it would come to about a quarter of the migrants with whom the returns deal. Secondly, ministers are likely to have had varying degrees of information about the type of help received. They are certain to have known about help from the poor funds or from general subscriptions which they probably helped to organise, and likely to have known about help from landowners: they probably under estimated the number of times help was provided through official bounties to go to Australia. Even if one inflates the total somewhat on this score, it is still probable that over two-thirds of the migrants found the whole of their passage money.

The one significant form of assistance reported here was that provided by landowners in the western Highlands, especially on Skye and the Outer Hebrides. Lord Macdonald, for instance, paid out £1159 in North Uist to send his 950 tenants to Canada, £1 a head to a 'considerable' number from the parish of Snizort and to four families from Sleat, and 'several hundred pounds to the poorest' to help 500 leaving Portree (see also above, p. 239). In Perthshire, Lord Breadalbane paid poor families in Killin between £5 and £25 to go to the U.S.A. and Canada (22.190). On the other hand, such help was far from universal. The 70 migrants from Barra received 'no assistance whatever for the purposes of emigration' from their tight-fisted landlord: nor did the migrants from Lewis.

In the Lowlands it was unusual in agricultural areas for more than the occasional family to receive help; thus the parochial funds at Chirnside in Berwickshire provided £7 to help a family of three to get to Canada, and at Mortlach in Banff 'one family got £1 who were on the poor roll'. Landowners here very seldom helped. In areas with more industry a general subscription was also sometimes used to provide funds for the unemployed to go away: thus 20 weavers and 10 labourers at Beith in Ayrshire were helped with 'about £25 by subscription and a collection' to emigrate to Canada and the U.S.A. What we cannot know, however, is the number of times the passage out was paid by relatives or friends on either side of the sea. That may have been of substantially greater importance than the charitable funds mentioned in these returns.

If there is one conclusion we can draw about Scottish migration at this period it must be that it was not simple. At the one extreme there was a strong Highland migration, largely directed to Canada, of people who were land-hungry, extremely poor, and often unwilling to go. At the other there were numbers of ambitious Lowlanders seeking higher incomes, often skilled workers, probably drawn particularly to the United States or Canada. In between there were small farmers going to Australia and Lowland weavers going to Canada – large numbers of people falling outside either of the stereotypes. Much migration was of a coagulated nature, drawing away a heavy percentage of the population from a small number of parishes, sometimes without affecting the parish next door. Much migration was of an opposite type, thin and diffuse, bringing away a family from this parish and a family from that parish without any very obvious or dramatic demographic effect. But migration was extraordinarily widespread – over two-thirds of the parishes that answered the question had had someone leave for a colony or a foreign country in the space of the previous three years, and few occupations at least of working men were not represented among those who left. This universality of the migration experience needs, perhaps, special emphasis if the historian is to attempt to understand the common mental horizons of the ordinary Scot in the parishes in early Victorian Scotland. Manifestly, it stretched beyond the local kailyard and the market town, even beyond the big city and the rest of the United Kingdom, to the empty lands, the cities and the outback of the New World and Australia: all over the country, those who did not or could not make a satisfactory living for themselves at home were very ready to try to do so abroad.

REFERENCES

1. Charlotte Erickson, *Invisible Immigrants, the Adaptation of English and Scottish Immigrants in Nineteenth-Century America* (London, 1972), p. 1.
2. M. W. Flinn (ed.), *Scottish Population History from the Seventeenth Century to the 1930s* (Cambridge, 1977), pp. 441–55.
3. N. H. Carrier and J. R. Jeffery, *External Migration, a Study of the Available Statistics 1815–1950 (Studies on Medical and Population Subjects)*, number 6, H.M.S.O. 1953, tables C(1), D/F/G(1).
4. *Ibid.*, table E(1).
5. D. S. Macmillan, *Scotland and Australia, 1788–1850* (Oxford, 1967), especially pp. 271–303, and for the period 1815–32, pp. 71–131.
6. Aberdeen provides an answer which we have disregarded because it looks like a copy of the official statistics drawn from the muster rolls rather than an attempt to delineate who had migrated from the town. Greenock, on the other hand, makes an honest effort to reply in terms of its citizens who emigrated.
7. Macmillan, *op. cit.*, p. 295.
8. Carrier and Jeffery, *op. cit.*
9. See J. E. Handley, *The Irish in Scotland, 1798–1845* (Cork, 1943), p. 135.
10 In 1853 when figures on the birthplace of British emigrants first became available those sailing to North America from Scottish ports were about as numerous as those sailing to North America of Scottish birth – though Irishmen sailed from the Clyde, they were exceeded (slightly) by the numbers of Scotsmen sailing from England. On the other hand more than 6000 Scots sailed from England to Australia compared to 4000 people who left Scottish ports for Australia. 1853 was, however, a boom year for Australian traffic, and there is no reason at all to assume this would be true in the early 1840s. Carrier and Jeffery, *op. cit.*, table 4.
11. *Ibid.*, tables D/F/G(1), D/F/G(2).

12. We know, however, that substantial numbers of Scots did emigrate from the cities them-
    selves. See Macmillan, *op. cit. First Report of the Select Committee on Emigration,
    Scotland*, P.P. 1841, vol. 6, p. 86.
13. *First Report of the Select Committee on Emigration, Scotland, 1841*, p. 202.
14. *Ibid.*, p. 199.
15. *Ibid.*, p. 821. Dr. Macleod's description of the Mull of Kintyre in the same terms, however,
    seems to need qualification.
16. See *N.S.A*, Argyll, and notes to the 1841 census, P.P. 1843, vol. 23(2), pp. 6–7.
17. See Ingrid Semmingsen, 'Emigration from Scandinavia', *Scandinavian Economic History
    Review*, vol. XX (1972), pp. 49–50, for close Scandinavian parallels to the propensity
    of Islemen to migrate overseas, and those close to towns to move to them.
18. For evidence of the anxiety of the Irish to move on, see Handley, *op. cit.*, pp. 135, 142. See
    also Semmingsen, *loc. cit.*, p. 54.
19. *First Report of the Select Committee on Emigration, Scotland, 1841*, p. 163.
20. *Ibid.*, p. 202.
21. *Ibid.*, p. 27.
22. *Ibid.*, p. 141.
23. See D. L. Jones, 'The Background and Motives of Scottish Emigration to the United States
    of America in the Period 1815–61', unpublished Ph.D. thesis, University of Edinburgh,
    1970, p. 103.
24. R. K. Vedder and L. E. Gallaway, 'The Geographical Distribution of British and Irish
    Emigrants to the United States after 1800', *Scottish Journal of Political Economy*, vol.
    XIX (1972), pp. 19–35; R. Everest, 'On the Distribution of the Emigrants from Europe
    over the Surface of the United States', *Journal of the Royal Statistical Society*, vol.
    XIX (1856), pp. 49–59.
25. Compare in Carrier and Jeffery, *op. cit.*, tables D(1) and E(1), pp. 94–5.
26. *Ibid.*, table C(1), p. 92.
27. Macmillan, *op. cit.*, especially Tables XI and XII, pp. 294–5.
28. R.A.C.S. Balfour, 'Emigration from the Highlands and Western Isles of Scotland to Aus-
    tralia during the Nineteenth Century', unpublished M.Litt. thesis, University of Edin-
    burgh, 1973, Chapter 3.
29. Brinley Thomas, *Migration and Economic Growth* (Cambridge, 1954), p. 64.

TABLE 10.A
Numbers of Emigrants leaving Scotland, 1840–2, by District

	Emigrant numbers reported	Emigrants as % of reporting population
1. Shetland	40	0·15
2. Orkney	139	0·49
3. Caithness	239	1·73
4. East Sutherland	268	1·58
5. East Ross	107	0·73
6. N.-E. Inverness	93	0·34
7. North-west coast	203	1·23
8. Skye and Outer Hebrides	2,831	7·42
9. West Argyll	382	1·71
10. North Argyll	103	0·50
11. South Argyll	1,144	3·44
12. Highland Inverness, Banff, Moray	185	1·51
13. Highland Perth, Aberdeenshire	77	0·78
14. N.-W. Perth	154	1·32
15. Nairn, Lowland Moray	77	0·28
16. Lowland Banff	229	0·57
17. Buchan	201	0·38
18. S.-E. Aberdeenshire	82	0·40
19. Inner Aberdeenshire	75	0·39
20. Kincardine	31	0·12
21. Inner Angus	349	0·58
22. Coastal Angus	115	0·30
23. East Perthshire	124	0·61
24. South Perthshire	178	0·66
25. East Fife	217	0·42
26. West Fife	157	0·26
27. North Stirling-Clackmannan	136	0·32
28. West Lothian, East Stirling	88	0·21
29. Edinburgh area	24	0·08
30. Dunbarton, Renfrewshire	742	0·76
31. North Ayrshire	346	0·71
32. South Ayrshire	158	0·42
33. North Lanarks.	535	0·85
34. South Lanarks.	86	0·31
35. Peeblesshire	85	0·34
36. Dunbar area	57	0·30
37. South Berwick	147	0·52
38. Kelso area	96	0·56
39. Hawick area	307	2·11
40. Inner Dumfries, Kirkcudbright	210	0·96
41. South Dumfries	579	1·34
42. South Kirkcudbright	217	0·90
43. Wigtown and south tip of Ayr	94	0·35
SCOTLAND	11,707	0·90

TABLE 10.B

Destinations of Emigrants, by Economic Type of Community

| | % of parishes of each type reporting emigration to: | | | | |
| | a | b | c | d | |
	Canada	U.S.A.	'America'[1]	Australia	N
1.1. Urban-industrial: large towns	56	15	19	48	27
1.2. Urban-industrial: smaller towns, etc.	38	28	29	35	109
2.1. Mixed economy: rural parishes	23	12	25	29	179
2.2. Mixed economy: country towns	28	13	26	21	39
3.1. Agricultural: farming parishes	31	13	24	19	341
3.2. Agricultural: crofting parishes	52	7	19	11	98
SCOTLAND	34	14	24	24	793

[1] I.e., all parishes described as having emigrants to 'America', but not specifically to 'Canada' or 'U.S.A.'

TABLE 10.C

Occupations of Emigrants, All Scotland

Occupation reported	No. of parishes reporting
Middle class[1]	24
Farmers or tenants	46
Crofters, cottars or small tenants	20
Farm-workers or farm labourers[2]	148
Unspecified labourers	84
Unspecified artizans or tradesmen	78
Weavers	25
Shoemakers and tailors	12
Carpenters or wrights	31
Masons	14
Smiths	11
Millers and millwrights	11
Colliers and quarrymen	4
Bakers	3
Clerks	3
Seamen	4
Others[3]	42

[1] Breakdown as follows: 'gentlemen's sons', 4; 'of small property', 1; 'of middle rank', 2; managers, 3; shopkeepers, 3; dealers, 2; teachers, 5; ministers of religion, 3; surgeon, 1.
[2] Breakdown as follows: 110 agricultural labourers or 'agriculturalists'; 19 'farm servants'; 13 shepherds; 4 ploughmen; 2 gardeners.
[3] Breakdown as follows: 17 unspecified members of the labouring classes, 10 unspecified servants, 10 unspecified females; 3 female children; a pauper and a dressmaker.

TABLE 10.D
Assistance to Emigrants, All Scotland

Assistance paid by	No. of parishes in which assistance was paid	No. of emigrants known to have been so assisted[1]
Government or colonial bounty	18	133
Landowners	19	1380
General subscription	12	112
Poor funds	15	38
Unspecified[2]	27	220
Total	91	1883

[1] Only 49 parishes gave particulars of numbers.

[2] We have disregarded six instances in which help was given by neighbours or relatives on the grounds that such assistance was probably not known or reported systematically.

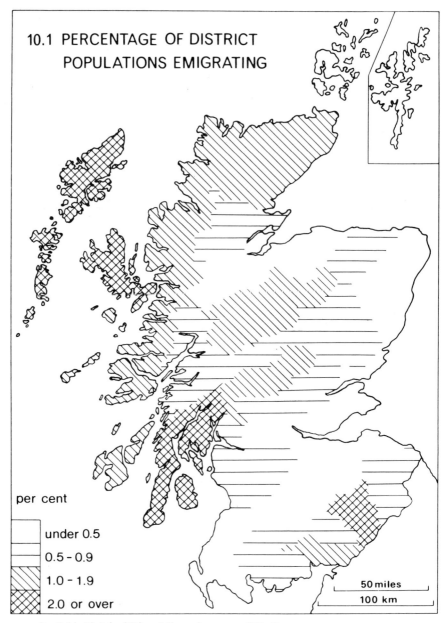

10.1 PERCENTAGE OF DISTRICT
POPULATIONS EMIGRATING

per cent

under 0.5
0.5 - 0.9
1.0 - 1.9
2.0 or over

50 miles
100 km

See Table 10.A (p. 251) and discussion on pp. 237–42.

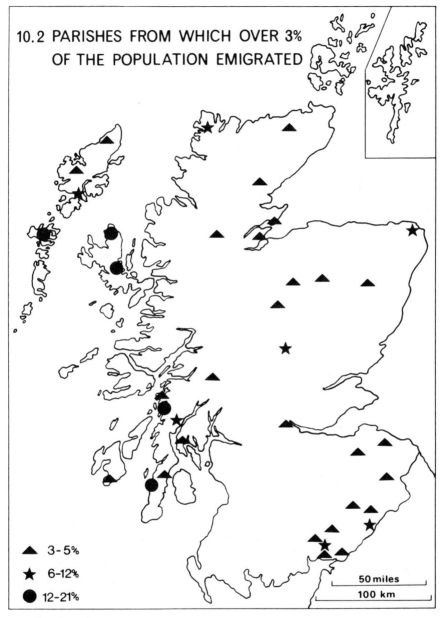

10.2 PARISHES FROM WHICH OVER 3%
OF THE POPULATION EMIGRATED

▲ 3-5%

★ 6-12%

● 12-21%

50 miles

100 km

See discussion on pp. 241–2.

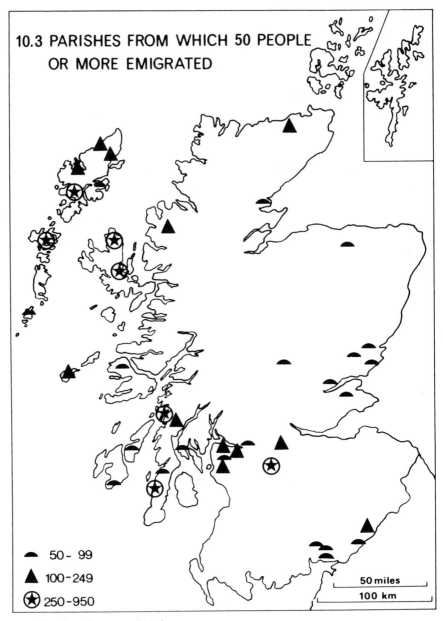

10.3 PARISHES FROM WHICH 50 PEOPLE
OR MORE EMIGRATED

50- 99
100-249
250-950

50 miles
100 km

See discussion on pp. 241–2.

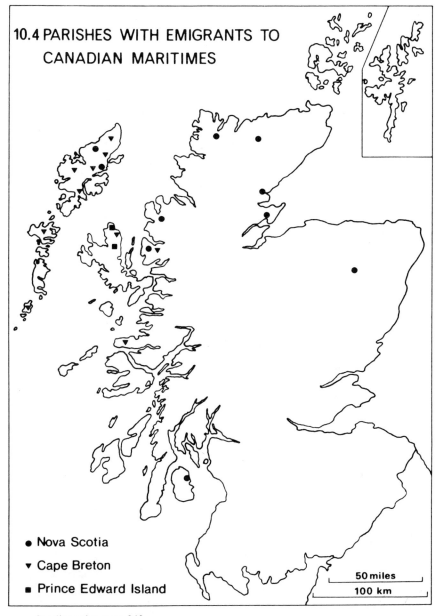

10.4 PARISHES WITH EMIGRANTS TO
CANADIAN MARITIMES

● Nova Scotia
▼ Cape Breton
■ Prince Edward Island

50 miles
100 km

See discussion on p. 243.

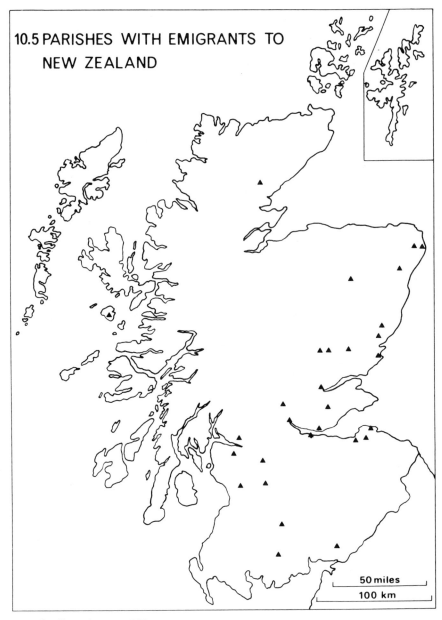

10.5 PARISHES WITH EMIGRANTS TO
     NEW ZEALAND

50 miles
100 km

See discussion on p. 246.

Chapter 11

CONCLUSION

It is not easy to attempt a conclusion to a study of the many aspects of working-class life which were touched upon in the 1843 questionnaire: the material is so rich and the spatial variations so complex that any summary may serve rather to confuse or oversimplify than to illuminate. Nevertheless we have devised a final table (Table 11.A) in an attempt to show in a very broad way how certain partial indicators of working-class welfare varied from district to district. The percentage of parishes in each district reporting meat-eating as an item of working-class diet, and the wage rates of farm servants and artizans, in the first three columns, are chosen to reflect living standards and income: we have, however, to remember awkward complications such as the fact that the high percentage of meat-eating in some areas (e.g., Shetland or Orkney) might reflect nothing more than a local abundance of pigs, rabbits and seabirds within a subsistence framework, and that the relatively high wages of artizans in the western Highlands did not represent an income for many individuals. Column 4, the ratio of drink sellers to population, measures working-class disposable income and amenity – in the sense that drink was the main consumer good for the workers once subsistence needs had been satisfied, and drinking their favourite recreation: again, however, we have to recall the complicating factors at play – for example, the large number of licensed premises in South Dumfries compared to Inner Dumfries and Kirkcudbright probably reflects the presence of little towns and villages free of landowner control rather than much larger working-class incomes (you could live in one district and drink in another). Column 5 concerns the percentage of parishes with friendly societies, which indicates concentrations of well-paid workers able to afford the subscriptions. Column 6 deals with poor-law income per capita – as a measure of the income available for the amenity of social welfare. The final column refers to the percentage of the population that emigrated, on the grounds that those who leave may do so because they are dissatisfied with welfare at home and they find their income and amenity insufficient – though, as pointed out in the last chapter, the propensity to emigrate had to do with knowledge, opportunity and funds to reach the outside world as well as with incentive and dissatisfaction.

For each variable in each district we awarded a score between 1 and 6 based on their position in the rank order for each column. A score of 6 indicates a position in the top 7 districts (i.e., respectively among the most meat-eating, best paid, most full of pubs or friendly societies, with most poor relief available, or having the least propensity to emigrate); a score of 5 indicates a position in the next band of 7 districts, a score of 4 in the next 7 – all these are in the top half of the overall rank order. A score of 3 indicates a place among the first 7 districts in the bottom half of the overall rank order, a score of 2 in the next 7, and a score of 1 indicates a position in the bottom 8 districts. To illustrate by a specific example from the table, Shetland (at the head) was among the 8 districts in Scotland with lowest pay for farm servants and artizans and least provision with pubs, friendly societies or poor law income, but was in the band just below the median position for meat-eating and actually among those 7 districts with least inclination to emigrate. At the foot of the table is Wigtown which was, by contrast, never in the top 7 or bottom 8 for anything; but it did achieve the top half of the rank order for every variable except provision of friendly societies and poor law income.

A study of Table 11.A shows at once two poles of poverty and prosperity (see also Map 11.1). The Highland north and the north-west (districts 1–13) formed a zone of deprivation with Skye and the Outer Hebrides as its epicentre, and the remainder of the Highland west coast much the same. Caithness and the Northern Isles were a little better and North-east Inverness and the two districts of Argyll away from its harsh western fringe a little better again – but East Ross for all its fertility and the inland central Highland bloc were scarcely as well off as most of Argyll. This is the misery of the periphery, of poverty in deep rural areas without the resources to support a population that had been rising for a hundred years and without towns large enough or near enough to force up the rate of wages in the countryside around. It is no accident that the Inverness and Argyll districts (6, 10 and 11) are partial exceptions to this rule.

The other extreme – the pole of prosperity – was a zone formed by the industrial central belt along with the most advanced areas of capitalist farming in the south-east (districts 25–39, except 32). If the districts round Edinburgh and the Lothians appear to score higher than the districts immediately adjoining Glasgow it is only because workers in the former were less likely to emigrate. Affluence fades a little as distance from the largest towns increases – in East Fife and North Ayrshire, and around Kelso, Peebles, Hawick and South Lanarks., though it is compensated for in the Borders by better standards of poor relief.

To claim – as we are doing – that the average working-class person was better off in material terms in this area than anywhere else in Scotland is not, of course, to claim that the sum of human suffering was necessarily greater in Shetland or Skye than in the Edinburgh district and North Lanarks. This conclusion would be untenable on at least three grounds: firstly, the cities of Edinburgh and Glasgow are themselves missing from our data; secondly, far more Scots lived in the industrial central belt than on the islands, so far more poor people would be found there even though *average* working-class incomes might be much higher; thirdly, suffering is subjective – a man and his wife might be content on a croft but miserable in a slum for all sorts of reasons unconnected with those aspects of income and amenity which we can measure.

What we can fairly conclude, however, is that those central and southern districts which were most industrialised and urbanised or most developed along the lines of capitalist farming contained, on average, workers who were better fed, better paid, better provided with pubs, friendly societies and social welfare payments and less likely to emigrate than those at a greater distance from such active markets for labour. Such general gains from the industrial and agricultural revolutions are important: they can be forgotten by dwelling too long on the drama and pathos of the accompanying slums.

Two other zones can be described, intermediate in character between the Highlands and the central belt. One stretches down the Lowland plain from Nairn to southern Perthshire (districts 14–24), and can perhaps be sub-divided into two parts north and south of Kincardine. The districts to the north have worse conditions in terms of diet and poor relief, but a low propensity to emigrate – this is the more purely agricultural area, still with pronounced peasant characteristics such as the presence of many small family farms and crofts. To the south lie the textile districts and larger arable farms of Angus and Perthshire. Despite quite large towns in the zone (Aberdeen, Dundee and Perth) wages even in the southern half did not reach the heights of the central belt. Probably this was because expensive coal (see Chapter 3) in an area remote from minerals led to high operating costs and a low level of mechanis-ation. Manufacturers only stayed in business by utilising pools of cheap labour in the manufacture of coarse linen. Had the reward to labour risen too high, textile firms, at least inland where fuel costs were highest, would simply have gone out of business.

The last zone is in the south-west, comprising Dumfriesshire, Galloway and parts of Ayrshire (districts 32, 40–3). This was also a country of fairly small farms, and again it contained textile manufactures, especially of cotton and muslin sewing, though the latter were coming to their last days. Wages and the standard of diet, though certainly inferior to the districts immediately to the north and east, were rather better than over most of the zone north of the Tay. The south-west was an area surrounded by external temptations to migrate, and labour shifted out of it readily, either abroad, or within Scotland, or possibly even to the industrial districts round Carlisle and Belfast. This mobility, or willingness of the population to vote with their feet, may have tended to keep wages above what they would otherwise have been. On the other hand, the proximity of Wigtownshire to Ireland was often blamed for the lower wages of the south-west compared to the eastern Border counties, on the grounds that Scottish labour on the farms was too readily replaced by cheaper immigrant labour from across the Irish Sea. It was a complex situ-ation which it would be interesting to investigate by local demographic studies.

Our work is a snapshot of Scotland at one point in time, and the nature of the data makes it impossible to compare the picture from 1843 closely or systematically with different kinds of data from other points in time. But what is the dynamic historical process illustrated by our one still photograph of regional variation discussed throughout this book? It is, briefly, the spatial effects of rapid economic growth in a free market economy. A hundred years before 1843 population was, we know, more evenly distributed, and the available evidence suggests less regional variation in working-class income – in pre-industrial society people were poorer but more equal. Fifty years after 1843 we know that population was still more unevenly distributed, since the demographic history of the rural counties of all the north, the south-west and the Borders was one of decline in contrast to the continuing advance of the industrial core in the central belt. It is reasonable, however, to suppose that in per capita terms working-class regional inequalities were somewhat less. We have been able to show that this was indeed the case with respect to agricultural wage rates (see above pp. 80–1), and evidence in government reports on welfare in the Hebrides, for example, suggests a narrowing (but not an abolition) of the gap between the periphery and the core by the end of the nineteenth century.

If this supposition is true we are seeing what economists and historians like Williamson and Easterlin predict in their models – economic growth causing an initial widening gap in income per capita between regions, followed by a protracted period of convergence in which they slowly grow more alike again. In theory this is due to the migration of the factors of production towards each other, of labour towards capital and capital towards labour: in fact, because labour is much more mobile than capital, and because firms prefer to stay close to the existing concentrations of population in order to enjoy advantages in transport costs when buying and selling, any convergence of per capita incomes under free market conditions is usually still accompanied by a continuing population fall in the periphery.

Finally, if we take our standpoint from the present day we find the inequality of population distribution has been in no way rectified since the start of the twentieth century, and is therefore still much more unequal than it was in 1843 (let alone 1743). Rural areas continue to lose population and towns to grow, though these may now be new towns or old middle-sized towns rather than Glasgow or Edinburgh. It is also evident that some of the indicators of regional working-class differences in welfare that we used for 1843 have now converged completely, not because of market forces but for institutional reasons. Trade unions have now decreed that minimum wage rates shall be the same across the country; the welfare state fixes a level of social security payments (the successor to poor relief) that is the same for everyone. Nevertheless regional differences are certainly not done away with. It is common knowledge that it is usually much less difficult for a working-class person to 'get on' – to get a job at all, to get a well-paid job, to get promotion, to get a house – in an urban location than in a deeply rural one, so the drain from periphery to core continues. It is the aim of modern regional policy – manifested in the Highlands and Islands Development Board, for example – to throw a still heavier institutional counterweight on the side of convergence. How successful such intervention can be (and at what cost) remains to be seen.

Perhaps the most surprising feature of the present day, as indeed of 1843, is that so many people continue to live with poor prospects in remote and beautiful places. It only goes to prove what every economic historian knows, that man does not live by economic considerations alone.

TABLE 11.A

Rank Order (in Bands) of Districts in Respect to Certain Variables measuring Working-class Welfare

	% of parishes reporting meat in working-class diet (1 = lowest)	Farm servant's wage (money plus kind) (1 = lowest)	Artizan's wage (1 = lowest)	Ratio of licensed outlets to population (1 = lowest)	% of parishes reporting friendly societies (1 = lowest)	Poor law income per head (1 = lowest)	% of population emigrating (1 = highest)
1. Shetland	3	1	1	1	1	1	6
2. Orkney	4	1	1	2	1	2	4
3. Caithness	3	1	1	2	6	3	1
4. East Sutherland	2	1	2	1	4	2	1
5. East Ross	1	2	1	2	1	2	1
6. N.-E. Inverness	1	1	3	4	3	1	5
7. North-west coast	1	1	3	1	1	1	2
8. Skye and Outer Hebrides	1	1	2	1	1	1	1
9. West Argyll	2	1	3	1	1	1	1
10. North Argyll	2	2	4	1	2	1	4
11. South Argyll	3	2	3	4	2	2	1
12. Highland Inverness, Banff, Moray	2	2	2	1	1	2	1
13. Highland Perth, Aberdeenshire	3	3	1	2	2	2	2
14. N.-W. Perth	5	3	1	4	4	4	2
15. Nairn, Lowland Moray	1	2	4	3	3	2	6
16. Lowland Banff	1	2	2	4	3	3	3
17. Buchan	2	3	3	3	5	4	5
18. S.-E. Aberdeenshire	1	2	4	2	4	3	4
19. Inner Aberdeenshire	1	3	3	2	4	2	4
20. Kincardine	2	3	2	3	5	5	6

21.	Inner Angus	2	3	1	5	3	5	3
22.	Coastal Angus	3	3	2	6	3	4	5
23.	East Perthshire	4	4	4	3	1	5	3
24.	South Perthshire	4	4	1	5	3	4	3
25.	East Fife	6	4	3	6	4	4	4
26.	West Fife	5	5	4	6	5	3	6
27.	North Stirling-Clackmannan	5	5	6	6	5	3	5
28.	West Lothian, East Stirling	5	6	6	5	6	4	6
29.	Edinburgh area	5	6	6	6	6	6	6
30.	Dunbarton, Renfrewshire	5	6	6	6	6	5	2
31.	North Ayrshire	4	5	5	5	6	4	3
32.	South Ayrshire	3	5	2	3	6	3	4
33.	North Lanarks.	6	6	6	5	6	3	2
34.	South Lanarks.	6	5	5	2	5	5	5
35.	Peeblesshire	5	5	5	4	5	6	5
36.	Dunbar area	6	6	6	5	6	6	5
37.	South Berwick	6	6	5	4	5	6	4
38.	Kelso area	6	6	5	2	2	6	3
39.	Hawick area	6	5	6	3	4	6	1
40.	Inner Dumfries, Kirkcudbright	3	4	4	1	2	5	2
41.	South Dumfries	4	4	4	6	3	6	1
42.	South Kirkcudbright	3	4	5	4	2	5	2
43.	Wigtown and south tip of Ayr	4	4	5	4	2	3	5

11.1 ZONES OF POVERTY AND
     PROSPERITY

1   poverty zone ⊠⊠ centre
2   prosperity ·· ▨ ··
3 ⎫
  ⎬ intermediate zones
4 ⎭

50 miles
100 km

See Table 11.A (pp. 264–5) and discussion on pp. 259–61.

Appendix I

LIST OF PARISHES

For key to districts see Map 1.1.

Parishes in square brackets had no information on them in the answers to the Poor Law Commission questionnaire.

Parish	District	Parish	District	Parish	District
Abbey St. Bathans	37	Applegarth	40	Ballingry	26
Abbotshall	26	Arbroath	22	Balmaclellan	40
Abdie	25	Arbuthnott	20	Balmaghie	42
Abercorn	28	Ardchattan	10	Balmerino	25
Aberdalgie	23	Ardclach	15	Balquhidder	14
Aberdeen	18	[Ardersier	6]	Banchory-Devenick	20
Aberdour (Fife)	26	Ardgour	10	Banchory-Ternan	20
Aberdour (Ab.)	17	Ardnamurchan	9	Banff	16
Aberfoyle	24	Ardoch	24	Barr	43
Aberlady	36	Ardrossan	31	Barra	8
Aberlemno	21	Arisaig	9	Barry	22
[Aberlour	16]	Arngask	23	Barvas	8
Abernethy (Perth)	23	Arrochar	14	Bathgate	28
Abernethy (Inv.)	12	[Ashkirk	39]	[Beath	26]
Abernyte	23	[Assynt	7]	Bedrule	38
Abirlot	22	[Athelstaneford	36]	Beith	31
Aboyne	19	Auchindoir	19	Belhelvie	18
Airlie	21	Auchinleck	32	Bellie	15
Airth	28	Auchterarder	24	[Bendochy	21]
Aithsting	1	Auchterderran	26	Benholm	20
Alford	19	Auchtergaven	24	Berriedale	3
Alloa	27	Auchterhouse	22	Bervie	20
Alness	5	Auchterlees	17	Biggar	34
Alva	27	Auchtermuchty	25	Birnie	15
Alvah	16	Auchtertool	26	[Birsay	2]
Alves	15	[Auldearn	15]	Birse	19
Alvie	12	Avoch	6	Blackford	24
Alyth	21	Avondale	33	Blair Atholl	13
Ancrum	38	Ayr	31	Blairgowrie	21
Annan	41	Ayton	37	Blantyre	33
Anstruther Easter	25	Baldernock	27	Boharm	16
Anstruther Wester	25	Balfron	27	Boleskine and	
Anworth	42	Ballachullish	10	Abertarff	12
Applecross	7	Ballantrae	43	Bolton	36

Parish	District	Parish	District	Parish	District
Bo'ness	28	Chapel of Garioch	18	Culross	26
Bonhill	30	Chirnside	37	Culsalmond	18
Borgue	42	Clackmannan	27	Culter	34
[Borthwick	29]	Clatt	19	Cults	25
Bothwell	33	Cleish	26	Cumbernauld	33
Botriphnie	16	Closeburn	40	Cumbrae	11
Bourtie	18	Clunie	21	Cumlodden	11
Bowden	38	Cluny	19	Cummertrees	41
Bower	3	[Clyne	4]	Cunningsburgh	1
Boyndie	16	Cockburnspath	36	Cupar	25
[Bracadale	8]	[Cockpen	29]	Currie	29
Brechin	21	Coldingham	37	Dailly	32
Bressay	1	Coldstream	37	Dairsie	25
Broughton	35	Colinton	29	Dalgety	26
Buchanan	14	Coll	9	Dalkeith	29
Buittle	42	Collace	23	[Dallas	15]
Bunkle and Preston	37	Collessie	25	Dalmellington	32
[Burntisland	26]	Colmonell	43	Dalmeny	28
Burra	1	Colonsay	9	Dalry (Ayr)	31
Cabrach	16	Colvend	42	Dalry (Kirk.)	40
Cadder	33	Comrie	14	Dalrymple	32
Caddonfoot	39	Contin	5	Dalserf	33
Caerlaverock	41	Corstorphine	29	Dalton	41
Cairnie	16	Cortachy and Clova	13	Dalziel	33
Callander	24	Coull	19	Daviot	18
Cambuslang	33	Coupar Angus	21	Daviot and	
Cambusnethan	33	Covington	34	Dunlichity	6
[Cameron	25]	Coylton	32	Deerness	2
Campbeltown	11	Craig	22	Delting	1
Campsie	27	Craigie	31	[Denny	27]
Canisbay	3	Craignish	10	Deskford	16
Canonbie	41	[Crail	25]	Dingwall	5
Caputh	21	Crailing	38	Dirleton	36
Cardross	30	Cramond	29	Dollar	27
Careston	21	Cranshaws	37	Dolphinton	34
Cargill	21	Cranston	29	Dores	6
Carluke	34	[Crathie and Braemar	13]	Dornoch	4
Carmichael	34	Crawford	34	Dornock	41
Carmunnock	33	Crawfordjohn	34	Douglas	34
Carmyllie	22	Creich (Fife)	25	Dowally	14
Carnach	6	Creich (Suth.)	4	Drainie	15
Carnbee	25	Crichton	29	Dreghorn	31
Carnock	26	Crieff	24	Dron	23
Carnwath	34	Crimond	17	Drumblade	16
Carriden	28	Croick	5	Drumelzier	35
Carrington	29	Cromarty	6	Drumoak	18
Carsphairn	40	Cromdale	15	Dryfesdale	41
Carstairs	34	Cross	8	Drymen	27
Castleton	39	Cross and Burness	2	Duddingston	29
Cathcart	30	Crosshill	33	Duffus	15
Cavers	39	Crossmichael	42	Duirnish	8
Cawdor	15	[Croy	6 and 15]	Dull	14
[Ceres	25]	Cruden	17	Dumbarton	30
Channelkirk	37	Cullen	16	Dumfries	41

Parish	District	Parish	District	Parish	District
Dun	22	Ettrick	39	[Glasgow	33]
Dunbar	36	Evie	2	Glass	16
Dunbarney	23	Ewes	40	Glassary	11
Dunblane	24	Eyemouth	37	Glasserton	43
Dunbog	25	Fala	35	Glassford	33
Dundee	22	Falkirk	28	Glenbervie	20
Dundonald	31	Falkland	25	Glenbuchat	19
Dunfermline	26	Farnell	22	Glencairn	40
Dunino	25	Farr	4	Glencorse	29
Dunipace	27	Fearn	5	Glendevon	24
Dunkeld	14	Fenwick	31	Glenelg	9
Dunlop	31	Fern	21	Glenisla	13
Dunnet	3	Ferryport	25	Glenlyon	13
Dunnichen	21	Fetlar	1	Glenmuick, Tullich	
Dunning	24	Fettercairn	20	and Glencairn	13
[Dunnottar	20]	Fetteresso	20	Glenorchy	10
[Dunoon	11]	Fintray	18	Glenshiel	7
Dunrossness	1	Fintry	27	Golspie	4
Duns	37	Firth	2	Gordon	37
Dunscore	41	Flisk	25	[Govan	33]
Dunsyre	34	Flotta	2	Grange	16
Durisdeer	32	Fodderty	5	Grangemouth	28
Durness	7	Fogo	37	Greenlaw	37
Durris	20	Fordoun	20	Greenock	30
Duthill and		Fordyce	16	Gretna	41
Rothiemurchus	12	Forfar	21	Guthrie	21
Dyce	18	Forgan	25	Haddington	36
Dyke	15	Forgandenny	23	Half Morton	41
Dysart	26	Forglen	16	Halkirk	3
Eaglesham	30	Forgue	16	Hamilton	33
Earlston	37	[Forres	15]	[Harray	2]
Eassie and Nevay	21	[Forteviot	23]	Harris	8
East Kilbride	33	Fortingall	13	Hawick	39
Eastwood	30	Fossoway	26	Heriot	35
Eccles	37	Foulden	37	Hobkirk	39
Ecclesmachan	28	[Foveran	17]	Hoddom	41
Echt	18	Fowlis Easter	22	Holm	2
Eckford	38	Fowlis Wester	24	Holywood	41
Eday	2	Fraserburgh	17	Houston	30
[Edderton	5]	Fyvie	17	Hownam	38
Eddleston	35	Gairloch	7	Hoy	2
Eddrachillis	7	[Galashiels	39]	Humbie	36
[Edinburgh	29]	Galston	31	Hume	37
Edinkillie	15	Gamrie	16	Huntly	16
Ednam	38	Gargunnock	27	Hutton	37
Edrom	37	Gartly	16	Hutton and Corrie	40
Edzell	21	Garvald	36	Inch	43
Elgin	15	Garvock	20	Inchinnan	30
Elie	25	Gask	24	Inchture	23
Ellon	17	Gigha	11	Innerleithen	35
Enzie	21	Girthon	42	Innerwick	36
Errol	23	Girvan	32	Insch	18
Erskine	30	Gladsmuir	29	Insh	12
Eskdalemuir	40	Glamis	21	Inverarity	21

Parish	District	Parish	District	Parish	District
Inveraray	11	Kilmadock	24	Kirkcolm	43
Inveravon	12	Kilmallie	10	Kirkconnel	32
Inverbrothock	22	Kilmany	25	Kirkcowan	43
Inverchaolain	11	Kilmarnock	31	Kirkcudbright	42
Inveresk	29	Kilmaronock	30	Kirkden	21
Inverkeillor	22	Kilmartin	10	Kirkgunzeon	42
Inverkeithing	26	Kilmaurs	31	Kirkhill	6
Inverkeithney	16	Kilmeny	9	Kirkhope	39
[Inverkip	30]	Kilmodan	11	Kirkinner	43
Inverness	6	Kilmonivaig	12	Kirkintilloch	33
Inverurie	18	Kilmorack	6	Kirkliston	28 and 29
Iona	9	Kilmore and		Kirkmabreck	42
Irvine	31	Kilbride	10	Kirkmahoe	41
[Jedburgh	38]	Kilmory	11	Kirkmaiden	43
Johnstone	40	Kilmuir	8	Kirkmichael (Ayr)	32
Jura	9	[Kilmuir Easter	5]	Kirkmichael (Ban.)	12
Keig	19	Kilninian and		Kirkmichael (Per.)	13
Keir	40	Kilmore	9	Kirkmichael (Dum.)	41
Keiss	3	[Kilninver and		Kirknewton	28
Keith	16	Kimelfort	10]	Kirkoswald	32
Keithall and Kinkell	18	Kilspindie	23	Kirkpatrick-Durham	42
Kells	40	Kilsyth	27	Kirkpatrick-Fleming	41
Kelso	38	[Kiltarlity	6]	Kirkpatrick-Irongray	42
Kelton	42	Kiltearn	5	Kirkpatrick-Juxta	40
[Kemback	25]	Kilwinning	31	Kirkton	39
Kemnay	18	Kincardine (Ross)	5	Kirkurd	35
Kenmore	14	Kincardine (Perth)	24	Kirkwall	2
Kennethmont	19	Kincardine O'Neil	19	Kirriemuir	21
Kennoway	26	Kinclaven	21	Knock	8
Kettins	22	Kinfauns	23	Knockando	15
Kettle	25	Kingarth	11	Knockbairn	6
Kilarrow	9	King Edward	17	Lady	2
Kilbarchan	30	Kinghorn	26	Ladykirk	37
Kilbirnie	31	Kinglassie	26	Laggan	12
Kilbrandon and		Kingoldrum	21	Lairg	4
Kilchattan	10	Kingsbarns	25	Lanark	34
Kilbride	11	Kingussie	12	Langholm	41
Kilcalmonell	11	Kinloch	21	Langton	37
Kilchoman	9	Kinlochbervie	4	[Larbert	28]
Kilchrenan and		Kinlochluichart	5	Largo	25
Dalavich	10	Kinlochspelvie	9	Largs	31
Kilconquhar	25	Kinloss	15	Lasswade	29
Kildalton	9	Kinnaird	23	Latheron	3
[Kildonan	4]	Kinneff	20	Lauder	37
Kildrummy	19	Kinnell	22	Laurencekirk	20
Kilfinan	11	Kinnellar	18	Legerwood	37
[Kilfinichen and		Kinnetles	21	[Leith	29]
Kilvickeon	9]	Kinnoull	23	Leochel-Cushnie	19
Killean and		Kinross	26	Lerwick	1
Kilchenzie	11	Kintail	7	Leslie	26
Killearn	27	Kintore	18	Leslie	18
[Killearnan	6]	Kippen	27	Lesmahagow	34
Killin	14	Kirkbean	42	Leswalt	43
Kilmacolm	30	Kirkcaldy	26	Lethendy	21

Parish	District	Parish	District	Parish	District
Lethnot	21	Mauchline	31	Newhills	18
Leuchars	25	Maxton	38	New Kilpatrick	30
Libberton	34	Maybole	32	Newlands	35
Liberton	29	[Mearns	30]	New Luce	43
Liff	22	Meigle	21	New Machar	18
Lilliesleaf	38	Meldrum	18	New Monkland	33
Linlithgow	28	Melrose	38	Newton	29
Linton	38	Menmuir	21	Newton-on-Ayr	31
Lintrathen	21	Mertoun	37	Newtyle	22
Lismore and		Methlick	17	Nigg (Crom.)	5
Appin	10	Methven	24	Nigg (Kinc.)	20
Little Dunkeld	14	Mid Calder	28	North Berwick	36
Livingston	28	Middlebie	41	North Bute	11
Lochalsh	7	Midmar	19	North Knapdale	11
Lochbroom	7	Minnigaff	40	Northmaven	1
Lochcarron	7	Minto	38	North Ronaldsay	2
Lochgilphead	11	Mochrum	43	North Uist	8
Lochgoilhead	11	Moffat	40	Oa	9
Lochlee	13	Moneydie	24	Oathlaw	21
Lochmaben	41	Monifieth	22	Ochiltree	32
Lochrutton	42	Monikie	22	Old Cumnock	32
Lochs	8	Monimail	25	Old Deer	17
Lochwinnoch	30	Monkton	31	Oldhamstocks	36
Logie (Fife)	25	Monquhitter	17	Old Kilpatrick	30
Logie (Perth)	27	Montrose	22	Old Luce	43
Logiealmond	24	Monymusk	18	Old Machar	18
Logie-Buchan	17	Monzievaird and		Old Monkland	33
Logie-Coldstone	19	Strowan	14	Olrig	3
Logie-Easter	5	Moonzie	25	Ordiquhill	16
Logie-Pert	22	Mordington	37	[Ormiston	29]
Logierait	14	[Morebattle	38]	Orphir	2
Longforgan	23	Morham	36	Orwell	26
Longformacus	37	Mortlach	16	Oxnam	38
Longside	17	Morton	40	Oyne	18
Lonmay	17	[Morvern	9]	[Paisley	30]
Loth	4	Moulin	13	Panbride	22
[Loudon	31]	Mousewald	41	Papa Stour	1
Lumphanan	19	Moy	12	Papa Westray	2
Lunan	22	Muckairn	10	Parton	40
Lunnalasting	1	Muckhart	24	Peebles	35
Lundie	22	Muiravonside	28	Pencaitland	29
Luss	30	Muirkirk	32	Penicuik	29
Lyne	35	Murroes	22	Penninghame	43
Madderty	24	Muthill	24	Penpont	40
Mains and		Nairn	15	[Perth	23]
Strathmartine	22	Neilston	30	Peterculter	18
Makerston	38	Nenthorn	37	Peterhead	17
Manor	35	Nesting	1	Pettinain	34
Markinch	26	New Abbey	42	Petty	6
Marnoch	16	Newbattle	29	Pitsligo	17
Maryburgh	5	Newburgh	25	Pittenweem	25
Maryculter	20	Newburn	25	Plockton	7
Marykirk	20	New Cumnock	32	Polmont	28
Maryton	22	New Deer	17	Polwarth	37

Parish	District	Parish	District	Parish	District
Poolewe	7	St. Mungo	41	[Strath	8]
Port Glasgow	30	St. Ninians	27	Strathblane	27
Portmoak	26	St. Quivox	31	Strathdon	13
[Port of Menteith	24]	St. Vigeans	22	Strathfillan	14
[Portpatrick	43]	Saline	26	Strathmiglo	25
Portree	8	Salton	36	Strathy	4
Portsoy	16	Sandness	1	Strichen	17
Premnay	18	Sandsting	1	Stromness	2
Prestonkirk	36	Sandwick (Ork.)	2	Stronsay	2
Prestonpans	29	Sandwick (Shet.)	1	Swinton	37
Queensferry	28	Sanquhar	32	Symington (Ayr)	31
Rafford	15	Scone	23	Symington (Lan.)	34
Rathen	17	Scoonie	26	Tain	5
Ratho	29	Selkirk	39	Tannadice	21
Rathven	16	Shapinsay	2	[Tarbat	5]
Rattray	21	Shotts	33	Tarbolton	31
Rayne	18	Skene	18	Tarland	19
Reay	3	Skirling	35	Tarves	17
Redgorton	24	Slains	17	Tealing	22
Rendall	2	Slamannan	28	Temple	29
[Renfrew	30]	Sleat	8	Terregles	42
Rerrick	42	Smailholm	38	Teviothead	39
Rescobie	21	Small Isles	9	Thurso	3
Resolis	6	Snizort	8	Tibbermore	23
Rhu	30	Sorbie	43	Tillicoultry	27
Rhynd	23	Sorn	31	Tingwall	1
Rhynie	16	Southdean	38	Tinwald	41
Riccarton	31	[Southend	11]	Tiree	9
Roberton	39	South Knapdale	11	Tomintoul	12
Rogart	4	South Ronaldsay	2	[Tongland	42]
Rosemarkie	6	[South Uist	8]	Tongue	4
Roseneath	30	Speymouth	15	Torosay	9
Rosskeen	5	Spott	36	Torphichen	28
Rothes	15	Sprouston	38	Torryburn	26
[Rothesay	11]	Spynie	15	Torthorwald	41
Rothiemay	16	Stair	31	Tough	19
Rousay	2	Stanley	24	Towie	19
Roxburgh	38	Stenness	2	Tranent	29
Rutherglen	33	Stenton	36	Traquair	35
Ruthven	21	[Stevenston	31]	Trinity Gask	24
[Ruthwell	41]	Stewarton	31	Troqueer	42
Saddell	11	Stichill	38	Tulliallan	26
St. Andrews	25	Stirling	27	Tullynessie and	
St. Andrews and		Stobo	35	Forbes	19
Deerness	2	Stonehouse	33	Tundergarth	41
St. Andrews		Stoneykirk	43	Turriff	17
Lhanbryde	15	Stornoway	8	Tweedsmuir	35
St. Boswells	38	Stow	35	Twynholm	42
St. Cyrus	20	Stracathro	21	Tynron	40
St. Fergus	17	Strachan	20	Tyrie	17
St. Leonards	25	Strachur	11	Udny	17
St. Madoes	23	Straiton	32	Uig	8
St. Martins	23	Stralachlan	11	Ullapool	7
St. Monance	25	Stranraer	43	Ulva	9

Parish	District	Parish	District	Parish	District
Unst	1	Wandel and		Whitekirk	36
Uphall	28	Lamington	34	Whiteness	1
Urquhart (Mor.)	15	Watten	3	Whithorn	43
Urquhart and		Weem	14	Whitsome	37
Glenmoriston	6	Weisdale	1	Whittinghame	36
Urquhart and Logie		Wemyss	26	Wick	3
Wester	6	West Calder	28	Wigtown	43
Urr	42	Westerkirk	40	Wilton	39
Urray	6	[West Kilbride	31]	Wiston and	
Walls (Foula)	1	West Linton	35	Roberton	34
Walls (Ork.)	2	Westray	2	Yarrow	39
Walls (Shet.)	1	Westruther	37	Yell	1
Walston	34	Whalsay	1	Yester	36
Wamphray	40	Whitburn	28	Yetholm	38

Appendix II

THE 'DRYFESDALE STANDARD'

The budgetary details below are drawn from the evidence of Mr. David Stuart, Distributor of Stamps at Dumfries, who had investigated working-class budgets at Dryfesdale in Dumfriesshire (22.613). The family described in the first paragraph has been used for the cost of living calculations in Chapter 5.

'The next subject of inquiry was as to the standard of living and the rate of expenditure common among the labouring classes. To arrive at this, I first took an individual instance. A hired servant with a yearly income of £26, and having a wife and four children under twelve years of age. His expenditure was, house rent, £2; fuel about £2, food, sixty five stone of oatmeal at 1s. 10d. the stone (the average price of ten years), £5. 17s. 6d.; ten stone of barley meal at 1s. 8d., 16s. 8d.; fifty cwt. of potatoes at 1s. 2d., £2. 18s. 4d.; two quarts of skimmed milk daily, £1 10s.; probable outlay in tea, sugar, ham, etc. £2; whisky 3s.; tobacco, 12s.; the food, in all, amounting to £13 17s. 6d.; the probable cost of clothes for the man, £2 10s.; for the wife, £1 15s.; for the children, £1.15s.; in all £23 17s. 6d.; various items, soap, candles, doctor's attendance, school fees, £2 2s. annually. From this it appears that the yearly consumption by a family of oatmeal and barleymeal is seventy five stones; being nearly one and a half stone per week, or three pounds per day. Of this two pounds of oatmeal are consumed each day in making porridge for breakfast, from nine to ten ounces, making a moderate sized dishful for a working man. Their dinner is constituted principally of potatoes, of which they appear to consume nearly one cwt. per week, or fourteen pounds per day. Of this nine pounds or ten pounds weight may be consumed at dinner; supper consisting sometimes of potatoes, sometimes of oatmeal. At dinner, along with potatoes they may use occasionally a little milk, or herring, or a little ham, or inferior meat; but this latter only for a short period of the year, – the expenditure in these extra articles being necessarily exceedingly small, not above 8d. or 9d. a week. The yearly income of this family viz. £26, is somewhat about the average of ordinary labourers, which may not exceed from £20 to £22. To counterbalance this, however, there are four children under twelve, which is more than the average number; and therefore, the style of living here represented, may be considered as the common standard, or nearly so. A cheaper diet is of course sometimes effected by substituting potatoes entirely for oatmeal, potatoes being generally more than one half cheaper as an article of food.

'To take the case of a single woman's expense, the most important in regard to the allowances from public charity, as being much the most frequent: − House rent as before 25s. yearly, or 5¾d. weekly; food, eight ounces of oatmeal daily, making 5½d. per week; three pounds of potatoes, making 2½d. per week; about ½d. per day for extras, making 4d. per week, in all 52s. yearly, or 1s. a week; fuel, about half a cwt. of coals per week, 5d., with a few peats, say 1d., making 26s. a year, or 6d. a week; clothes, including 10s. or 12s. for shoes or clogs, 30s. yearly, 7d. weekly; various items, soap, candles, etc., 10s. yearly, 2¼d. weekly; making her expenses in all about £7 yearly, or 2s. 8d. or 2s. 9d. weekly. Though meal and potatoes are taken above as representative of the staple article of food, it is not meant that they are exclusively so in every case, loaf bread and tea being sometimes used, but then they must be in proportionally smaller quantities. And so also if oatmeal be exclusively used in place of potatoes, then only four ounces or five ounces can be had in lieu of the three pounds of potatoes.'

Appendix III

LIST OF VERBAL QUESTIONS ADDRESSED TO PRINCIPAL RURAL PARISH WITNESSES

These questions appear to be the ones normally addressed verbally to the person responsible for filling in the 72-part written questionnaire. That person was usually the man who had been the minister of the established church before the Disruption, or the session clerk. Not all the questions were asked of one witness and some were asked of other witnesses. Generally they were used to lead the discussion, and witnesses would often labour at length on one topic.

1. You are . . .?
2. How long have you been in that situation?
3. Have you received the printed queries from the Commission?
4. Is it correct, to the best of your knowledge and belief?
5. How many resident heritors have you?
6. Do the heritors take any charge of the distribution of the poor funds?
7. What is the usual allowance to people aged, and infirm and unable to work?
8. What is the largest sum given to any person on the roll throughout the year?
9. Do you consider that those allowances, which you make, are adequate for the relief of the poor?
10. Do any of them suffer destitution from want of food?
11. In what condition do you find the poor in point of clothing?
12. In what state are their houses?
13. What kind of beds and bedding have they?
14. Does the maintenance of the poor depend on the voluntary contributions of their neighbours?
15. How are those who are bed-ridden provided for?
16. How are widows and young children provided for?
17. Are there any lunatics on the parish at present?
18. Are there any orphans on the parish at present?
19. Are there any deaf and dumb on the parish at present?
20. Are there any blind on the parish at present?
21. Do you give any extra diet to the poor when sick, or furnish them with cordials such as wine or porter?
22. Do you provide a doctor for the poor from the poor funds?

23. Do you provide coffins for deceased paupers?
24. Are the children generally vaccinated?
25. Do you think that some further provision is necessary for medical attendance and proper food for the poor when sick?
26. Are you satisfied with the means of education in your parish?
27. Is there much begging in your parish?
28. Are there any stranger beggars in your parish?
29. Is the population in your parish superabundant?
30. Is there any desire amongst the people to emigrate?
31. Are there any manufactures in the parish?
32. Are there many in your parish who depend entirely on day labour?
33. Are the parishioners in general temperate and industrious in their habits?
34. How are the people in the country, compared with those in the village (or town)?
35. What is the general food of those just above the paupers?
36. Are the paupers on the roll worse off in your opinion than the lowest class of labourers?
37. Have you any poor people who are relieved occasionally, and are not on the poor roll?
38. Are the funds in your parish continuing pretty steady, or have they been affected by the late movement in the church?
39. Do you think any additional provision will be necessary for the poor by assessment or otherwise?
40. Are there any able-bodied men suffering from want of work in the parish?
41. Would it be necessary or proper to introduce a legal provision for able-bodied men when out of employment, by assessment?
42. Have you had applications from other parishes for payment of allowances to paupers belonging to your parish?
43. When you find persons belonging to other parishes in distress in your parish, do you give them temporary relief?

Appendix IV

LIST OF VERBAL QUESTIONS ADDRESSED TO WITNESSES FROM THE PRINCIPAL TOWNS

These questions appear to be the main types of questions asked verbally of the witnesses from large towns. They represent the broad subject areas in which the commissioners sought to understand the operation of the Poor Law. As the witnesses varied in background, so too did the type of question. No single witness ever answered all of them, and of course, a great number of supplementary questions were asked of each.

1. You are . . .?
2. What is your duty as . . . (with details)?
3. Are you well acquainted with the situation and habits of the lower class in . . . (elaborate)?
4. Has it appeared to you that the provision for the poor has been adequate to their needful sustentation?
5. Is there much difference in regard to those on the Poor's Roll, in their habits of cleanliness?
6. Are there any cases of (a) mothers with illegitimate children (b) deserted families (c) able-bodied single women under 60 (d) able-bodied men (e) Irish (f) orphans (g) lunatics, receiving relief?
7. Have you known instances of people applying for relief whom you conceived entitled by law and refused?
8. What is the largest allowances to a . . . (categories of poor)?
9. Do you find that their allowance is supplemented from other sources?
10. What is the number of poor at present?
11. Is there much begging in this parish?
12. Do you approve of the system of licensed begging?
13. What is the effect of begging on the character of the paupers – does it raise or demoralise them?
14. What would you think a sufficient allowance for a . . . (categories of poor)?
15. Would you propose to increase the allowance, and give it to the poor in a different manner from that in which it is given them now?
16. Do you think that the smallness of the allowance has any particular effect on the religious habits and other morals of the pooor?
17. Does it lead to a weakening of their friendly feelings towards each other?

18. Does it lead them into habits of crime?
19. Do you think that the (proposed) increased allowances would stop up the resources coming from the upper ranks?
20. Do you think it would be practicable to abolish assessments and leave the poor maintained by the collection at the church doors?
21. Would not entrusting the poor to the establishment of the kirk-session have a moral effect on the people?
22. Do you think providing for them by an assessment and giving them a claim to relief, would increase their improvident habits?
23. Have you considered the bearing of the Poor Laws on the population, either as giving a stimulus to its increase, or to the contrary?
24. Is there much intemperance amongst the poor?
25. Would you attribute early marriages to the want of means, or the improvident character of the person who is without means?
26. When parties come from the country to . . . , and make application for relief, what do you find are the causes (obtaining relief from the charities, old farm servants, difficulty of obtaining cottages etc.) that bring them here?
27. If a party applies for relief who has not a settlement, what does the parish do?
28. Do you object to the principle of residence on conferring a settlement?
29. Would it be desirable to alter the law of settlement?
30. Would you (or do you), initiate Poor Law inquiry by paid or unpaid agents?
31. Would it be right to give any appeal (to the Sheriff or Court of Session) from the decision of the parish?
32. Would it not be desirable to have a law a removal?
33. Are you of the opinion that the provision of medical relief for the poor is sufficiently ample?
34. Is the parish surgeon paid a salary?
35. Have the surgeons the power of ordering nutritious diets?
36. Are they allowed anything extra for operations, midwife cases, etc.?
37. Do you think that the town is well ventilated and the sewerage good?
38. It has been stated that the crowding of the poor together is a main cause of the diffusion of fever, and that intemperance and destitution have nothing to do with fever?
39. Are patients of all classes requiring use of the hospital/house of recovery admitted without restriction?
40. Have you any difficulty in raising funds for its maintenance?
41. Have you had an opportunity of seeing any of the lunatics who are maintained by the parish?
42. Is there any class of persons for whom a public institution or hospital or workhouse would be desirable?
43. Are there many persons (numbers and class) inclined to be industrious in ordinary times, out of employment?
44. Judging from your experience during previous years, do you think the

distress on this occasion was of unprecedented duration?

45. Will you explain your machinery for the operation of the unemployed relief fund?

46. Did you receive any money from the Manufacturers' Relief Committee in London in 1842?

47. Were the funds raised sufficient to relieve the destitution?

48. Were there paid inspectors of the fund and/or relief work?

49. Was there an unwillingness on the part of the operatives to come on the fund?

50. How much can they earn doing relief work in a day?

51. Do you know whether their goods were pawned to a very great amount?

52. Would you interfere with the present system of regular pawnbreaking?

53. Have you reason to believe that educational means are deficient in . . .?

54. Do you think that proper education would be the main measure for preventing improvidence?

55. During a period of distress, would you give relief by affording facilities for emigration?

56. Would you state what institutions exist among the working-class by which when they are sick, they manage not to come on the parish?

57. Do the working-classes generally belong to some of these friendly societies?

58. Have receipts and depositors of savings banks been generally increasing?

59. Have you found that the savings banks exercise a very beneficial influence on the habits of the poor?

60. Are there particular descriptions of persons amongst the working-classes who deposit more than others?

N.B. The questions listed in Appendices III and IV are not, of course, the ones systematically analysed in the tables. The latter are drawn from the written answers to the questionnaire and detailed individually in the discussion in each chapter.

INDEX